Microservices

Microservices

Flexible Software Architecture

Eberhard Wolff

Addison-Wesley

Boston • Columbus • Indianapolis • New York • San Francisco
Amsterdam • Cape Town • Dubai • London • Madrid • Milan
Munich • Paris • Montreal • Toronto • Delhi • Mexico City
São Paulo • Sydney • Hong Kong • Seoul • Singapore • Taipei • Tokyo

Library of Congress Control Number: 2016952028

Copyright © 2017 Pearson Education, Inc.

ISBN-13: 978-0-134-60241-7
ISBN-10: 0-134-60241-2

Text printed in the United States on recycled paper at RR Donnelley in Crawfordsville, Indiana.
1   16

Editor-in-Chief
Mark Taub

Acquisitions Editor
Chris Guzikowski

Development Editor
Chris Zahn

Managing Editor
Sandra Schroeder

Project Editor
Lori Lyons

Production Manager
Dhayanidhi

Copy Editor
Warren Hapke

Indexer
Erika Millen

Proofreader
Sudhakaran

Editorial Assistant
Olivia Basegio

Cover Designer
Chuti Prasertsith

Compositor
codeMantra

To my family and friends for their support.

And to the computing community for all the fun it has provided to me.

Contents at a Glance

Contents

Preface

Although "microservices" is a new term, the concepts that it represents have been around for long time. In 2006, Werner Vogels (CTO at Amazon) gave a talk at the JAOO conference presenting the Amazon Cloud and Amazon's partner model. In his talk he mentioned the CAP theorem, today the basis for NoSQL. In addition, he spoke about small teams that develop and run services with their own databases. Today this structure is called DevOps, and the architecture is known as micro services.

Later I was asked to develop a strategy for a client that would enable them to integrate modern technologies into their existing application. After a few attempts to integrate the new technologies directly into the legacy code, we finally built a new application with a completely different modern technology stack alongside the old one. The old and the new application were only coupled via HTML links and via a shared database. Except for the shared database, this is in essence a microservices approach. That happened in 2008.

In 2009, I worked with another client who had divided his complete infrastructure into REST services, each being developed by individual teams. This would also be called microservices today. Many other companies with a web-based business model had already implemented similar architectures at that time. Lately, I have also realized how continuous delivery influences software architecture. This is another area where microservices offer a number of advantages.

This is the reason for writing this book—a number of people have been pursuing a microservices approach for a long time, among them some very experienced architects. Like every other approach to architecture, microservices cannot solve every problem. However, this concept represents an interesting alternative to existing approaches.

Overview of the Book

This book provides a detailed introduction to microservices. Architecture and organization are the main topics. However, technical implementation strategies are not neglected. A complete example of a microservice-based system demonstrates a concrete technical implementation. The discussion of technologies for nanoservices illustrates that modularization does not stop with microservices. The book provides all the necessary information for readers to start using microservices.

For Whom Is the Book Meant?

The book addresses managers, architects, and developers who want to introduce microservices as an architectural approach.

Managers

Microservices work best when a business is organized to support a microservices-based architecture. In the introduction, managers understand the basic ideas behind microservices. Afterwards they can focus on the organizational impact of using microservices.

Developers

Developers are provided with a comprehensive introduction to the technical aspects and can acquire the necessary skills to use microservices. A detailed example of a technical implementation of microservices, as well as numerous additional technologies, for example for nanoservices, helps to convey the basic concepts.

Architects

Architects get to know microservices from an architectural perspective and can at the same time deepen their understanding of the associated technical and organizational issues.

The book highlights possible areas for experimentation and additional information sources. These will help the interested reader to test their new knowledge practically and delve deeper into subjects that are of relevance to them.

Structure and Coverage

The book is organized into four parts.

Part I: Motivation and Basics

The first part of the book explains the motivation for using microservices and the foundation of the microservices architecture. Chapter 1, "Preliminaries," presents the basic properties as well as the advantages and disadvantages of microservices. Chapter 2, "Microservice Scenarios," presents two scenarios for the use of microservices: an e-commerce application and a system for signal processing. This section provides some initial insights into microservices and points out contexts for applications.

Part II: Microservices—What, Why, and Why Not?

Part II not only explains microservices in detail but also deals with their advantages and disadvantages:

- Chapter 3, "What Are Microservices," investigates the definition of the term "microservices" from three perspectives: the size of a microservice, Conway's Law (which states that organizations can only create specific software architectures), and finally a technical perspective based on domain-driven Design and Bounded Context.

- The reasons for using microservices are detailed in Chapter 4, "Reasons for Using Microservices." Microservices have not only technical but also organizational advantages, and there are good reasons for turning to microservices from a business perspective.

- The unique challenges posed by microservices are discussed in Chapter 5, "Challenges." Among these are technical challenges as well as problems related to architecture, infrastructure, and operation.

- Chapter 6, "Microservices and SOA," aims at defining the differences between microservices and SOA (service-oriented architecture). At first sight both concepts seem to be closely related. However, a closer look reveals plenty of differences.

Part III: Implementing Microservices

Part III deals with the application of microservices and demonstrates how the advantages that were described in Part II can be obtained and how the associated challenges can be solved.

- Chapter 7, "Architecture of Microservice-Based Systems," describes the architecture of microservices-based systems. In addition to domain architecture, technical challenges are discussed.

- Chapter 8, "Integration and Communication," presents the different approaches to the integration of and the communication between microservices. This includes not only communication via REST or messaging but also the integration of UIs and the replication of data.

- Chapter 9, "Architecture of Individual Microservices," shows possible architectures for microservices such as CQRS, Event Sourcing, or hexagonal architecture. Finally, suitable technologies for typical challenges are addressed.

- Testing is the main focus of Chapter 10, "Testing Microservices and Microservice-Based Systems." Tests have to be as independent as possible to enable the independent deployment of the different microservices. However, the tests need to not only check the individual microservices, but also the system in its entirety.

- Operation and Continuous Delivery are addressed in Chapter 11, "Operations and Continuous Delivery of Microservices." Microservices generate a huge number of deployable artifacts and thus increase the demands on the infrastructure. This is a substantial challenge when introducing microservices.

- Chapter 12, "Organizational Effects of a Microservices-Based Architecture," illustrates how microservices also influence the organization. After all, microservices are an architecture, which is supposed to influence and improve the organization.

Part IV: Technologies

The last part of the book shows in detail and at the code level how microservices can be implemented technically:

- Chapter 13, "Example of a Microservices-Based Architecture," contains an exhaustive example for a microservices architecture based on Java, Spring Boot, Docker, and Spring Cloud. This chapter aims at providing an application, which can be easily run, that illustrates the concepts behind microservices in practical terms and offers a starting point for the implementation of a microservices system and experiments.

- Even smaller than microservices are nanoservices, which are presented in Chapter 14, "Technologies for Nanoservices." Nanoservices require specific technologies and a number of compromises. The chapter discusses different technologies and their related advantages and disadvantages.

- Chapter 15, "Getting Started with Microservices," demonstrates how microservices can be adopted.

Essays

The book contains essays that were written by experts of various aspects of micro-services. The experts were asked to record their main findings about microservices on approximately two pages. Sometimes these essays complement book chapters, sometimes they focus on other topics, and sometimes they contradict passages in the book. This illustrates that there is, in general, no single correct answer when it comes to software architectures, but rather a collection of different opinions and possibilities. The essays offer the unique opportunity to get to know different viewpoints in order to subsequently develop an opinion.

Paths through the Book

The book offers content suitable for each type of audience. Of course, everybody can and should read the chapters that are primarily meant for people with a different type of job. However, the chapters focused on topics that are most relevant for a certain audience are indicated in Table P.1.

Table P.1 *Paths through the Book*

Chapter	Developer	Architect	Manager
1 - Preliminaries	X	X	X
2 - Microservice Scenarios	X	X	X
3 - What Are Microservices?	X	X	X
4 - Reasons for Using Microservices	X	X	X
5 - Challenges	X	X	X
6 - Microservices and SOA		X	X
7 - Architecture of Microservice-Based Systems		X	
8 - Integration and Communication	X	X	
9 - Architecture of Individual Microservices	X	X	
10 - Testing Microservices and Microservice-Based Systems	X	X	
11 - Operations and Continuous Delivery of Microservices	X	X	

(Continued)

Table P.1 *Continued*

Chapter	Developer	Architect	Manager
12 - Organizational Effects of a Microservices-Based Architecture			X
13 - Example of a Microservice-Based Architecture	X		
14 - Technologies for Nanoservices	X	X	
15 - Getting Started with Microservices	X	X	X

Readers who only want to obtain an overview are advised to concentrate on the summary section at the end of each chapter. People who want to gain practical knowledge should commence with Chapters 13 and 14, which deal with concrete technologies and code.

The instructions for experiments, which are given in the sections "Try and Experiment," help deepen your understanding by providing practical exercises. Whenever a chapter is of particular interest to you, you are encouraged to complete the related exercises to get a better grasp of the topics presented in that chapter.

Supplementary Materials

Errata, links to examples, and additional information can be found at http://microservices-book.com/. The example code is available at https://github.com/ewolff/microservice/.

Register your copy of *Microservices* at informit.com for convenient access to downloads, updates, and corrections as they become available. To start the registration process, go to informit.com/register and log in or create an account. Enter the product ISBN 9780134602417 and click Submit. Once the process is complete, you will find any available bonus content under "Registered Products."

Acknowledgments

I would like to thank everybody with whom I have discussed microservices and all the people who asked questions or worked with me—way too many to list them all. The interactions and discussions were very fruitful and fun!

I would like to mention especially Jochen Binder, Matthias Bohlen, Merten Driemeyer, Martin Eigenbrodt, Oliver B. Fischer, Lars Gentsch, Oliver Gierke, Boris Gloger, Alexander Heusingfeld, Christine Koppelt, Andreas Krüger, Tammo van Lessen, Sascha Möllering, André Neubauer, Till Schulte-Coerne, Stefan Tilkov, Kai Tödter, Oliver Wolf, and Stefan Zörner.

As a native speaker, Matt Duckhouse has added some significant improvements to the text and improved its readability.

My employer, innoQ, has also played an important role throughout the writing process. Many of the discussions and suggestions of my innoQ colleagues are reflected in the book.

Finally, I would like to thank my friends and family—especially my wife, whom I have often neglected while working on the book. In addition, I would like to thank her for the English translation of the book.

Of course, my thanks also go to all the people who have been working on the technologies that are mentioned in the book and thus have laid the foundation for the development of microservices. Special thanks also due to the experts who shared their knowledge of and experience with microservices in the essays.

Leanpub has provided me with the technical infrastructure to create the translation. It has been a pleasure to work with it, and it is quite likely that the translation would not exist without Leanpub.

Addison-Wesley enabled me to take the English translation to the next level. Chris Zahn, Chris Guzikowski, Lori Lyons and Dhayanidhi Karunanidhi provided excellent support for that process.

Last but not least, I would like to thank dpunkt.verlag and René Schönfeldt, who supported me very professionally during the genesis of the original German version.

About the Author

Eberhard Wolff, a Fellow at innoQ in Germany, has more than 15 years of experience as an architect and consultant working at the intersection of business and technology. He has given talks and keynote addresses at several international conferences, served on multiple conference program committees, and written more than 100 articles and books. His technological focus is on modern architectures—often involving cloud, continuous delivery, DevOps, microservices, or NoSQL.

PART I

Motivation and Basics

Part I explains what microservices are, why they are interesting, and where they are useful. Practical examples demonstrate the impact of microservices in different scenarios.

Chapter 1, "Preliminaries," start to define microservices.

To illustrate the importance of microservices, Chapter 2, "Microservice Scenarios," contains detailed scenarios illustrating where microservices can be used.

Chapter 1

Preliminaries

This chapter provides an overview of the concept of a microservice. The first section defines microservices. The second section answers the question "Why microservices?" Finally, the chapter ends by discussing the challenges associated with microservices.

1.1 Overview of Microservice

The focus of this book is microservices—an approach to the modularization of software. Modularization in itself is nothing new. For quite some time, large systems have been divided into small modules to facilitate the implementation, understanding, and further development of the software.

Microservices are a new approach to modularization. However, the term "microservice" is not really well defined, so the chapter starts with a definition of the term and describes how microservices are different from the usual deployment monoliths.

Microservice: Preliminary Definition

The new aspect is that microservices use modules that run as distinct processes. This approach is based on the philosophy of UNIX, which can be reduced to three aspects:

- One program should fulfill only one task, but it should perform this task really well.

- Programs should be able to work together.

- A universal interface should be used. In UNIX this is provided by text streams.

The term microservice is not firmly defined. Chapter 3, "What Are Microservices," provides a more detailed definition. However, the following criteria can serve as a first approximation:

- Microservices are a modularization concept. Their purpose is to divide large software systems into smaller parts. Thus they influence the organization and development of software systems.

- Microservices can be deployed independently of each other. Changes to one microservice can be taken into production independently of changes to other microservices.

- Microservices can be implemented in different technologies. There is no restriction on the programming language or the platform for each microservice.

- Microservices possess their own data storage: a private database or a completely separate schema in a shared database.

- Microservices can bring their own support services along, for example a search engine or a specific database. Of course, there is a common platform for all microservices—for example virtual machines.

- Microservices are self-contained processes or virtual machines, e.g., to bring the supporting services along.

- Microservices have to communicate via the network. To do so microservices use protocols that support loose coupling, such as REST or messaging.

Deployment Monoliths

Microservices are the opposite of deployment monoliths. A deployment monolith is a large software system that can only be deployed in one piece. It has to pass, in its entirety, through all phases of the continuous delivery pipeline, such as development, the test stages, and release. Due to the size of deployment monoliths, these processes take longer than for smaller systems. This reduces flexibility and increases process costs. Internally, deployment monoliths can have a modular structure; however, all modules have to be brought into production simultaneously.

1.2 Why Microservices?

Microservices enable software to be divided into modules, making it easier to change the software.

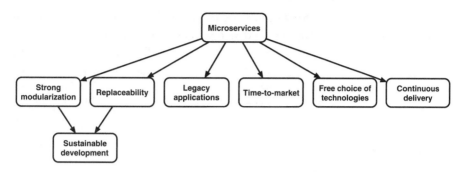

Figure 1.1 *Advantages of Microservices*

As illustrated in Figure 1.1, microservices offer a number of important advantages.

Strong Modularization

Microservices offer a strong modularization concept. Whenever a system is built from different software components, such as Ruby GEMs, Java JARs, .NET assemblies or Node.js NPMs, undesirable dependencies can easily creep in. For example, imagine that somebody references a class or function in a place where it is not supposed to be used. This use creates a dependency that the developers of the class or function are not aware of. Any changes they make to their class or function could cause unexpected failures in another part of the system. After a short while, so many dependencies will have accumulated and the problem has worsened so much that the system can no longer be serviced or further developed.

Microservices, in contrast, communicate only via explicit interfaces, which are realized using mechanisms such as messages or REST. This makes the technical hurdles for the use of microservices higher, and thus unwanted dependencies are less likely to arise. In principle, it should be possible to achieve a high level of modularization in deployment monoliths. However, practical experience teaches us that the architecture of deployment monoliths deteriorates over time.

Easy Replaceability

Microservices can be replaced more easily than modules in a deployment monolith. Other components utilize a microservice via an explicit interface. If a new service offers the same interface, it can replace the existing microservice. The new microservice can use a different code base and even different technologies as long as it presents the same interface. This can often be impossible or difficult to achieve in legacy systems.

Small microservices further facilitate replacement. The need to replace code in the future is often neglected during the development of software systems. Who wants to consider how a newly built system can be replaced in the future? In addition, the easy replaceability of microservices reduces the costs of incorrect decisions. When the decision for a technology or approach is limited to a microservice, this microservice can be completely rewritten if the need arises.

Sustainable Development

Strong modularization and easy replaceability enable sustainable software development. Most of the time, working on a new project is straightforward, but over longer projects productivity decreases. One of the reasons is the erosion of architecture. Microservices counteract this erosion by enforcing strong modularization. Being bound to outdated technologies and the difficulties associated with the removal of old system modules constitute additional problems with deployment monoliths. Microservices, which are not linked to a specific technology, can be replaced one by one to overcome these problems.

Further Development of Legacy Applications

Starting with a microservices-based architecture is easy and provides immediate advantages when working with old systems: Instead of having to add to the old and hard to understand code base, the system can be enhanced with a microservice. The microservice can act on specific requests while leaving all others to the legacy system. It can also modify requests before they are processed by the legacy system. With this approach, it is not necessary to replace the legacy system completely. In addition, the microservice is not bound to the technology stack of the legacy system but can be developed using modern approaches.

Time-to-Market

Microservices enable shorter time-to-market. As mentioned previously, microservices can be brought into production on a one-by-one basis. If teams working on a large system are responsible for one or more microservices and if features require changes only to these microservices, each team can develop and bring features into production without time-consuming coordination with other teams. This enables many teams to work on numerous features in parallel and bring more features into production in less time than would have been possible with a deployment monolith.

Microservices help with scaling agile processes to large teams by dividing the large team into small teams, each dealing with its own microservices.

Independent Scaling

Each microservice can be scaled independently of other services. This removes the need to scale the entire system when only a few pieces of functionality are used intensely. This will often be a significant simplification for the infrastructure and operations.

Free Choice of Technologies

When microservices are used in development, there are no restrictions with regards to the usage of technologies. This gives the ability to test a new technology within a single microservice without affecting other services. The risk associated with the introduction of new technologies and new versions of already used technologies is decreased, as these new technologies are introduced and tested in a confined environment keeping costs low. In addition, it is possible to use specific technologies for specific functions, for example a specific database. The risk is small, as the microservice can easily be replaced or removed if problems arise. The new technology is confined to one or a small number of microservices. This reduces the potential risk and enables independent technology decisions for different microservices. More importantly, it makes the decision to try out and evaluate new, highly innovative technologies easier. This increases the productivity of developers and prevents the technology platform from becoming outdated. In addition, the use of modern technologies will attract well-qualified developers.

Continuous Delivery

Microservices are advantageous for continuous delivery. They are small and can be deployed independently of each other. Realizing a continuous delivery pipeline is simple due to the size of a microservice. The deployment of a single microservice is associated with less risk than the deployment of a large monolith. It is also easier to ensure the safe deployment of a microservice, for instance by running different versions in parallel. For many microservice users, continuous delivery is the main reason for the introduction of microservices.

All these points are strong arguments for the introduction of microservices. Which of these reasons is the most important will depend on the context. Scaling agile processes and continuous delivery are often crucial from a business perspective. Chapter 4, "Reasons for Using Microservices," describes the advantages of microservices in detail and also deals with prioritization.

1.3 Challenges

However, there is no light without shadow. Chapter 5, "Challenges," discusses the challenges posed by the introduction of microservices and how to deal with them. In short, the main challenges are the following:

- **Relationships are hidden**—The architecture of the system consists of the relationships between the services. However, it is not evident which microservice calls which other microservice. This can make working on the architecture challenging.

- **Refactoring is difficult**—The strong modularization leads to some disadvantages: refactoring, if it requires functionality to move between microservices, is difficult to perform. And, once introduced, it is hard to change the microservices-based modularization of a system. However, these problems can be reduced with smart approaches.

- **Domain architecture is important**—The modularization into microservices for different domains is important, as it determines how teams are divided. Problems at this level also affect the organization. Only a solid domain architecture can ensure the independent development of microservices. As it is difficult to change the modularization once established, mistakes can be hard to correct later on.

- **Running microservices is complex**—A system composed of microservices has many components that have to be deployed, controlled, and run. This increases the complexity of operations and the number of runtime infrastructures used by the system. Microservices require that operations are automated to make sure that operating the platform does not become laborious.

- **Distributed systems are complex**—Developers face increased complexity: a microservice-based system is a distributed system. Calls between microservices can fail due to network problems. Calls via the network are slower and have a smaller bandwidth than calls within a process.

1.4 Conclusion

This chapter provided an overview of the concept of a microservice. It started with a definition of microservices. Then it answered the question "Why microservices?" Finally, the chapter ended with a discussion of the challenges associated with microservices.

Chapter 2

Microservice Scenarios

This chapter presents a number of scenarios in which microservices can be useful. Section 2.1 focuses on the modernization of a legacy web application. This is the most common use case for microservices. A very different scenario is discussed in section 2.2. A signaling system is being developed as a distributed system based on microservices. Section 2.3 draws some conclusions and invites the reader to judge the usefulness of microservices in the scenarios presented for themselves.

2.1 Modernizing an E-Commerce Legacy Application

Migrating from a legacy deployment monolith is the most common scenario for microservices. This section starts with a general description of such a scenario and then gets into the details of the legacy application and how to modularize it into microservices.

Scenario

Big Money Online Commerce Inc. runs an e-commerce shop, which is the main source of the company's revenue. It's a web application that offers many different functions, such as user registration and administration, product search, an overview of orders, and, of course, the ordering process, the central feature of any e-commerce application.

The application is a deployment monolith: it can only be deployed in its entirety. Whenever a feature is changed, the entire application needs to be deployed anew. The e-commerce shop works together with other systems—for example, with accounting and logistics.

Reasons to Use Microservices

The deployment monolith started out as a well-structured application. However, over the years, more and more dependencies between the individual modules have crept in. This has led to the application becoming very difficult to maintain and update. In addition, the original architecture is no longer suited to the current requirements of the business. Product search, for instance, has been greatly modified as the Big Money Online Commerce Inc. attempts to outperform its competitors in this area. Also, clients have been given a number of self-service options that have helped the company to reduce costs. However, these two modules have become very large, with complex internal structures, and they have numerous dependencies on other modules that had not originally been intended.

Slow Continuous Delivery Pipeline

Big Money has decided to use continuous delivery and has established a continuous delivery pipeline. This pipeline is complicated and slow, as the entire deployment monolith needs to be tested and brought into production in one go. Some of the tests run for hours. A faster pipeline would be highly desirable.

Parallel Work Is Complicated

There are teams working on different new features. However, the parallel work is complicated: the software structure just doesn't really support it. The individual modules are not separated well enough and have too many interdependencies. As everything can only be deployed together, the entire deployment monolith has to be tested. The deployment and testing phases are a bottleneck. Whenever a team has a problem in the deployment pipeline, all other teams have to wait until the problem has been fixed and the change has been successfully deployed. Also, access to the continuous delivery pipeline has to be coordinated. Only one team can be doing testing and deployment at a time. There has to be coordination between the teams to determine the order in which teams will bring their changes into production.

Bottleneck During Testing

In addition to deployment, tests also have to be coordinated. When the deployment monolith runs an integration test, only the changes made by one team are allowed to be contained in the test. There were attempts to test several changes at once. This meant it was very hard to discern the origin of errors and led to error analyses that were long and complex.

One integration test requires approximately one hour. About six integration tests are feasible per working day, because errors have to be fixed and the environment has to be set up again for the next test. If there are ten teams, one team can bring one change into production every two days, on average. However, often a team also has to do error analysis, which lengthens integration. For that reason, some teams use feature branches in order to separate themselves from integration; they perform their changes on a separate branch in the version control system. Integrating these changes into the main branch later on often causes problems; changes are erroneously removed upon merging, or the software suddenly contains errors that are caused by the separated development process and that only show up after integration. These errors can only be eliminated in lengthy processes after integration.

Consequently, the teams slow each other down due to the testing (see Figure 2.1). Although each team develops its own modules, they all work on the same code base so that they impede each other. As a consequence of the shared continuous delivery pipeline and the ensuing need for coordination, the teams are unable to work either independently of each other or in parallel.

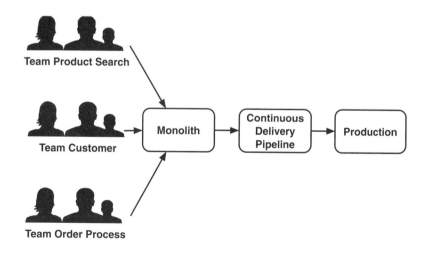

Figure 2.1 *Teams Slow Each Other Down due to the Deployment Monolith*

Approach

Because of the many problems being experienced, Big Money Online Commerce Inc. decided to split off small microservices from the deployment monolith. The microservices each implement one feature, such as the product search, and are developed by individual teams. Each team has complete responsibility for an individual microservice, starting from requirements engineering up to running the application in production. The microservices communicate with the monolith and other microservices via REST. The client GUI is also divided between the individual microservices based on use cases. Each microservice delivers the HTML pages for its use cases. Links are allowed between the HTML pages of the microservices. However, access to the database tables of other microservices or the deployment monolith is not allowed. Integration of services is exclusively done via REST or via links between the HTML pages.

The microservices can be deployed independently of each other. This enables changes in a microservice to be deployed without the need to coordinate with other microservices or teams. This greatly facilitates parallel work on features while reducing coordination efforts.

The deployment monolith is subject to far fewer changes due to the addition of microservices. For many features, changes to the monolith are no longer necessary. Thus, the deployment monolith is changed and deployed less often. Originally, the plan was to completely replace the deployment monolith at some point. However, in the meantime it seems more likely that the deployment monolith will just be deployed less and less frequently because most changes take place within the microservices. Thus the deployment monolith does not disturb work anymore. To replace it entirely is not necessary and also does not appear sensible in economic terms.

Challenges

Implementing microservices creates additional complexity at the start; all the microservices need their own infrastructure, and at the same time, the Monolith has to be supported.

The microservices require a lot more servers and therefore pose very different challenges. Monitoring and log file processing has to deal with the fact that data originates from different servers. As a result, information has to be centrally consolidated. A substantially larger number of servers must be handled, not only in production, but also in the different test stages and team environments. This is only possible with good infrastructure automation. It is necessary to support different types of infrastructure for the monolith and the microservices, and this leads to substantially more servers overall.

Entire Migration Lengthy

The added complexity due to the two different software types will persist for a long time, as it is a very lengthy process to completely migrate away from the monolith. If the monolith is never entirely replaced, the additional infrastructure costs will remain as well.

Testing Remains a Challenge

Testing is an additional challenge; previously, the entire deployment monolith was tested in the deployment pipeline. These tests are complex and take a long time, as all the functions of the deployment monolith have to be tested. If every change to every microservice is sent through these tests, it will take a long time for each change to reach production. Additionally, the changes have to be coordinated, because each change should be tested in isolation so that errors can be easily linked back to the change that caused them. In that scenario, a microservices-based architecture does not seem to have major advantages over a deployment monolith; while microservices can in principle be deployed independently of each other, the test stages preceding deployment still have to be coordinated, and each change still has to pass through them individually.

Current Status of Migration

Figure 2.2 presents the current status; product search works as an independent microservice and is completely independent of the deployment monolith. Coordination with other teams is hardly ever necessary. Only in the last stage of the deployment do the deployment monolith and the microservices have to be tested together. Each change to the monolith or any microservice has to run through this step. This causes a bottleneck. The team "Customer" works together with the team "Order Process" on the deployment monolith. In spite of microservices, these teams still have to closely coordinate their work. For that reason, the team "Order Process" has implemented its own microservice, which forms part of the order process. In this part of the system, changes can be introduced faster than in the deployment monolith, not only due to the younger code base, but also because it is no longer necessary to coordinate with the other teams.

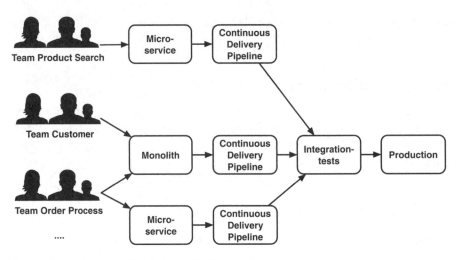

Figure 2.2 *Independent Work through Microservices*

Creating Teams

For the teams to be able to work independently on features, it is important to create teams that match to functionalities such as product search, customer processing, or order processing. If teams correspond to technical layers such as the UI, middle tier, or database instead, each feature requires the involvement of all the teams, because a feature normally comprises changes to the UI, middle tier, and database. Thus, to minimize coordination efforts between the teams, the best approach is to create teams that center around features like product search. Microservices support the independence of the teams by their own technical independence from each other. Consequently, teams need to coordinate less in respect to basic technologies and technical designs.

The tests also need to be modularized. Each test should ideally deal with a single microservice so that it is sufficient to perform the test when changes are made in the respective microservice. In addition, it might be possible to implement the test as unit test rather than as an integration test. This progressively shortens the test phase in which all microservices and the monolith have to be tested together. This reduces the coordination problems for the final test phase.

Migrating to a microservices-based architecture created a number of performance problems and also some problems due to network failures. However, these problems were solved over time.

Advantages

Thanks to the new architecture, changes can be deployed much faster. A team can bring a change into production within 30 minutes. The deployment monolith, on the other hand, is deployed only weekly because the tests are not yet fully automated.

Deploying the microservices is not only much faster, but also much less risky: less coordination is required. Errors are more easily found and fixed because developers still know what they have been working on well, as it was only 30 minutes ago.

In summary, the goal was attained; the developers can introduce more changes to the e-commerce shop. This is possible because the teams need to coordinate their work less and because the deployment of a microservice can take place independently of the other services.

The option of using different technologies was only sparingly used by the teams. The previously used technology stack proved sufficient, and the teams wanted to avoid the additional complexity caused by the use of different technologies. However, the long-needed search engine for the product search was introduced. The team responsible for product search was able to implement this change on its own. Previously, the introduction of this new technology had been prohibited because the associated risk had been considered too great. In addition, some teams have new versions of the libraries of the technology stack in production because they needed the bug fixes included in the more recent version. This did not require any coordination with the other teams.

Conclusion

Replacing a monolith via the implementation of microservices is a very common scenario for the introduction of microservices. It requires a lot of effort to keep developing a monolith and to add new features to it. The complexity of the monolith and the associated problems caused by it progressively increase over time. It is often very difficult and risky to completely replace an existing system with a newly written one.

Rapid and Independent Development of New Features

In the case of companies like Big Money Online Commerce Inc., the rapid development of new features and the ability to do parallel work on several features are vital for the success of the business. Only by providing state-of-the-art features can new customers be won and existing customers be kept from switching to other companies. The promise of being able to develop more features faster makes microservices compelling in many use cases.

Influence on the Organization

The presented example illustrates the influence of microservices on the organization. The teams work on their own microservices. As the microservices can be developed and deployed independently of each other, the work of the different teams is no longer linked. In order to keep it that way, a microservice should not be changed by more than one team at any time. The microservices architecture requires a team organization corresponding to the different microservices. Each team is responsible for one or several microservices, each of which implements an isolated piece of functionality. This relationship between organization and architecture is especially important in the case of microservices-based architectures. Each team takes care of all issues concerning "its" microservices from requirements engineering up to operation monitoring. Of course, for operation, the teams can use common infrastructure services for logging and monitoring.

And finally, if the goal is to achieve a simple and fast deployment in production, just including microservices in the architecture will not be sufficient. The entire continuous delivery pipeline has to be checked for potential obstacles, and these have to be removed. This is illustrated by the tests in the presented example; the testing of all microservices together should be reduced to the essential minimum. Each change has to run through an integration test with the other microservices, but this test must run quickly to avoid a bottleneck in integration tests.

Amazon Has Been Doing It for a Long Time

The example scenario presented here is very similar to what Amazon has been doing for a very long time, and for the discussed reasons: Amazon wants to be able to quickly and easily implement new features on its website. In 2006, Amazon not only presented its Cloud platform, but also discussed how it develops software. Essential features are:

- The application is divided into different services.
- Each service provides a part of the website. For instance, there is a service for searching, and another one for recommendations. In the end, the individual services are presented together in the UI.

- There is always one team responsible for one service. The team takes care of developing new features as well as operating the service. The idea is: "You build it—you run it!"

- The Cloud platform (i.e., virtual machines) acts as the common foundation of all services. Apart from that, there are no other standards. As a result of this, each team is very free in their choice of technologies.

By introducing this type of architecture, Amazon implemented the fundamental characteristics of microservices back in 2006. Moreover, Amazon introduced DevOps by having teams consisting of operation experts and developers. This approach means that deployments occur largely in an automated fashion, as the manual construction of servers is not feasible in Cloud environments. Therefore, Amazon also implemented at least one aspect of continuous delivery.

In conclusion, some companies have been using microservices for a number of years already—especially companies with an Internet-based business model. This approach has already proven its practical advantages in real life. In addition, microservices work well with other modern software practices such as continuous delivery, Cloud, and DevOps.

2.2 Developing a New Signaling System

Greenfield applications can also be built using microservices. In some cases, that is the much more natural approach. This section starts with a general description of a greenfield scenario and then gets into the details of the example—a new signaling system.

Scenario

Searching for airplanes and ships that have gone missing is a complex task. Rapid action can save lives. Therefore, different systems are required. Some provide signals such as radio or radar signals. These signals have to be recorded and processed. Radio signals, for example, can be used to obtain a bearing, which subsequently has to be checked against radar-based pictures. Finally, humans have to further analyze the information. The data analyses, as well as the raw data, have to be provided to the different rescue teams. Figure 2.3 provides an overview of the signaling system. Signal Inc. builds systems for exactly these use cases. The systems are individually assembled, configured, and adapted to the specific needs of the respective client.

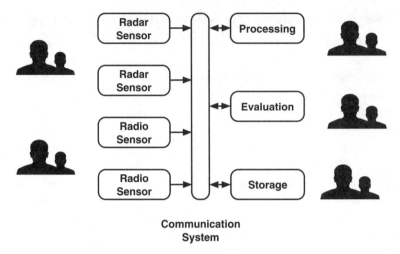

Figure 2.3 *Overview of the Signaling System*

Reasons to Use Microservices

The system is composed of different components that run on different computers. The sensors are distributed all over the area to be monitored and are provided with their own servers. However, these computers are not supposed to handle the more detailed data processing or store the data. Their hardware is not sufficiently powerful for that. Data privacy considerations would also render such an approach very undesirable.

Distributed System

For these reasons, the system has to be a distributed system. The different pieces of functionality are distributed within the network. The system is potentially unreliable, as individual components and the communication between components can fail.

It would be possible to implement a large part of the system within a deployment monolith. However, upon closer consideration, the different parts of the system have to fulfil very different demands. Data processing requires a substantial CPU and an approach that enables numerous algorithms to process the data. For such purposes, there are solutions that read events out of a data or event stream and process them. Data storage requires a very different focus. Basically, the data has to be maintained within a data structure that is suitable for different data analyses. Modern NoSQL databases are well suited for this. Recent data is more important than old data. It has to be accessible faster, while old data can even be deleted at some point. For final analysis by experts, the data has to be read from the database and processed.

Technology Stack per Team

Each of the discussed tasks poses different challenges. Consequently, each requires not only a well-adapted technology stack, but also a dedicated team consisting of technical experts on the respective task. Additionally, people are needed to decide which features Signal Inc. will bring to the market and to define new requirements for the systems. Systems for processing and sensors are individual products that can be positioned on the market independently of each other.

Integration of Other Systems

An additional reason for the use of microservices is the opportunity to easily integrate other systems. Sensors and computing units are also provided by other companies. The ability to integrate such solutions is a frequent requirement in client projects. Microservices enable the easy integration of other systems, as the integration of different distributed components is already a core feature of a microservices-based architecture.

For these reasons, the architects of Signal Inc. decided to implement a distributed system. Each team must implement its respective domain in several small microservices. This approach should ensure that microservices can be easily exchanged, and the integration of other systems will be straightforward.

Only the communication infrastructure to be used by all services for their communication is predetermined. The communication technology supports many programming languages and platforms so that there are no limitations as to which concrete technology is used. To make flawless communication possible, the interfaces between the microservices have to be clearly defined.

Challenges

A failure of communication between the different microservices presents an important challenge. The system has to stay usable even if network failures occur. This requires the use of technologies that can handle such failures. However, technologies alone will not solve this problem. It has to be decided as part of the user requirements what should happen if a system fails. If, for instance, old data is sufficient, caches can be helpful. In addition, it may be possible to use a simpler algorithm that does not require calls to other systems.

High Technological Complexity

The technological complexity of the entire system is very high. Different technologies are employed to satisfy the demands of the different components. The teams working on the individual systems can make largely independent technology decisions. This enables them to always implement the most suitable solution.

Unfortunately, this also means that developers can no longer easily switch between teams. For example, when there was a lot of work for the data storage team, developers from other teams could hardly help out, as they were not even proficient in the programming languages the data storage team was using and did not know the specific technologies, such as the used database.

It can be a challenge to run a system made up of so many technologies. For this reason, there is one standardization in this area: all microservices must be able to be run in a largely identical manner. They are virtual machines so that their installation is fairly simple. Furthermore, the monitoring is standardized, which determines data formats and technologies. This makes the central monitoring of the applications possible. In addition to the typical operational monitoring, there is also monitoring of application-specific values, and finally an analysis of log files.

Advantages

In this context, the main advantage offered by microservices is good support for the distributed nature of the system. The sensors are at different locations, so a centralized system is not sensible. The architecture has adapted to this fact by further dividing the system into small microservices that are distributed within the network. This enhances the exchangeability of the microservices. The microservices approach supports the technology diversity, which characterizes this system.

In this scenario, time-to-market is not as important as in the e-commerce scenario. It would also be hard to implement, as the systems are installed for different clients and cannot be easily reinstalled. However, some ideas from the continuous delivery field are used: for instance, the largely uniform installation and the central monitoring.

Verdict

Microservices are a suitable architectural pattern for this scenario. The system can benefit from the fact that typical problems can be solved during implementation by established approaches from the microservices field: for example, technology complexity and platform operation.

Still, this scenario wouldn't be immediately associated with the term "microservice." This leads to the following conclusions:

- Microservices have a wider application than is apparent at first glance. Outside of web-based business models, microservices can solve many problems, even if those issues are very different from the ones found in web companies.

- Indeed, many projects from different fields have been using microservice-based approaches for some time, even if they do not call them by this name or only implement them partially.

- With the help of microservices, these projects can use technologies that are currently being created in the microservice field. In addition, they can benefit from the experiences of others who have worked in this field, for instance in regards to architecture.

2.3 Conclusion

This chapter presented two very different scenarios from two completely distinct business areas: a web system with a strong focus on rapid time-to-market, and a system for signal processing that is inherently distributed. The architectural principles are very similar for the two systems, although they originate from different reasons.

In addition, there are a number of common approaches, among those the creation of teams according to microservices and the demands in regards to infrastructure automatization, as well as other organizational topics. However, in other areas, there are also differences. For the signaling system, it is essential to have the option to use different technologies, as this system has to employ a number of different technologies. For the web system, this aspect is not as important. Here, the independent development, the fast and easy deployment, and finally the better time-to-market are the critical factors.

Essential Points

- Microservices offer a significant number of advantages.

- In the case of web-based applications, continuous delivery and short time-to-market can be important motivations for the use of microservices.

- However, there are also very different use cases for which microservices as distributed systems are extremely well suited.

PART II

Microservices: What, Why, and Why Not?

Part II discusses the different facets of microservice-based architectures to present the diverse possibilities offered by microservices. Advantages as well as disadvantages are addressed so that the reader can evaluate what can be gained by using microservices and which points require special attention and care during the implementation of microservice-based architectures.

Chapter 3, "What Are Microservices," explains the term "**microservice**" in detail. The term is dissected from different perspectives, which is essential for an in-depth understanding of the microservice approach. Important issues are the size of a microservice, Conway's Law as organizational influence, and domain-driven design particularly with respect to *Bounded Context* from a domain perspective. Furthermore, the chapter addresses the question of whether a microservice should contain a UI.

Chapter 4, "**Reasons for Using Microservices**," focuses on the advantages of microservices, taking alternatingly technical, organizational, and business perspectives.

Chapter 5, "**Challenges**," deals with the associated challenges in the areas of technology, architecture, infrastructure, and operation.

Chapter 6, "**Microservices and SOA**," distinguishes microservices from service-oriented architecture (SOA). By making this distinction microservices are viewed from a new perspective, which helps to further clarify the microservices approach. Besides, microservices have been frequently compared to SOAs.

Chapter 3

What Are Microservices?

Section 1.1 provided an initial definition of the term microservice. However, there are a number of different ways to define microservices. The different definitions are based on different aspects of microservices. They also show for which reasons the use of microservices is advantageous. At the end of the chapter the reader should have his or her own definition of the term microservice—depending on the individual project scenario.

The chapter discusses the term microservice from different perspectives:

- Section 3.1 focuses on the size of microservices.

- Section 3.2 explains the relationship between microservices, architecture, and organization by using the Conway's Law.

- Section 3.3 presents a domain architecture of microservices based on domain-driven design (DDD) and bounded context.

- Section 3.5 explains why microservices should contain a user interface (UI).

3.1 Size of a Microservice

The name "microservices" conveys the fact that the size of the service matters; obviously, microservices are supposed to be small.

One way to define the size of a microservice is to count the lines of code (LOC).[1] However, such an approach has a number of problems:

- It depends on the programming language used. Some languages require more code than others to express the same functionality—and microservices are explicitly not supposed to predetermine the technology stack. Therefore, defining microservices based on this metric is not very useful.

- Finally, microservices represent an architecture approach. Architectures, however, should follow the conditions in the domain rather than adhering to technical metrics such as LOC. Also for this reason attempts to determine size based on code lines should be viewed critically.

In spite of the voiced criticism, LOC can be an indicator for a microservice. Still, the question as to the ideal size of a microservice remains. How many LOC may a microservice have? Even if there are no absolute standard values, there are nevertheless influencing factors, which may argue for larger or smaller microservices.

Modularization

One factor is modularization. Teams develop software in modules to be better able to deal with its complexity; instead of having to understand the entire software package, developers only need to understand the module(s) they are working on as well as the interplay between the different modules. This is the only way for a team to work productively in spite of the enormous complexity of a typical software system. In daily life there are often problems as modules get larger than originally planned. This makes them hard to understand and hard to maintain, because changes require an understanding of the entire module. Thus it is very sensible to keep microservices as small as possible. On the other hand, microservices, unlike many other approaches to modularization, have an overhead.

Distributed Communication

Microservices run within independent processes. Therefore, communication between microservices is distributed communication via the network. For this type of system, the "First Rule of Distributed Object Design"[2] applies. This rule states that systems should not be distributed if it can be avoided. The reason for this is that

---

a call on another system via the network is orders of magnitude slower than a direct call within the same process. In addition to the pure latency time, serialization and deserialization of parameters and results are time consuming. These processes not only take a long time, but also cost CPU capacity.

Moreover, distributed calls might fail because the network is temporarily unavailable or the called server cannot be reached—for instance due to a crash. This increases complexity when implementing distributed systems, because the caller has to deal with these errors in a sensible manner.

Experience[3] teaches us that microservice-based architectures work in spite of these problems. When microservices are designed to be especially small, the amount of distributed communication increases and the overall system gets slower. This is an argument for larger microservices. When a microservice contains a UI and fully implements a specific part of the domain, it can operate without calling on other microservices in most cases, because all components of this part of the domain are implemented within one microservice. The desire to limit distributed communication is another reason to build systems according to the domain.

Sustainable Architecture

Microservices also use distribution to design architecture in a sustainable manner through distribution into individual microservices: it is much more difficult to use a microservice than a class. The developer has to deal with the distribution technology and has to use the microservice interface. In addition, he or she might have to make preparations for tests to include the called microservice or replace it with a stub. Finally, he has to contact the team responsible for the respective microservice.

To use a class within a deployment monolith is much simpler—even if the class belongs to a completely different part of the monolith and falls within the responsibility of another team. However, because it is so simple to implement a dependency between two classes, unintended dependencies tend to accumulate within deployment monoliths. In the case of microservices dependencies are harder to implement, which prevents the creation of unintended dependencies.

Refactoring

However, the boundaries between microservices also create challenges, for instance during refactoring. If it becomes apparent that a piece of functionality does not fit well within its present microservice, it has to be moved to another microservice. If the target microservice is written in a different programming language, this transfer

---

3. http://martinfowler.com/articles/distributed-objects-microservices.html

inevitably leads to a new implementation. Such problems do not arise when functionalities are moved within a microservice. This consideration may argue for larger microservices, and this topic is the focus of section 7.3.

Team Size

The independent deployment of microservices and the division of the development effort into teams result in an upper limit for the size of an individual microservice. A team should be able to implement features within a microservice and deploy those features into production independently of other teams. By ensuring this, the architecture enables the scaling of development without requiring too much coordination effort between the teams.

A team has to be able to implement features independently of the other teams. Therefore, at first glance it seems like the microservice should be large enough to enable the implementation of different features. When microservices are smaller, a team can be responsible for several microservices, which together enable the implementation of a domain. A lower limit for the microservice size does not result from the independent deployment and the division into teams.

However, an upper limit does result from it: when a microservice has reached a size that prevents its further development by a single team, it is too large. For that matter a team should have a size that is especially well suited for agile processes, which is typically three to nine people. Thus a microservice should never grow so large that a team of three to nine people cannot develop it further by themselves. In addition to the sheer size, the number of features to be implemented in an individual microservice plays an important role. Whenever a large number of changes is necessary within a short time, a team can rapidly become overloaded. Section 12.2 highlights alternatives that enable several teams to work on the same microservice. However, in general a microservice should never grow so large that several teams are necessary to work on it.

Infrastructure

Another important factor influencing the size of a microservice is the infrastructure. Each microservice has to be able to be deployed independently. It must have a continuous delivery pipeline and an infrastructure for running the microservice, which has to be present not only in production but also during the different test stages. Also databases and application servers might belong to infrastructure. Moreover, there has to be a build system for the microservice. The code for the microservice has to be versioned independently of that for other microservices. Thus a project within version control has to exist for the microservice.

Depending on the effort that is necessary to provide the required infrastructure for a microservice, the sensible size for a microservice can vary. When a small microservice size is chosen, the system is distributed into many microservices, thus requiring more infrastructure. In the case of larger microservices, the system overall contains fewer microservices and consequently requires less infrastructure.

Build and deployment of microservices should anyhow be automated. Nevertheless, it can be laborious to provide all necessary infrastructure components for a microservice. Once setting up the infrastructure for new microservices is automated, the expenditure for providing infrastructures for additional microservices decreases. This automation enables further reduction of the microservice size. Companies that have been working with microservices for some time usually simplify the creation of new microservices by providing the necessary infrastructure in an automated manner.

Additionally, some technologies enable reduction of the infrastructure overhead to such an extent that substantially smaller microservices are possible—however, with a number of limitations in such cases. Such nanoservices are discussed in Chapter 14, "Technologies for Microservices."

Replaceability

A microservice should be as easy to replace as possible. Replacing a microservice can be sensible when its technology becomes outdated or if the microservice code is of such bad quality that it cannot be developed any further. The replaceability of microservices is an advantage when compared to monolithic applications, which can hardly be replaced at all. When a monolith cannot be reasonably maintained anymore, its development has either to be continued in spite of the associated high costs or a similarly cost-intensive migration has to take place. The smaller a microservice is, the easier it is to replace it with a new implementation. Above a certain size a microservice may be difficult to replace, for it then poses the same challenges as a monolith. Replaceability thus limits the size of a microservice.

Transactions and Consistency

Transactions possess the so-called ACID characteristics:

- **Atomicity** indicates that a given transaction is either executed completely or not at all. In case of an error, all changes are reversed.

- **Consistency** means that data is consistent before and after the execution of a transaction—database constraints, for instance, are not violated.

- **Isolation** indicates that the operations of transactions are separated from each other.

- **Durability** indicates permanence: changes to the data are stored and are still available after a crash or other interruption of service.

Within a microservice, changes to a transaction can take place. Moreover, the consistency of data in a microservice can be guaranteed very easily. Beyond an individual microservice, this gets difficult, and overall coordination is necessary. Upon the rollback of a transaction all changes made by all microservices would have to be reversed. This is laborious and hard to implement, for the delivery of the decision that changes have to be reversed has to be guaranteed. However, communication within networks is unreliable. Until it is decided whether a change may take place, further changes to the data are barred. If additional changes have taken place, it might no longer be possible to reverse a certain change. However, when microservices are kept from introducing data changes for some time, system throughput is reduced.

However, when communications occur via messaging systems, transactions are possible (see section 8.4). With this approach, transactions are also possible without a close link between the microservices.

Consistency

In addition to transactions, data consistency is important. An order, for instance, also has to be recorded as revenue. Only then will revenue and order data be consistent. Data consistency can be achieved only through close coordination. Data consistency can hardly be guaranteed across microservices. This does not mean that the revenue for an order will not be recorded at all. However, it will likely not happen exactly at the same point of time and maybe not even within one minute of order processing because the communication occurs via the network—and is consequently slow and unreliable.

Data changes within a transaction and data consistency are only possible when all data being processed is part of the same microservice. Therefore, data changes determine the lower size limit for a microservice: when transactions are supposed to encompass several microservices and data consistency is required across several microservices, the microservices have been designed too small.

Compensation Transactions across Microservices

At least in the case of transactions there is an alternative: if a data change has to be rolled back in the end, compensation transactions can be used for that.

A classic example for a distributed transaction is a travel booking, which consists of a hotel, a rental car, and a flight. Either everything has to be booked together or nothing at all. Within real systems and also within microservices, this functionality is divided into three microservices because the three tasks are very different. Inquiries are sent to the different systems whether the desired hotel room, rental car, and flight are available. If all are available, everything is reserved. If, for instance, the hotel room suddenly becomes unavailable, the reservations for the flight and the rental car have to be cancelled. However, in the real world the concerned companies will likely demand a fee for the booking cancellation. Due to that, the cancellation is not only a technical event happening in the background like a transaction rollback but also a business process. This is much easier to represent with a compensation transaction. With this approach, transactions across several elements in microservice environments can also be implemented without the presence of a close technical link. A compensation transaction is just a normal service call. Technical as well as business reasons can lead to the use of mechanisms such as compensation transactions for microservices.

Summary

In conclusion, the following factors influence the size of a microservice (see Figure 3.1):

- The team size sets an upper limit; a microservice should never be so large that one very large team or several teams are required to work on it. Eventually, the teams are supposed to work and bring software into production independently of each other. This can only be achieved when each team works on a separate deployment unit—that is, a separate microservice. However, one team can work on several microservices.

- Modularization further limits the size of a microservice: The microservice should preferably be of a size that enables a developer to understand all its aspects and further develop it. Even smaller is of course better. This limit is below the team size: whatever one developer can still understand, a team should still be able to develop further.

- Replaceability reduces with the size of the microservice. Therefore, replaceability can influence the upper size limit for a microservice. This limit lies below the one set by modularization: when somebody decides to replace a microservice, this person has first of all to be able to understand the microservice.

- A lower limit is set by infrastructure: if it is too laborious to provide the necessary infrastructure for a microservice, the number of microservices should be kept rather small; consequently the size of each microservice will be larger.

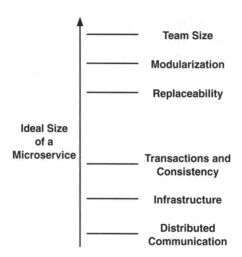

Figure 3.1 *Factors Influencing the Size of a Microservice*

- Similarly, distributed communication overhead increases with the number of microservices. For this reason, the size of microservices should not be set too small.

- Consistency of data and transactions can only be ensured within a micro-service. Therefore, microservices should not be so small that consistency and transactions must be ensured across several microservices.

These factors not only influence the size of microservices but also reflect a certain idea of microservices. According to this idea, the main advantages of microservices are independent deployment and the independent work of the different teams, along with the replaceability of microservices. The optimal size of a microservice can be deduced from these desired features.

However, there are also other reasons for microservices. When microservices are, for instance, introduced because of their independent scaling, a microservice size has to be chosen that ensures that each microservice is a unit, which has to scale independently.

How small or large a microservice can be, cannot be deduced solely from these criteria. This also depends on the technology being used. Especially the effort necessary for providing infrastructure for a microservice and the distributed commu-nication depends on the utilized technology. Chapter 14 looks at technologies, which make the development of very small services possible—denoted as nanoservices. These nanoservices have different advantages and disadvantages to microservices, which, for instance, are implemented using technologies presented in Chapter 13, "Example of a Microservice-based Architecture."

Thus, there is no ideal size. The actual microservice size will depend on the technology and the use case of an individual microservice.

Try and Experiment

How great is the effort required for the deployment of a microservice in your language, platform, and infrastructure?

- Is it just a simple process? Or is it a complex infrastructure containing application servers or other infrastructure elements?

- How can the effort for the deployment be reduced so that smaller microservices become possible?

Based on this information you can define a lower limit for the size of a microservice. Upper limits depend on team size and modularization, so you should also think of appropriate limits in those terms.

3.2 Conway's Law

Conway's Law[4] was coined by the American computer scientist Melvin Edward Conway and indicates the following:

> Any organization that designs a system (defined broadly) will produce a design whose structure is a copy of the organization's communication structure.

It is important to know that this law is meant to apply not only to software but to any kind of design. The communication structures that Conway mentions, do not have to be identical to the organization chart. Often there are informal communication structures, which also have to be considered in this context. In addition, the geographical distribution of teams can influence communication. After all it is much simpler to talk to a colleague who works in the same room or at least in the same office than with one working in a different city or even in a different time zone.

---

4. http://www.melconway.com/research/committees.html

Reasons for the Law

Conway's Law derives from the fact that each organizational unit designs a specific part of the architecture. If two architectural parts have an interface, coordination in regards to this interface is required—and, consequently, a communication relationship between the organizational units that are responsible for the respective parts of the architecture.

From Conway's Law it can also be deduced that design modularization is sensible. Via such a design, it is possible to ensure that not every team member has to constantly coordinate with every other team member. Instead the developers working on the same module can closely coordinate their efforts, while team members working on different modules only have to coordinate when they develop an interface—and even then only in regards to the specific design of the external features of this interface.

However, the communication relationships extend beyond that. It is much easier to collaborate with a team within the same building than with a team located in another city, another country, or even within a different time zone. Therefore, architectural parts having numerous communication relationships are better implemented by teams that are geographically close to each other, because it is easier for them to communicate with each other. In the end, the Conway's Law focuses not on the organization chart but on the real communication relationships.

By the way, Conway postulated that a large organization has numerous communication relationships. Thus communication becomes more difficult or even impossible in the end. As a consequence, the architecture can be increasingly affected and finally break down. In the end, having too many communication relationships is a real risk for a project.

The Law as Limitation

Normally Conway's Law is viewed as a limitation, especially from the perspective of software development. Let us assume that a project is modularized according to technical aspects (see Figure 3.2). All developers with a UI focus are grouped into one team, the developers with backend focus are put into a second team, and data bank experts make up the third team. This distribution has the advantage that all three teams consist of experts for the respective technology. This makes it easy and transparent to create this type of organization. Moreover, this distribution also appears logical. Team members can easily support each other, and technical exchange is also facilitated.

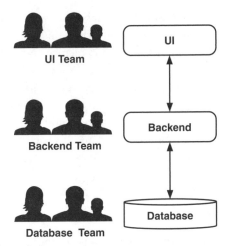

Figure 3.2 *Technical Project Distribution*

According to Conway's Law, it follows from such a distribution that the three teams will implement three technical layers: a UI, a backend, and a database. The chosen distribution corresponds to the organization, which is in fact sensibly built. However, this distribution has a decisive disadvantage: a typical feature requires changes to UI, backend, and database. The UI has to render the new features for the clients, the backend has to implement the logic, and the database has to create structures for the storage of the respective data. This results in the following disadvantages:

- The person wishing to have a feature implemented has to talk to all three teams.

- The teams have to coordinate their work and create new interfaces.

- The work of the different teams has to be coordinated in a manner that ensures that their efforts temporally fit together. The backend, for instance, cannot really work without getting input from the database, and the UI cannot work without input from the backend.

- When the teams work in sprints, these dependencies cause time delays: The database team generates in its first sprint the necessary changes, within the second sprint the backend team implements the logic, and in the third sprint the UI is dealt with. Therefore, it takes three sprints to implement a single feature.

In the end this approach creates a large number of dependencies as well as a high communication and coordination overhead. Thus this type of organization does not make much sense if the main goal is to implement new features as rapidly as possible.

Many teams following this approach do not realize its impact on architecture and do not consider this aspect further. This type of organization focuses instead on the notion that developers with similar skills should be grouped together within the organization. This organization becomes an obstacle to a design driven by the domain like microservices, whose development is not compatible with the division of teams into technical layers.

The Law as Enabler

However, Conway's Law can also be used to support approaches like microservices. If the goal is to develop individual components as independently of each other as possible, the system can be distributed into domain components. Based on these domain components, teams can be created. Figure 3.3 illustrates this principle: There are individual teams for product search, clients, and the order process. These teams work on their respective components, which can be technically divided into UI, back-end, and database. By the way, the domain components are not explicitly named in the figure, for they are identical to the team names. Components and teams are synonymous. This approach corresponds to the idea of so-called cross-functional teams, as proposed by methods such as Scrum. These teams should encompass different roles so that they can cover a large range of tasks. Only a team designed along such principles can be in charge of a component—from engineering requirements via implementation through to operation.

The division into technical artifacts and the interface between the artifacts can then be settled within the teams. In the easiest case, developers only have to talk to developers sitting next to them to do so. Between teams, coordination is more complex. However, inter-team coordination is not required very often, since features are ideally implemented by independent teams. Moreover, this approach creates thin interfaces between the components. This avoids laborious coordination across teams to define the interface.

Ultimately, the key message to be taken from Conway's Law is that architecture and organization are just two sides of the same coin. When this insight is cleverly put to use, the system will have a clear and useful architecture for the project. Architecture and organization have the common goal to ensure that teams can work in an unobstructed manner and with as little coordination overhead as possible.

The clean separation of functionality into components also facilitates maintenance. Since an individual team is responsible for individual functionality and component, this distribution will have long-term stability, and consequently the system will remain maintainable.

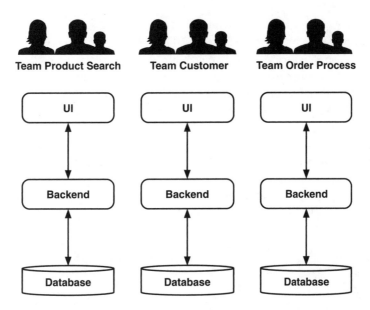

Figure 3.3 *Project by Domains*

   The teams need requirements to work upon. This means that the teams need to contact people who define the requirements. This affects the organization beyond the projects, for the requirements come from the departments of the enterprise, and these also according to Conway's Law have to correspond to the team structures within the project and the domain architecture. Conway's Law can be expanded beyond software development to the communication structures of the entire organization, including the users. To put it the other way round: the team structure within the project and consequently the architecture of a microservice system can follow from the organization of the departments of the enterprise.

The Law and Microservices

The previous discussion highlighted the relationship between architecture and organization of a project only in a general manner. It would be perfectly conceivable to align the architecture along functionalities and devise teams, each of which are in charge for a separate functionality without using microservices. In this case the project would develop a deployment monolith within which all functionalities are implemented. However, microservices support this approach. Section 3.1 already discussed that microservices offer technical independence. In conjunction with the division by domains, the teams become even more independent of each other and have even less need to coordinate their work. The technical coordination as well as the coordination concerning the domains can be reduced to the absolute minimum. This makes it far easier to work in parallel on numerous features and also to bring the features in production.

Microservices as a technical architecture are especially well suited to support the approach to devise a Conway's Law–based distribution of functionalities. In fact, exactly this aspect is an essential characteristic of a microservices-based architecture.

However, orienting the architecture according to the communication structures entails that a change to the one also requires a change of the other. This makes architectural changes between microservices more difficult and makes the overall process less flexible. Whenever a piece of functionality is moved from one microservice to another, this might have the consequence that another team has to take care of this functionality from that point on. This type of organizational change renders software changes more complex.

As a next step this chapter will address how the distribution by domain can best be implemented. Domain-driven design (DDD) is helpful for that.

Try and Experiment

Have a look at a project you know:

- What does the team structure look like?
  - Is it technically motivated, or is it divided by domain?
  - Would the structure have to be changed to implement a microservices-based approach?
  - How would it have to be changed?
- Is there a sensible way to distribute the architecture onto different teams? Eventually each team should be in charge of independent domain components and be able to implement features relating to them.
  - Which architectural changes would be necessary?
  - How laborious would the changes be?

3.3 Domain-Driven Design and Bounded Context

In his book of the same title, Eric Evans formulated domain-driven design (DDD)[5] as pattern language. It is a collection of connected design patterns and supposed to support software development especially in complex domains. In the following text, the names of design patterns from Evan's book are written in *italics*.

---

5. Eric Evans. 2003. *Domain-Driven Design: Tackling Complexity in the Heart of Software*. Boston: Addison-Wesley.

Domain-driven design is important for understanding microservices, for it supports the structuring of larger systems according to domains. Exactly such a model is necessary for the division of a system into microservices. Each microservice is meant to constitute a domain, which is designed in such a way that only one microservice has to be changed in order to implement changes or to introduce new features. Only then is the maximal benefit to be derived from independent development in different teams, as several features can be implemented in parallel without the need for extended coordination.

Ubiquitous Language

DDD defines a basis for how a model for a domain can be designed. An essential foundation of DDD is *Ubiquitous Language*. This expression denotes that the software should use exactly the same terms as the domain experts. This applies on all levels: in regards to code and variable names as well as for database schemas. This practice ensures that the software really encompasses and implements the critical domain elements. Let us assume for instance that there are express orders in an e-commerce system. One possibility would be to generate a Boolean value with the name "fast" in the order table. This creates the following problem: domain experts have to translate the term "express order," which they use on a daily basis, into "order with a specific Boolean value." They might not even know what Boolean values are. This renders any discussion of the model more difficult, for terms have to be constantly explained and related to each other. The better approach is to call the table within the database scheme "express order." In that case it is completely transparent how the domain terms are implemented in the system.

Building Blocks

To design a domain model, DDD identifies basic patterns:

- *Entity* is an object with an individual identity. In an e-commerce application, the customer or the items could be examples for *Entities*. *Entities* are typically stored in databases. However, this is only the technical implementation of the concept *Entity*. An *Entity* belongs in essence to the domain modeling like the other DDD concepts.

- *Value Objects* do not have their own identity. An address can be an example of a *Value Object*, for it makes only sense in the context of a specific customer and therefore does not have an independent identity.

- *Aggregates* are composite domain objects. They facilitate the handling of invariants and other conditions. An order, for instance, can be an *Aggregate* of order lines. This can be used to ensure that an order from a new customer does not exceed a certain value. This is a condition that has to be fulfilled by calculating values from the order lines so that the order as *Aggregate* can control these conditions.

- *Services* contain business logic. DDD focuses on modeling business logic as *Entities, Value Objects*, and *Aggregates*. However, logic accessing several such objects cannot be sensibly modeled using these objects. For these cases there are *Services*. The order process could be such a *Service*, for it needs access to items and customers and requires the *Entity* order.

- *Repositories* serve to access all *Entities* of a type. Typically, there is a persistency technology like a database behind a *Repository*.

- *Factories* are mostly useful to generate complex domain objects. This is especially the case when these contain for instance many associations.

Aggregates are of special importance in the context of microservices: within an *Aggregate* consistency can be enforced. Because consistency is necessary, parallel changes have to be coordinated in an *Aggregate*. Otherwise two parallel changes might endanger consistency. For instance, when two order positions are included in parallel into an order, consistency can be endangered. The order has already a value of €900 and is maximally allowed to reach €1000. If two order positions of €60 each are added in parallel, both might calculate a still acceptable total value of €960 based on the initial value of €900. Therefore, changes have to be serialized so that the final result of €1020 can be controlled. Accordingly, changes to *Aggregates* have to be serialized. For this reason, an *Aggregate* cannot be distributed across two microservices. In such a scenario consistency cannot be ensured. Consequently, *Aggregates* cannot be divided between microservices.

Bounded Context

Building blocks such as *Aggregate* represent for many people the core of DDD. DDD describes, along with strategic design, how different domain models interact and how more complex systems can be built up this way. This aspect of DDD is probably even more important than the building blocks. In any case it is the concept of DDD, which influences microservices.

The central element of strategic designs is the *Bounded Context*. The underlying reasoning is that each domain model is only sensible in certain limits within a system. In e-commerce, for instance, number, size, and weight of the ordered items are of interest in regards to delivery, for they influence delivery routes and costs. For accounting on the other hand prices and tax rates are relevant. A complex system consists of several *Bounded Contexts*. In this it resembles the way complex biological organisms are built out of individual cells, which are likewise separate entities with their own inner life.

Bounded Context: An Example

The customer from the e-commerce system shall serve as an example for a *Bounded Context* (see Figure 3.4). The different *Bounded Contexts* are Order, Delivery, and Billing. The component Order is responsible for the order process. The component Delivery implements the delivery process. The component Billing generates the bills.

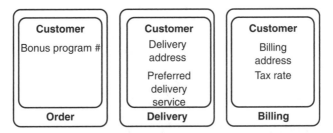

Figure 3.4 *Project by Domains*

Each of these Bounded Contexts requires certain customer data:

• Upon ordering the customer is supposed to be rewarded with points in a bonus program. In this Bounded Context the number of the customer has to be known to the bonus program.

• For Delivery the delivery address and the preferred delivery service of the customer are relevant.

• Finally, for generating the bill the billing address and the tax rate of the customer have to be known.

In this manner each *Bounded Context* has its own model of the customer. This renders it possible to independently change microservices. If for instance more information regarding the customer is necessary for generating bills, only changes to the *Bounded Context* billing are necessary.

It might be sensible to store basic information concerning the customer in a separate *Bounded Context*. Such fundamental data is probably sensible in many *Bounded Contexts*. To this purpose the *Bounded Contexts* can cooperate (see below).

(continued)

A universal model of the customer, however, is hardly sensible. It would be very complex since it would have to contain all information regarding the customer. Moreover, each change to customer information, which is necessary in a certain context, would concern the universal model. This would render such changes very complicated and would probably result in permanent changes to the model.

To illustrate the system setup in the different *Bounded Contexts* a *Context Map* can be used (see section 7.2). Each of the *Bounded Contexts* then can be implemented within one or several microservices.

Collaboration between *Bounded Contexts*

How are the individual *Bounded Contexts* connected? There are different possibilities:

- In case of a *Shared Kernel* the domain models share some common elements; however, in other areas they differ.

- *Customer/Supplier* means that a subsystem offers a domain model for the caller. The caller in this case is the client who determines the exact setup of the model.

- This is very different in the case of *Conformist*: The caller uses the same model as the subsystem, and the other model is thereby forced upon him. This approach is relatively easy, for there is no need for translation. One example is a standard software for a certain domain. The developers of this software likely know a lot about the domain since they have seen many different use cases. The caller can use this model to profit from the knowledge from the modeling.

- The *Anticorruption Layer* translates a domain model into another one so that both are completely decoupled. This enables the integration of legacy systems without having to take over the domain models. Often data modeling is not very meaningful in legacy systems.

- *Separate Ways* means that the two systems are not integrated, but stay independent of each other.

- In the case of *Open Host Service*, the *Bounded Context* offers special services everybody can use. In this way everybody can assemble their own integration. This is especially useful when an integration with numerous other systems is necessary and when the implementation of these integrations is too laborious.

- *Published Language* achieves similar things. It offers a certain domain modeling as a common language between the *Bounded Contexts*. Since it is widely used, this language can hardly be changed anymore afterwards.

Bounded Context and Microservices

Each microservice is meant to model one domain so that new features or changes have only to be implemented within one microservice. Such a model can be designed based on *Bounded Context.*

One team can work on one or several *Bounded Contexts*, which each serve as a foundation for one or several microservices. Changes and new features are supposed to concern typically only one *Bounded Context*—and thus only one team. This ensures that teams can work largely independently of each other. A *Bounded Context* can be divided into multiple microservices if that seems sensible. There can be technical reasons for that. For example, a certain part of a *Bounded Context* might have to be scaled up to a larger extent than the others. This is simpler if this part is separated into its own microservice. However, designing microservices that contain multiple *Bounded Contexts* should be avoided, for this entails that several new features might have to be implemented in one microservice. This interferes with the goal to develop features independently.

Nevertheless, it is possible that a special requirement comprises many *Bounded Contexts*—in that case additional coordination and communication will be required.

The coordination between teams can be regulated via different collaboration possibilities. These influence the independence of the teams as well: *Separate Ways, Anticorruption Layer* or *Open Host Service* offer a lot of independence. *Conformist* or *Customer/Supplier* on the other hand tie the domain models very closely together. For *Customer/Supplier* the teams have to coordinate their efforts closely: the supplier needs to understand the requirements of the customer. For *Conformist*, however, the teams do not need to coordinate: one team defines the model that the other team just uses unchanged (see Figure 3.5).

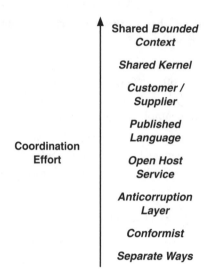

Figure 3.5 *Communication Effort of Different Collaborations*

As in the case of Conway's Law from section 3.2, it becomes very apparent that organization and architecture are very closely linked. When the architecture enables a distribution of the domains in which the implementation of new features only requires changes to a defined part of the architecture, these parts can be distributed to different teams in such a way that these teams can work largely independently of each other. DDD and especially *Bounded Context* demonstrate what such a distribution can look like and how the parts can work together and how they have to coordinate.

Large-Scale Structure

With large-scale structure, DDD also addresses the question how the system in its entirety can be viewed from the different *Bounded Contexts* with respect to microservices.

- A *System Metaphor* can serve to define the fundamental structure of the entire system. For example, an e-commerce system can orient itself according to the shopping process: the customer starts out looking for products, then he/she will compare items, select one item, and order it. This can give rise to three microservices: search, comparison, and order.

- A *Responsibility Layer* divides the system into layers with different responsibilities. Layers can call other layers only if those are located below them. This does not refer to a technical division into database, UI and logic. In an e-commerce system, domain layers might be (for example) the catalog, the order process, and billing. The catalog can call on the order process, and the order process can call on the generation of the bill. However, calls into the other direction are not permitted.

- *Evolving Order* suggests it is best not to determine the overall structure too rigidly. Instead, the order should arise from the individual components in a stepwise manner.

These approaches can provide an idea how the architecture of a system, which consists of different microservices, can be organized (see also Chapter 7, "Architecture of Microservice-based Systems").

Try and Experiment

Look at a project you know:

- Which *Bounded Contexts* can you identify?

- Generate an overview of the *Bounded Contexts* in a *Context Map*. Compare section 7.2.

- How do the Bounded Contexts cooperate? (Anticorruption Layer Customer/ Supplier etc.). Add this information to the Context Map.

- Would other mechanisms have been better at certain places? Why?

- How could the *Bounded Contexts* be sensibly distributed to teams so that features are implemented by independent teams?

These questions might be hard to answer because you need to get a new perspective on the system and how the domains are modeled in the system.

3.4 Why You Should Avoid a Canonical Data Model (Stefan Tilkov)

by Stefan Tilkov, innoQ

In recent times, I've been involved in a few architecture projects on the enterprise level again. If you've never been in that world, that is, if you've been focusing on individual systems so far, let me give you the gist of what this kind of environment is like. There are lots of meetings, more meetings, and even more meetings; there's an abundance of slide decks, packed with text and diagrams—none of that Presentation Zen nonsense, please. There are conceptual architecture frameworks, showing different perspectives; there are guidelines and reference architectures, enterprise-wide layering approaches, a little bit of SOA and EAI and ESB and portals and (lately) API talk thrown in for good measure. Vendors and system integrators and (of course) consultants all see their chance to exert influence on strategic decisions, making their products or themselves an integral part of the company's future strategy. It can be a very frustrating but (at least sometimes) also very rewarding experience: those wheels are very big and really hard to turn, but if you manage to turn them, the effect is significant.

It's also amazing to see how many of the things that cause problems when building large systems are repeated on the enterprise level. (We don't often make mistakes ... but if we do, we make them big!) My favorite one is the idea of establishing a canonical data model (CDM) for all of your interfaces.

If you haven't heard of this idea before, a quick summary is: Whatever kind of technology you're using (an ESB, a BPM platform, or just some assembly of services of some kind), you standardize the data models of the business objects you exchange. In its extreme (and very common) form, you end up with having just one kind of Person, Customer, Order, Product, etc., with a set of IDs, attributes, and associations everyone can agree on. It isn't hard to understand why that might seem a very compelling thing to attempt. After all, even a nontechnical manager will understand that the conversion from one data model to another whenever systems need to talk to each other is a complete waste of time. It's obviously a good idea to standardize. Then, anyone who happens to have a model that differs from the canonical one will have to implement a conversion to and from it just once, new systems can just use the CDM directly, and everyone will be able to communicate without further ado!

In fact, it's a horrible, horrible idea. Don't do it.

In his book on domain-driven design, Eric Evans gave a name to a concept that is obvious to anyone who has actually successfully built a larger system: the *Bounded Context*. This is a structuring mechanism that avoids having a single huge model for all of your application, simply because that (a) becomes unmanageable and (b) makes no sense to begin with. It recognizes that a Person or a Contract are different things in different contexts on a *conceptual level*. This is not an implementation problem—it's reality.

If this is true for a large system—and trust me, it is—it's infinitely more true for an enterprise-wide architecture. Of course you can argue that with a CDM, you're only standardizing the interface layer, but that doesn't change a thing. You're still trying to make everyone agree what a concept means, and my point is that you should recognize that not every single system has the same needs.

But isn't this all just pure theory? Who cares about this, anyway? The amazing thing is that organizations are excellent in generating a huge amount of work based on bad assumptions. The CDM (in the form I've described it here) requires coordination between all the parties that use a particular object in their interfaces (unless you trust that people will be able to just design the right thing from scratch on their own, which you should never do). You'll have meetings with some enterprise architect and a few representatives for specific systems, trying to agree what a customer is. You'll end up with something that has tons of optional attributes because all the participants insisted theirs need to be there, and with lots of things that are kind of weird because they reflect some system's internal restrictions. Despite the fact that it'll take you ages to agree on it, you'll end up with a zombie interface model will be universally hated by everyone who has to work with it.

So is a CDM a universally bad idea? Yes, unless you approach it differently. In many cases, I doubt a CDM's value in the first place and think you are better off with a different and less intrusive kind of specification. But if you want a CDM, here are a number of things you can do to address the problems you'll run into:

- Allow independent parts to be specified independently. If only one system is responsible for a particular part of your data model, leave it to the people to specify what it looks like canonically. Don't make them participate in meetings. If you're unsure whether the data model they create has a significant overlap with another group's, it probably hasn't.

- Standardize on formats and possibly fragments of data models. Don't try to come up with a consistent model of the world. Instead, create small buildings blocks. What I'm thinking of are e.g. small XML or JSON fragments, akin to microformats, that standardize small groups of attributes (I wouldn't call them business objects).

- Most importantly, don't push your model from a central team downwards or outwards to the individual teams. Instead, it should be the teams who decide to "pull" them into their own context when they believe they provide value. It's not you who's doing the really important stuff (even though that's a common delusion that's attached to the mighty Enterprise Architect title). Collect the data models the individual teams provide in a central location, if you must, and make them easy to browse and search. (Think of providing a big elastic search index as opposed to a central UML model.)

What you actually need to do as an enterprise architect is to get out of people's way. In many cases, a crucial ingredient to achieve this is to create as little centralization as possible. It shouldn't be your goal to make everyone do the same thing. It should be your goal to establish a minimal set of rules that enable people to work as independently as possible. A CDM of the kind I've described above is the exact opposite.

3.5 Microservices with a UI?

This book recommends that you equip microservices with a UI. The UI should offer the functionality of the microservice to the user. In this way, all changes in regards to one area of functionality can be implemented in one microservice—regardless of whether they concern the UI, the logic, or the database. However, microservice experts so far have different opinions in regards to the question of whether the integration of UI into microservices is really required. Ultimately, microservices should not be too large. And when logic is supposed to be used by multiple frontends, a microservice consisting of pure logic without a UI might be sensible. In addition, it is possible to implement the logic and the UI in two different microservices but to have them implemented by one team. This enables implementation of features without coordination across teams.

Focusing on microservices with a UI puts the main emphasis on the distribution of the domain logic instead of a distribution by technical aspects. Many architects are not familiar with the domain architecture, which is especially important for microservices-based architectures. Therefore, a design where the microservices contain the UI is helpful as a first approach in order to focus the architecture on the domains.

Technical Alternatives

Technically the UI can be implemented as Web UI. When the microservices have a RESTful-HTTP interface, the Web-UI and the RESTful-HTTP interface are very similar—both use HTTP as a protocol. The RESTful-HTTP interface delivers JSON or XML, the Web UI HTML. If the UI is a Single-Page Application, the JavaScript code is likewise delivered via HTTP and communicates with the logic via RESTful HTTP. In case of mobile clients, the technical implementation is more complicated. Section 8.1 explains this in detail. Technically a deployable artifact can deliver via an HTTP interface, JSON/XML, and HTML. In this way it implements the UI and allows other microservices to access the logic.

Self-Contained System

Instead of calling this approach "Microservice with UI" you can also call it "Self-Contained System" (SCS).[6] SCS define microservices as having about 100 lines of code, of which there might be more than one hundred in a complete project.

An SCS consists of many of those microservices and contains a UI. It should communicate with other SCSs asynchronously, if at all. Ideally each functionality should be implemented in just one SCS, and there should be no need for SCSs to communicate with each other. An alternative approach might be to integrate the SCSs at the UI-level.

In an entire system, there are then only five to 25 of these SCS. An SCS is something one team can easily deal with. Internally the SCS can be divided into multiple microservices.

The following definitions result from this reasoning:

- SCS is something a team works on and which represents a unit in the domain architecture. This can be an order process or a registration. It implements a sensible functionality, and the team can supplement the SCS with new features. An alternative name for a SCS is a vertical. The SCS distributes the architecture by domain. This is a vertical design in contrast to a horizontal design. A horizontal design would divide the system into layers, which are technically motivated—for instance UI, logic, or persistence.

- A microservice is a part of a SCS. It is a technical unit and can be independently deployed. This conforms with the microservice definition put forward in this book. However, the size given in the SCS world corresponds to what this book denotes as nanoservices (see Chapter 14).

- This book refers to nanoservices as units that are still individually deployable but make technical trade-offs in some areas to further reduce the size of the deployment units. For that reason, nanoservices do not share all technical characteristics of microservices.

SCS inspired the definition of microservices as put forward in this book. Still there is no reason not to separate the UI into a different artifact in case the microservice gets otherwise too large. Of course, it is more important that the microservice is small and thus maintainable than to integrate the UI. But the UI and logic should at least be implemented by the same team.

---

6. http://scs-architecture.org

3.6 Conclusion

Microservices are a modularization approach. For a deeper understanding of microservices, the different perspectives discussed in this chapter are very helpful:

- Section 3.1 focuses on the size of microservices. But a closer look reveals that the size of microservices itself is not that important, even though size is an influencing factor. However, this perspective provides a first impression of what a microservice should be. Team size, modularization, and replaceability of microservices each determine an upper size limit. The lower limit is determined by transactions, consistency, infrastructure, and distributed communication.

- Conway's Law (section 3.2) shows that the architecture and organization of a project are closely linked—in fact, they are nearly synonymous. Microservices can further improve the independence of teams and thus ideally support architectural designs that aim at the independent development of functionalities. Each team is responsible for a microservice and therefore for a certain part of a domain, so that the teams are largely independent concerning the implementation of new functionalities. Thus, in regards to domain logic there is hardly any need for coordination across teams. The requirement for technical coordination can likewise be reduced to a minimum because of the possibility for technical independence.

- In section 3.3 domain-driven design provides a very good impression as to what the distribution of domains in a project can look like and how the individual parts can be coordinated. Each microservice can represent a *Bounded Context*. This is a self-contained piece of domain logic with an independent domain model. Between the *Bounded Contexts* there are different possibilities for collaboration.

- Finally, section 3.5 demonstrates that microservices should contain a UI to be able to implement the changes for functionality within an individual microservice. This does not necessarily have to be a deployment unit; however, the UI and microservice should be in the responsibility of one team.

Together these different perspectives provide a balanced picture of what constitutes microservices and how they can function.

Essential Points

To put it differently: A successful project requires three components:

- an organization (This is supported by Conway's Law.)
- a technical approach (This can be microservices.)
- a domain design as offered by DDD and *Bounded Context*

The domain design is especially important for the long-term maintainability of the system.

Try and Experiment

Look at the three approaches for defining microservices: size, Conway's Law, and domain-driven design.

- Section 1.2 showed the most important advantages of microservices. Which of the goals to be achieved by microservices are best supported by the three definitions? DDD and Conway's Law lead, for instance, to a better time-to-market.

- Which of the three aspects is, in your opinion, the most important? Why?

Chapter 4

Reasons for Using Microservices

Microservices offer many benefits, and these are discussed in this chapter. A detailed understanding of the benefits enables a better evaluation of whether microservices represent a sensible approach in a given use case. The chapter continues the discussion from section 1.2 and explains the benefits in more detail.

Section 4.1 explains the technical benefits of microservices. However, microservices also influence the organization. This is described in section 4.2. Finally, section 4.3 addresses the benefits from a business perspective.

4.1 Technical Benefits

Microservices are an effective modularization technique. Calling one microservice from another requires the developer to consciously create code that communicates over the network. This does not happen by accident; a developer has to make that happen within the communication infrastructure. Consequently, dependencies between microservices do not creep in unintentionally; a developer has to generate them explicitly. Without microservices, it is easy for a developer to just use another class and unwittingly create a dependency that was not architecturally intended.

Let us assume, for instance, that in an e-commerce application the product search should be able to call the order process, but not the other way round. This ensures that the product search can be changed without influencing the order process, as the product search does not use the order process. Now a dependency between the product search and the order process is introduced, for example, because developers found a piece of functionality there that was useful for them. Consequently, the product search and order processes now depend on each other and can only be changed together.

Once undesired dependencies have started to creep into the system, additional dependencies rapidly accrue. The application architecture erodes. This erosion can normally only be prevented with the use of architecture management tools. Such tools have a model of the desired architecture and can discover when a developer has introduced an undesired dependency. The developer can then immediately remove the dependency before any harm is done and the architecture suffers. Appropriate tools are presented in section 7.2.

In a microservices-based architecture, the product search and order processes would be separate microservices. To create a dependency, the developer would have to explicitly implement it within the communication mechanisms. This presents a relatively high barrier and consequently does not normally happen unnoticed, even without architecture management tools. This reduces the chances that the architecture erodes because of dependencies between microservices. The microservice boundaries act like firewalls, which prevent architectural erosion. Microservices offer strong modularization because it is difficult to overstep the boundaries between modules.

Replacing Microservices

Working with old software systems poses a significant challenge in that further development of the software may be difficult due to poor code quality. It is often risky to replace the software. It may be unclear exactly how the software works, and the system may be very large. The larger the software system, the more effort is required to replace it. If the software is supporting important business processes, it may be nearly impossible to change it. The failure of these business processes can have a significant negative impact, and each software change risks a failure.

Although this is a fundamental problem, most software architectures are never really aimed at replacing software. However, microservices do support this goal; they can be replaced individually, since they are separate and small deployment units. Therefore, the technical prerequisites for a replacement are better. Eventually it is not necessary to replace a large software system, but only a small microservice. Whenever necessary, additional microservices can be replaced.

With the new microservices, the developers are not tied to the old technology stack, but free to use other technologies at will. If the microservice is also independent in a domain sense, the logic is easier to understand. The developer does not need to understand the entire system, just the functionality of an individual microservice. Knowledge regarding the domain is a prerequisite for the successful replacement of a microservice.

Moreover, microservices keep functioning when another microservice fails. Even if the replacement of a microservice leads to the temporary failure of one microservice, the system as a whole can keep operating. This reduces the risk associated with a replacement.

Sustainable Software Development

Starting a new software project is simple because there is not much code, the code structure is clean, and developers can make rapid progress. Over time, however, the architecture can erode and development becomes more difficult as its complexity increases. At some point, the software turns into a legacy system. As previously discussed, microservices prevent architectural erosion. When a microservice has turned into a legacy system, it can be replaced. This means that microservices can make sustainable software development possible and that a high level of productivity can be reached over the long term. However, in a microservice-based system, it can be the case that a lot of code has to be newly written. This will, of course, decrease productivity.

Handling Legacy

Replacing microservices is only possible if the system is already implemented in a microservice-based manner. However, the replacement and amendment of existing legacy applications can be made easier with microservices, too. The legacy applications only have to provide an interface that enables the microservice to communicate with the legacy application. Comprehensive code changes or the integration of new code components into the legacy system is not necessary. This can mean that code level integration can be avoided. Otherwise such integration is a big challenge in the case of legacy systems. Amending the system is particularly easy when a microservice can intercept the processing of all calls and process them itself. Such calls can be HTTP requests for the creation of web sites or REST calls.

In this situation, the microservice can complement the legacy system. There are different ways for this to happen:

- The microservice can process certain requests by itself while leaving others to the legacy system.

- Alternatively, the microservice can change the requests and then transfer them to the actual application.

This approach is similar to the SOA approach (see Chapter 6, "Microservices and SOA"), which deals with the comprehensive integration of different applications. When the applications are split into services, these services be orchestrated anew, and it is also possible to replace individual services with microservices.

An Example of Microservices and Legacy

The goal of a project was to modernize an existing Java e-commerce application. This involved the introduction of new technologies, for example new frameworks, to improve future software development productivity. After some time, it transpired that the effort required to integrate the new and old technologies would be huge. The new code had to be able to call the old one—and vice versa. This required technology integration in both directions. Transactions and database connections had to be shared, and security mechanisms had to be integrated. This integration would render the development of the new software more complicated and endanger the entire project.

Figure 4.1 shows the solution: the new system was developed completely independent of the old system. The only integration was provided by links that call certain behaviors in the old software—for instance, the addition of items to the shopping cart. The new system also had access to the same database as the old system. In hindsight, a shared database is not a good idea, as the database is an internal representation of the data of the old system. When this representation is placed at the disposal of another application, the principle of encapsulation[a] is violated (see section 9.1). The data structures will be difficult to change now that both the old system and the new system depend on them.

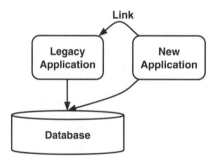

Figure 4.1 *Example of Legacy Integration*

The approach to develop the system separately solved the integration-related problems to a large extent. Developers could use new technological approaches without having to consider the old code and the old approaches. This enabled much more elegant solutions.

---

a. https://en.wikipedia.org/wiki/Encapsulation_(computer_programming)

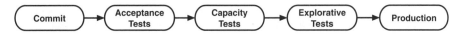

Figure 4.2 *Continuous Delivery Pipeline*

Continuous Delivery

Continuous delivery enables software to be brought into production regularly thanks to a simple, reproducible process. This is achieved via a continuous delivery pipeline (see Figure 4.2):

- In the commit phase, the software is compiled, the unit tests are run, and static code analysis might be performed.

- The automated acceptance tests in the next phase ensure that the software meets the business requirements and would be accepted by the customer.

- Capacity tests check that the software performs adequately to support the expected number of users. These tests are automated as well.

- Explorative tests, on the other hand, are performed manually and serve to test certain areas of the system such as new features or certain aspects like software security.

- Finally, the software is brought into production. Ideally, this process is also automated.

Software moves through the individual phases consecutively. For example, a build can successfully pass the acceptance tests. However, the capacity tests reveal that the software does not meet the requirements under the expected load. In this case, the software is never promoted to the remaining phases such as explorative tests or production.

A fully automated continuous delivery pipeline is ideal. However, software needs to get into production, and it may be necessary to optimize the current process step-by-step.

Continuous delivery is particular easy to realize with microservices.[1] Microservices are independent deployment units. Consequently, they can be brought into production independently of other services. This has a significant impact on the continuous delivery pipeline:

- The pipeline is faster as only small microservices have to be tested and brought into production at one time. This accelerates feedback. Rapid feedback is a

---

1. http://slideshare.net/ewolff/software-architecture-for-devops-andcontinuousdelivery

primary goal of continuous delivery. When it takes weeks for developers to know that their code has caused a problem in production, it will be difficult to become reacquainted with the code and to analyze the problem.

- The risk of deployment decreases. The deployed units are smaller and can therefore be more easily rolled back. Also microservice-based systems are designed to be resilient to failures in individual microservices. A failure in the deployment of a single microservice shouldn't impact the system as a whole.

- Measures to further reduce risk are easier to implement with smaller deployment units. For instance, in case of blue/green deployment, a new environment is built up with the new release. This is similar to canary releasing: in this approach, a single server is provided with the new software version. Only when this server runs successfully in production is the new version rolled out to the other servers. For a deployment monolith, this approach can be hard or nearly impossible to implement, as it requires a lot of resources for the large number of environments. With microservices, the required environments are much smaller, and the procedure is therefore easier.

- Test environments pose additional challenges. For instance, when a third-party system is used, the environment also has to contain a test version of this third-party system. With smaller deployment units, the demands on the environments are lower. The environments for microservices only have to integrate with the third-party systems that are necessary for the individual microservice. It is also possible to test the systems using mocks of the third-party systems. This helps with testing and is also an interesting method of testing microservices independently of each other.

Continuous delivery is one of the most important arguments for microservices. Many projects invest in migrating to microservices in order to facilitate the creation of a continuous delivery pipeline.

However, continuous delivery is also a prerequisite for microservices. Quickly bringing numerous microservices into production manually becomes unfeasible, and an automated approach is required. So microservices profit from continuous delivery and vice versa.[2]

---

2. http://slideshare.net/ewolff/continuous-delivery-and-micro-services-a-symbiosis

Scaling

Microservices are offered over network-reachable interfaces, which can be accessed, for instance, via HTTP or via a message solution. Each microservice can run on one server or on several. When the service runs on several servers, the load can be distributed across the different servers. It is also possible to install and run microservices on computers that perform differently. Each microservice can implement its own scaling.

In addition, caches can be placed in front of microservices. For REST-based microservices, it can be sufficient to use a generic HTTP cache. This significantly reduces the implementation effort for such a cache. The HTTP protocol contains comprehensive support for caching, which is very helpful in this context.

Furthermore, it might be possible to install microservices at different locations within the network in order to bring them closer to the caller. In the case of world-wide distributed cloud environments, it no longer matters in which computing center the microservices run. When the microservice infrastructure uses several computing centers and always processes calls in the nearest computing center, the architecture can significantly reduce the response times. Also, static content can be delivered by a CDN (content delivery network), whose servers are located even closer to the users.

However, improved scaling and support for caching cannot work miracles: microservices result in a distributed architecture. Calls via the network are a lot slower than local calls. From a pure performance perspective, it might be better to combine several microservices or to use technologies that focus on local calls (see Chapter 14, "Technologies for Nanoservices").

Robustness

Theoretically, a microservices-based architecture should be less reliable than other architectural approaches. Microservices are, after all, distributed systems, so there is an inherent risk of network failures adding to the usual sources of errors. Also, microservices run on several servers, increasing the likelihood of hardware failures.

To ensure high availability, a microservices-based architecture has to be correctly designed. The communication between microservices has to form a kind of firewall: The failure of a microservice should not propagate. This prevents problems from arising in an individual microservice and leading to a failure of the entire system.

To achieve this, a microservice which is calling another microservice has to somehow keep working when a failure occurs. One way to do this might be to assume some default values. Alternatively, the failure might lead to a graceful degradation such as some sort of reduced service.

How a failure is dealt with technically can be critical: the operating-system–level timeout for TCP/IP connections is often set to five minutes, for example. If, due to the failure of a microservice, requests run into this timeout, the thread is blocked for five minutes. At some point, all threads will be blocked. If that happens, the calling system might fail, as it cannot do anything else apart from wait for timeouts. This can be avoided by specifying shorter timeouts for the calls.

These concepts have been around much longer than the concept of microservices. The book *Release It*[3] describes, in detail, these sorts of challenges and approaches for solving them. When these approaches are implemented, microservice-based systems can tolerate the failure of entire microservices and therefore become more robust than a deployment monolith.

When compared to deployment monoliths, microservices have the additional benefit that they distribute the system into multiple processes. These processes are better isolated from each other. A deployment monolith only starts one process, and therefore a memory leak or a piece of functionality using up a lot of computing resources can make the whole system fail. Often, these sorts of errors are simple programming mistakes or slips. The distribution into microservices prevents such situations, as only a single microservice would be failing in such a scenario.

Free Technology Choice

Microservices offer technological freedom. Since microservices only communicate via the network, they can be implemented in any language and platform as long as communication with other microservices is possible. This free technology choice can be used to test out new technologies without running big risks. As a test, one can use the new technology in a single microservice. If the technology does not perform according to expectations, only this one microservice has to be rewritten. In addition, problems arising from the failure will be limited.

The free technology choice means that developers really can use new technologies in production. This can have positive effects on both motivation and recruitment because developers typically enjoy using new technologies.

This choice also enables the most appropriate technology to be used for each problem. A different programming language or a certain framework can be used to implement specific parts of the system. It is even possible for an individual

---

3. Michael T. Nygard. 2007. *Release It!: Design and Deploy Production-Ready Software*. Raleigh, N.C.: Pragmatic Programmers.

microservice to use a specific database or persistence technology, although in this situation, backup and disaster recovery mechanisms will need to be considered and implemented.

Free technology is an option—it does not have to be used. Technologies can also be imposed for all microservices in a project so that each microservice is bound to a specific technology stack. Compare this with a deployment monolith, which inherently narrows the choices developers have. For example, in Java applications, only one version of each library can be used. This means that not only the libraries used but even the versions used have to be set in a deployment monolith. Microservices do not impose such technical limitations.

Independence

Decisions regarding technology and putting new versions into production only concern individual microservices. This makes microservices very independent of each other, but there has to be some common technical basis. The installation of microservices should be automated, there should be a Continuous Delivery pipeline for each microservices, and microservices should adhere to the monitoring specifications. However, within these parameters microservices can implement a practically unlimited choice of technical approaches. Due to the greater technological freedom, less coordination between microservices is necessary.

4.2 Organizational Benefits

Microservices are an architectural approach, and you could be forgiven for thinking that they only benefit software development and structure. However, due to Conway's Law (see section 3.2), architecture also affects team communication, and thus the organization.

Microservices can achieve a high level of technical independence, as the last section (4.1) discussed. When a team within an organization is in full charge of a microservice, the team can make full use of this technical independence. However, the team also has the full responsibility if a microservice malfunctions or fails in production.

So, microservices support team independence. The technical basis enables teams to work on the different microservices with little coordination. This provides the foundation for the independent work of the teams.

In other projects, technology or architecture have to be decided centrally, since the individual teams and modules are bound to these decisions due to technical restrictions. It might just be impossible to use two different libraries or even two different versions of one library within one deployment monolith. Therefore, central coordination is mandatory. For microservices, the situation is different, and this makes self-organization possible. However, a global coordination might still be sensible so that, for example, a company is able to perform an update including all components because of a security problem with a library.

Teams have more responsibilities: they decide the architecture of their microservices. They cannot hand over this responsibility to a central function. This means they also have to take responsibility for the consequences, since they are responsible for the microservice.

The Scala Decision

In a project employing a microservice-based approach, the central architecture group was tasked with deciding whether one of the teams could use the Scala programming language. The group would have to decide whether the team could solve its problems more efficiently by using Scala, or whether the use of Scala might create additional problems. Eventually, the decision was delegated to the team, since the team has to take responsibility for its microservice. They have to deal with the consequences if Scala does not fulfill the demands of production or does not support efficient software development. They have the investment of getting familiar with Scala first and have to estimate whether this effort will pay off in the end. Likewise, they have a problem if suddenly all the Scala developers leave the project or switch to another team. To have the responsibility for this decision lie with the central architecture group is, strictly speaking, not even possible, since the group is not directly affected by the consequences. Therefore, the team just has to decide by itself. The team has to include all team members in the decision, including the product owner, who will suffer if the decision results in low productivity.

This approach represents a significant change to traditional forms of organization where the central architecture group enforces the technology stack to be used by everybody. In this type of organization, the individual teams are not responsible for decisions or nonfunctional requirements like availability, performance, or scalability. In a classical architecture, the nonfunctional properties can only be handled centrally, since they can only be guaranteed by the common foundations of the entire system. When microservices do not force a common foundation anymore, these decisions can be distributed to the teams, enabling greater self-reliance and independence.

Smaller Projects

Microservices enable large projects to be divided into a number of smaller projects. As the individual microservices are largely independent of each other, the need for central coordination is reduced. This reduces the need for a large, centralized project management function with its associated communication overhead. When microservices enable the division of a large organization into several smaller ones, the need for communication reduces. This makes it possible for teams to focus more of their efforts on the implementation of requirements.

Large projects fail more frequently than smaller projects, so it is better when a large project can be divided into multiple smaller projects. The smaller scope of the individual projects enables more precise estimations. Better estimations improve planning and decrease risk. Even if the estimation is wrong, the impact is lower. Added to the greater flexibility that microservices offer, this can speed up and facilitate the process of decision making, particularly because the associated risk is so much lower.

4.3 Benefits from a Business Perspective

The previously discussed organizational benefits also lead to business advantages; the projects are less risky, and coordination between teams needs to be less intense so the teams can work more efficiently.

Parallel Work on Stories

The distribution into microservices enables work on different stories to occur in parallel (see Figure 4.3). Each team works on a story that only affects their own microservice. Consequently, the teams can work independently, and the system as a whole can be simultaneously expanded in different places. This eventually scales the agile process. However, scaling does not take place at the level of the development processes, but is facilitated by the architecture and the independence of the teams. Changes and deployments of individual microservices are possible without complex coordination. Therefore, teams can work independently. When a team is slower or encounters obstacles, this does not negatively influence the other teams. Therefore, the risk associated with the project is further reduced.

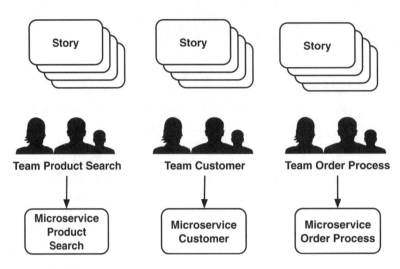

Figure 4.3 *Example of Legacy Integration*

An unambiguous domain-based design and the assignment of one developer team per microservice can scale the development or project organization with the number of teams.

It is possible that certain changes will impact several microservices and therefore several teams. For example, only certain customers are allowed to order certain types of product—for instance, because of age restrictions. In case of the architecture depicted in Figure 4.3, changes to all microservices would be necessary to implement this feature. The Customer microservice would have to store the data about whether a customer is of legal age. Product search should hide or label the products prohibited for underage customers. Finally, the order process has to prevent the ordering of prohibited products by underage customers. These changes have to be coordinated. Coordination is especially important when one microservice calls another. In that situation, the microservice being called has to be changed first so that the caller can use the new features.

This problem can certainly be solved, although one could argue that the outlined architecture is not optimal. If the architecture is geared to the business processes, the changes could be limited to just the order process. Eventually, only the ordering is to be prohibited, not searching. The information about whether a certain client is allowed to order or not should also be within the responsibility of the order process. Which architecture, and consequently which team distribution, is the right one depends on the requirements, microservices, and teams in question.

If the architecture has been selected appropriately, microservices can support agility well. This is certainly a good reason, from a business perspective, to use a microservice-based architecture.

4.4 Conclusion

In summary, microservices lead to the following technical benefits (section 4.1):

- **Strong modularization** ensures that dependencies between microservices cannot easily creep in.
- Microservices can be **easily replaced**.
- The strong modularization and the replaceability of microservices leads to a **sustained speed of development**: the architecture remains stable, and microservices that cannot be maintained any longer can be replaced. Thus, the quality of the system remains high in the long run, so that the system stays maintainable.
- **Legacy systems** can be supplemented with microservices without the need to carry around all the ballast that has accumulated in the legacy system. Therefore, microservices are good to use when dealing with legacy systems.
- Since microservices are small deployment units, a **continuous delivery pipeline** is much easier to set up.
- Microservices can be **scaled** independently.
- If microservices are implemented in line with established approaches, the system will end up more **robust**.
- Each microservice can be implemented in a different programming language and with a different **technology**.
- Therefore, microservices are largely **independent** of each other on a technical level.

The technical independence affects the organization (section 4.2) in that the teams can work independently and on their own authority. There is less need for central coordination. This means that large projects can be replaced by a collection of small projects, which positively affects both risk and coordination.

From a business perspective, just the effects on risk are already positive (section 4.3). However, it is even more attractive that the microservice-based architecture enables the scaling of agile processes without requiring an excessive amount of coordination and communication.

Essential Points

- There are a number of technical benefits that range from scalability and robustness to sustainable development.

- Technical independence results in benefits at an organizational level. Teams become independent.

- The technical and organizational benefits result in benefits at the business level: lower risk and faster implementation of more features.

Try and Experiment

Look at a project you know:

- Why are microservices useful in this scenario? Evaluate each benefit by assigning points (1 = no real benefit; 10 = significant benefit). The possible benefits are listed in the conclusion of this chapter.

- What would the project look like with or without the use of microservices?

- Develop a discussion of the benefits of microservices from the perspective of an architect, a developer, a project leader, and the customer for the project. The technical benefits will be more of interest to the developers and architects, while the organizational and business benefits matter more for project leaders and customers. Which benefits do you emphasize most for the different groups?

- Visualize the current domain design in your project or product.

  - Which teams are responsible for which parts of the project? Where do you see overlap?

  - How should teams be allocated to product features and services to ensure that they can operate largely independently?

Chapter 5

Challenges

The separation of a system into microservices makes the system as a whole more complex. This leads to challenges at the technical level (see section 5.1)—for instance, high latency times in the network or the failure of individual services. There are also a number of things to consider at the software architecture level—for instance, it can be difficult to move functionality between different microservices (section 5.2). Finally, there are many more components to be independently delivered—making operations and infrastructure more complex (section 5.3). These challenges have to be dealt with when introducing microservices. The measures described in the following chapters explain how to handle these challenges.

5.1 Technical Challenges

Microservices are distributed systems with calls between microservices going via the network. This can negatively impact both the response time and latency of microservices. The previously mentioned first rule for distributed objects[1] states that objects, where possible, should not be distributed (see section 3.1).

The reason for that is illustrated in Figure 5.1. A call has to go via the network to reach the server, is processed there, and has to then return to the caller. The latency just for network communication can be around 0.5 ms in a computing

---

1. http://martinfowler.com/bliki/FirstLaw.html

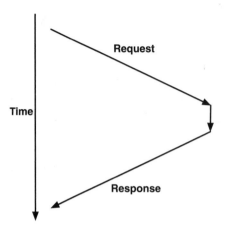

Figure 5.1 *Latency for a Call via the Network*

center (see here).[2] Within this period of time a processor running at 3 Ghz can process about 1.5 million instructions. When computation is redistributed to another node, it should be checked to find out whether local processing of the request might be faster. Latency can further increase because of parameter marshaling and unmarshaling for the call and for the result of the call. Network optimizations or connecting nodes to the same network switch can improve the situation.

The first rule for distributed objects and the warning to be aware of regarding the latency within the network dates back to the time when CORBA (Common Object Request Broker Architecture) and EJB (Enterprise JavaBeans) were used in the early two-thousands. These technologies were often used for distributed three-tier architectures (see Figure 5.2). For every client request the web tier only supplies the HTML for rendering the page. The logic resides on another server, which is called via the network. Data is stored in the database, and this is typically done on another server. When only data is to be shown, there is little happening in the middle tier. The data is not processed, just forwarded. For performance and latency reasons, it would be much better to keep the logic on the same server as the web tier. Although splitting the tiers between servers enables the independent scaling of the middle tier, the system does not get faster by doing this for situations where the middle tier has little to do.

---

2. https://www.cs.cornell.edu/projects/ladis2009/talks/dean-keynote-ladis2009.pdf

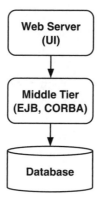

Figure 5.2 *Three-Tier Architecture*

For microservices the situation is different, as the UI is contained in the microservice. Calls between microservices only take place when microservices need the functionality offered by other microservices. If that is often the case, this might indicate that there are architectural problems, as microservices should be largely independent of each other.

In reality, microservice-based architectures function in spite[3] of the challenges related to distribution. However, in order to improve performance and reduce latency, microservices should not communicate with each other too much.

Code Dependencies

A significant benefit of a microservice-based architecture is the ability to independently deploy the individual services. However, this benefit can be undone by code dependencies. If a library is used by several microservices and a new version of this library is supposed to be rolled out, a coordinated deployment of several microservices might be required—a situation that should be avoided. This scenario can easily occur because of binary dependencies where different versions are not compatible any more. The deployment has to be timed such that all microservices are rolled out in a certain time interval and in a defined order. The code dependency also has to be changed in all microservices, a process that has to be prioritized and coordinated across all the teams involved. A binary-level dependency is a very tight technical coupling, which leads to a very tight organizational coupling.

---

3. http://martinfowler.com/articles/distributed-objects-microservices.html

Therefore, microservices should adhere to a "shared nothing" approach where microservices do not possess shared code. Microservices should instead accept code redundancy and resist the urge to reuse code in order to avoid a close organizational link.

Code dependencies can be acceptable in certain situations. For instance, when a microservice offers a client library that supports callers using the microservice, this does not necessarily have negative consequences. The library will depend on the interface of the microservice. If the interface is changed in a backward-compatible manner, a caller having an old version of the client library can still use the micro-service. The deployment remains uncoupled. However, the client library can be the starting point to a code dependency. For instance, if the client library contains domain objects, this can be a problem. In fact, if the client library contains the same code for the domain objects that is also used internally, then changes to the internal model will affect the clients. This might mean they have to be deployed again. If the domain object contains logic, this logic can only be modified when all clients are likewise deployed anew. This also violates the principle of independently deployable microservices.

Consequences of Code Dependencies

Here is an example of the effects of code dependencies: User authentication is a centralized function, which all services use. A project has developed the ser-vice implementing authentication. Nowadays there are open-source projects, which implement such things (section 7.14), so a home-grown implementa-tion is rarely sensible any more. In that project each microservice could use a library that makes it easier to use the authentication service. This means that all microservices have a code dependency on the authentication service. Changes to the authentication service might require that the library be rolled out again. This in turn means that all microservices have to be modified and rolled out again as well. In addition, the deployments of the microservices and the authentication service have to be coordinated. This can easily cost a two-digit number of work days. It becomes very difficult to modify the authentication service due to the code dependency. If the authentication ser-vice could be deployed quickly and if there were no code dependencies, which couple the deployment of the microservices and the authentication service, the problem would be solved.

Unreliable Communication

Communication between microservices occurs over the network and is therefore unreliable. Additionally, individual microservices can fail. To ensure that a microservice failure does not lead to a failure of the entire system, the remaining microservices must compensate for the failure and enable the system to continue. However, to achieve this goal, the quality of the services may have to be degraded, for example, by using default or cached values or limiting the usable functionality (section 9.5).

This problem cannot be completely solved on a technical level. For instance, the availability of a microservice can be improved by using hardware with high availability. However, this increases costs and is not a complete solution; in some respects, it can even increase risk. If the microservice fails despite highly available hardware and the failure propagates across the entire system, a complete failure occurs. Therefore, the microservices should still compensate for the failure of the highly available microservice.

In addition, the threshold between a technical and a domain problem is crossed. Take an automated teller machine (ATM) as an example: When the ATM cannot retrieve a customer's account balance, there are two ways to handle the situation. The ATM could refuse the withdrawal. Although this is a safe option, it will annoy the customer and reduce revenue. Alternatively, the ATM could hand out the money—maybe up to a certain upper limit. Which option should be implemented is a business decision. Somebody has to decide whether it is preferable to play it safe, even if it means foregoing some revenue and annoying customers, or to run a certain risk and possibly pay out too much money.

Technology Pluralism

The technology freedom of microservices can result in a project using many different technologies. The microservices do not need to have shared technology; however, the lack of common technology can lead to increasingly complexity in the system as a whole. Each team masters the technologies that are used in their own microservice. However, the large number of technologies and approaches used can cause the system to reach a level of complexity such that no individual developer or team can understand all of it any more. Often such a general understanding is not necessary since each team only needs to understand its own microservice. However, when it becomes necessary to look at the entire system—for example, from a certain limited perspective such as operations—this complexity might pose a problem. In this situation, unification can be a sensible countermeasure. This does not mean that the technology stack has to be completely uniform but that certain parts should be uniform or that the individual microservices should behave in a uniform manner. For instance, a uniform logging framework might be defined. The alternative is to define just a uniform format for logging. Then different logging frameworks could be used that implement the uniform format differently. Also a common technical basis like the JVM (Java Virtual Machine) can be decided upon for operational reasons without setting the programming languages.

5.2 Architecture

The architecture of a microservice-based system divides the domain-based pieces of functionality among the microservices. To understand the architecture at this level, dependencies and communication relationships between the microservices have to be known. Analyzing communication relationships is difficult. For large deployment monoliths there are tools that read source code or even executables and can generate diagrams visualizing modules and relationships. This makes it possible to verify the implemented architecture, adjust it towards the planned architecture, and follow the evolution of the architecture over time. Such overviews are central for architectural work; however, they are difficult to generate when using microservices as the respective tools are lacking—but there are solutions. Section 7.2 discusses these in detail.

Architecture = Organization

A key concept that microservices are based on is that organization and architecture are the same. Microservices exploit this situation to implement the architecture. The organization is structured in a way that makes the architecture implementation easy. However, the downside of this is that an architecture refactoring can require changes to the organization. This makes architectural changes more difficult. This is not only a problem of microservices; Conway's Law (section 3.2) applies to all projects. However, other projects are often not aware of the law and its implications. Therefore, they do not use the law productively and cannot estimate the organizational problems caused by architectural changes.

Architecture and Requirements

The architecture also influences the independent development of individual microservices and the independent streams of stories. When the domain-based distribution of microservices is not optimal, requirements might influence more than one microservice and therefore more than one team. This increases the coordination required between the different teams and microservices. This negatively influences productivity and undoes one of the primary reasons for the introduction of microservices.

With microservices the architecture influences not only software quality, but also the organization and the ability of teams to work independently and therefore productivity. Designing an optimal architecture is even more important since mistakes have far-reaching consequences.

Many projects do not pay sufficient attention to domain architecture, often much less than they pay to technical architecture. Most architects are not as experienced with domain architecture as with technical architecture. This situation can cause significant problems in the implementation of microservice-based approaches. The splitting of functionality into different microservices and therefore into the areas of responsibility for the different teams has to be performed according to domain criteria.

Refactoring

Refactoring a single microservice is straightforward since microservices are small. They can also be easily replaced and reimplemented.

Between microservices the situation is different. Transferring functionality from one microservice to another is difficult. The functionality has to be moved into a different deployment unit. This is always more difficult than moving functionality within the same unit. Technologies can be different between different microservices. Microservices can use different libraries and even different programming languages. In such cases, the functionality must be newly implemented in the technology of the other microservice and subsequently transferred into this microservice. However, this is far more complex than moving code within a microservice.

Agile Architecture

Microservices enable new product features to be rapidly delivered to end users and for development teams to reach a sustainable development speed. This is a particular benefit when there are numerous and hard-to-predict requirements. This is exactly the environment where microservices are at home. Changes to a microservice are also very simple. However, adjusting the architecture of the system, for instance, by moving around functionality, is not so simple.

Often the first attempt at the architecture of a system in not optimal. During implementation the team learns a lot about the domain. In a second attempt, it will be much more capable of designing an appropriate architecture. Most projects suffering from bad architecture had a good architecture at the outset based on the state of knowledge at that time. However, as the project progressed, it became clear that requirements were misunderstood, and new requirements arose to the point where the initial architecture stopped fitting. Problems arise when this does not lead to changes. If the project just continues with a more and more inappropriate architecture, at some point the architecture will not fit at all. This can be avoided by adjusting the architecture step by step, adapting to the changed requirements based on the current state of knowledge. The ability to change and adjust architecture in line with new requirements is central to this. However, the ability to change the architecture at the level of the entire system is a weakness of microservices while changes within microservices are very simple.

Summary

When using microservices, architecture is even more important than in other systems as it also influences the organization and the ability to independently work on requirements. At the same time, microservices offer many benefits in situations where requirements are unclear and architecture therefore has to be changeable. Unfortunately, the interplay between microservices is hard to modify since the distribution into microservices is quite rigid because of the distributed communication between them. Besides, as microservices can be implemented with different technologies, it gets difficult to move functionality around. On the other hand, changes to individual microservices or their replacement are very simple.

5.3 Infrastructure and Operations

Microservices are supposed to be brought into production independently of each other and should be able to use their own technology stacks. For these reasons each microservice usually resides on its own server. This is the only way to ensure complete technological independence. It is not possible to handle the number of systems required for this approach using hardware servers. Even with virtualization the management of such an environment remains difficult. The number of virtual machines required can be higher than might otherwise be used by the entire IT function of a business. When there are hundreds of microservices, there are also hundreds of virtual machines required, and for some of them, load balancing to distributed work across multiple instances. This requires automation and appropriate infrastructure that is capable of generating a large number of virtual machines.

Continuous Delivery Pipelines

Beyond what is required in production each microservice requires additional infrastructure; it needs its own continuous delivery pipeline so that it can be brought into production independently of other microservices. This means that appropriate test environments and automation scripts are necessary. The large number of pipelines brings about additional challenges: The pipelines have to be built up and maintained. To reduce expense, they also need to be largely standardized.

Monitoring

Each microservice also needs to be monitored. This is the only way to diagnose problems with the service at runtime. With a deployment monolith it is relatively straightforward to monitor the system. When problems arise, the administrator can log into the system and use specific tools to analyze errors. Microservice-based systems contain so many systems that this approach is no longer feasible. Consequently, there has to be a monitoring system that brings monitoring information from all the services together. This information should include not only the typical information from the operating system and the I/O to the hard disc and to the network, but also a view into the application should be possible based on application metrics. This is the only way for developers to find out where the application has to be optimized and where problems exist currently.

Version Control

Finally, every microservice has to be stored under version control independent of other microservices. Only software that is separately versioned can be brought into production individually. When two software modules are versioned together, they should always be brought into production together. If they are not, then a change might have affected both modules—meaning that both services should be newly delivered. Moreover, if an old version of one of the services is in production, it is not clear whether an update is necessary or whether the new version does not contain changes; after all, the new version might only have contained changes in the other microservice.

For deployment monoliths a lower number of servers, environments, and projects in version control would be necessary. This reduces complexity. Operation and infrastructure requirements are much higher in a microservices environment. Dealing with this complexity is the biggest challenge when introducing microservices.

5.4 Conclusion

This chapter discussed the different challenges associated with microservice-based architectures. At a technical level (section 5.1) the challenges mostly revolve around the fact that microservices are distributed systems, which makes ensuring good system performance and reliability more difficult. Technical complexity also increases because of the variety of technologies used. Furthermore, code dependencies can render the independent deployment of microservices impossible.

The architecture of a microservice-based system (section 5.2) is extremely important because of its impact on the organization and the ability to have parallel implementation of multiple stories. At the same time, changes to the interplay of microservices is difficult. Functionality cannot easily be transferred from one microservice to another. Classes within a project can often be moved with support from development tools, but in the case of microservices manual work is necessary. The interface to the code changes—from local calls to communication between microservices—and this increases the effort required. Finally, microservices can be written in different programming languages—in such situations moving code means that it has to be rewritten.

Changes to system architecture are often necessary because of unclear requirements. Even with clear requirements, the team continuously improves its knowledge about the system and its domain. In circumstances where the use of microservices is particularly beneficial because of rapid and independent deployments, architecture should be made especially easy to change. Within microservices changes are indeed easy to implement; however, between microservices they are very laborious.

Finally, infrastructure complexity increases because of the larger number of services (section 5.3) since more servers, more projects in version control, and more continuous delivery pipelines are required. This is a primary challenge encountered with microservice-based architectures.

Part III of the book will show solutions to these challenges.

Essential Points

- Microservices are distributed systems. This makes them technically complex.

- A good architecture is very important because of its impact on the organization. While the architecture is easy to modify within microservices, the interplay between microservices is hard to change.

- Due to the number of microservices, more infrastructure is required—for example, in terms of server environments, continuous delivery pipelines, and projects in version control.

Try and Experiment

- Choose one of the scenarios from Chapter 2, "Microservices Scenarios," or a project you know:

  - What are the likely challenges? Evaluate these challenges. The conclusion of this chapter highlights the different challenges in a compressed manner.

  - Which of the challenges poses the biggest risk? Why?

  - Are there ways to use microservices in a manner which maximizes the benefits and minimizes the downsides? For example, can heterogeneous technology stacks be avoided?

Chapter 6

Microservices and SOA

At first glance microservices and SOA (service-oriented architecture) seem to have a lot in common, for both approaches focus on the modularization of large systems into services. Are SOA and microservices actually the same or are there differences? Answering this question helps us to get an in-depth understanding of microservices, and some of the concepts from the SOA field are interesting for microservice-based architectures. An SOA approach can be advantageous when migrating to microservices. It separates the functionality of the old applications into services that can then be replaced or supplemented by microservices.

Section 6.1 defines the term "SOA" as well as the term "service" within the context of SOA. Section 6.2 extends this topic by highlighting the differences between SOA and microservices.

6.1 What Is SOA?

SOA and microservices have one thing in common: neither has a clear definition. This section looks only at one possible definition. Some definitions would suggest that SOA and microservices are identical. In the end, both approaches are based on services and the distribution of applications into services.

The term "service" is central to SOA.

An SOA service should have the following characteristics:

- It should implement an individual piece of the domain.

- It should be possible to use it independently.

- It should be available over the network.

- Each service has an interface. Knowledge about the interface is sufficient to use the service.

- The service can be used by different programming languages and platforms.

- To make it easy to use, the service is registered in a directory. To locate and use the service, clients search this directory at run time.

- The service should be coarse grained in order to reduce dependencies. Small services can only implement useful functionality when used in conjunction with other services. Therefore, SOA focuses on larger services.

SOA services do not need to be newly implemented; they may already be present in company applications. Introducing SOA requires these services to be made available outside of those applications. Splitting applications into services means they can be used in different ways. This is supposed to improve the flexibility of the overall IT and is the goal of SOA. By splitting applications into individual services it is possible to reuse services during the implementation of business processes. This simply requires the orchestration of the individual services.

Figure 6.1 shows a possible SOA landscape. Like the previous examples this one comes from the field of e-commerce. There are different systems in the SOA landscape:

- The *CRM* (customer relationship management) is an application that stores essential information about customers. This information includes not only contact details but also the history of all transactions with the

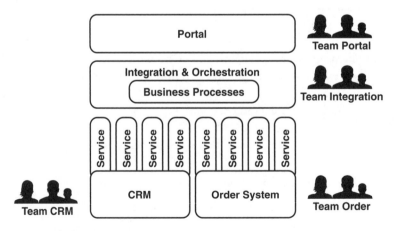

Figure 6.1 *Overview of an SOA Landscape*

customer—telephone calls as well as emails and orders. The CRM exposes services that, for instance, support the creation of a new customer, provide information about a customer, or generate reports for all customers.

- The *order system* is responsible for order processing. It can receive new orders, provide information about the status of an order, and cancel an order. This system provides access to the different pieces of functionality via individual services. These services may have been added as additional interfaces to the system after the first version was put into production.

- In the diagram the CRM and order system are the only systems. In reality there would certainly be additional systems that would, for example, provide the product catalog. However, to illustrate an SOA landscape these two systems will suffice.

- For the systems to be able to call each other there is an *integration platform*. This platform enables communication between the services. It can compose the services through orchestration. The orchestration can be controlled by a technology that models business processes and calls the individual services to execute the different processes.

- Therefore, *orchestration* is responsible for coordinating the different services. The infrastructure is intelligent and can react appropriately to different messages. It contains the model of the business processes and is therefore an important part of the business logic.

- The SOA system can be used via a *portal*. The portal is responsible for providing users with an interface for using the services. There can be different portals: one for the customers, one for the support, and one for internal employees, for instance. Also, the system can be called via rich client applications or mobile apps. From an architectural perspective this makes no difference: All such systems access the different services and make them usable for a user. They are effectively a universal UI—able to use all services in the SOA.

Each of these systems could be operated and developed by individual teams. In this example there could be one team for the CRM and another for the order system. Additional teams could be allocated for each portal, and finally one team could take care of integration and orchestration.

Figure 6.2 shows how communication is structured in an SOA architecture. Users typically work with the SOA via the portal. From here business processes can be initiated that are then implemented in the orchestration layer. These processes use the services. When migrating from a monolith to an SOA, users might still use a monolith through its own user interface. However, SOA usually aims to have a portal as the central user interface and an orchestration layer for implementing processes.

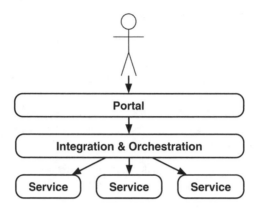

Figure 6.2 *Communication in an SOA Architecture*

Introducing SOA

Introducing SOA into a business is a strategic initiative involving different teams. The end game is to distribute the company's entire IT into separate services. Once separated, the services are easier to compose in new and different ways to create new functionality and processes. However, this is only possible when all systems in the entire organization have been modified. Only when enough services are available can business processes actually be implemented by simple orchestration. This is when SOA's advantages are really evident. Therefore, the integration and orchestration technology has to be used across the entire IT to enable service communication and integration. This involves high investment costs as the entire IT landscape has to be changed. This is one of the main points of criticism[1] of SOA.

The services can also be offered to other companies and users via the Internet or over private networks. This makes SOA well suited to support business concepts that are based on the outsourcing of services or the inclusion of external services. In an e-commerce application an external provider could, for instance, offer simple services like address validation or complex services like a credit check.

Services in an SOA

When introducing SOA based on old systems, the SOA services are simply interfaces of large deployment monoliths. One monolith offers several services. The services are built upon the existing applications. Often it is not even necessary to adjust the internals of a system in order to offer the services. Such a service typically does not have a UI; instead, it just offers an interface for other applications. A UI exists for all systems. It is not part of a service, but independent—for instance, in the portal.

---

1. http://apsblog.burtongroup.com/2009/01/soa-is-dead-long-live-services.html

In addition, it is possible to implement smaller deployment units in an SOA. The definition of an SOA service does not limit the size of the deployment units, which is quite different from microservices where the size of the deployment units is a defining feature.

Interfaces and Versioning

Service versioning in SOA is a particular challenge. Service changes have to be coordinated with the users of the respective service. Because of this coordination requirement, changes to the interface of the services can be laborious. Service users are unlikely to adjust their own software if they do not benefit from the new interface. Therefore, old interface versions frequently have to be supported as well. This means that numerous interface versions probably have to be supported if a service is used by many clients. This increases software complexity and makes changes more difficult. The correct functioning of the old interfaces has to be ensured with each new software release. If data is added, challenges arise because the old interfaces do not support this new data. This is not a problem during reading. However, when writing, it can be difficult to create new data sets without the additional data.

External Interfaces

If there are external users outside the company using the service, interface changes get even more difficult. In a worst case the provider of the service may not even know who is using it if it is available to anonymous users on the Internet. In that situation it is very difficult to coordinate changes. Consequently, switching off an old service version can be unfeasible. This leads to a growing number of interface versions, and service changes get more and more difficult. This problem can occur with microservices as well (see section 8.6).

The interface users also face challenges: If they need an interface modification, they have to coordinate this with the team offering the service. Then the changes have to be prioritized in relation to all the other changes and wishes of other teams. As discussed previously, an interface change is no easy task. This can lead to it taking a long time before changes are, in fact, implemented. This further hampers the development of the system.

Interfaces Enforce a Coordination of Deployments

After a change to the interface the deployment of the services has to be coordinated. First the service has to be deployed to offer the new version of the interface. Only then can the service that uses the new interface be deployed. Since applications are mostly deployment monoliths in the case of SOA, several services can sometimes only be deployed together. This makes the coordination of services more difficult. In addition, the deployment risk increases as the release of a monolith takes a long time and is hard to undo—just because the changes are so extensive.

Coordination and Orchestration

Coordinating an SOA system via orchestration in the integration layer poses a number of challenges. In a way, a monolith is generated: All business processes are reflected in this orchestration. This monolith is often even worse than the usual monoliths as it is using all the systems within the enterprise IT. In extreme cases it can end up that the services only perform data administration while all the logic is found in the orchestration. In such situations the entire SOA can deteriorate to being nothing other than a monolith that has its entire logic in the orchestration.

However, even in other settings, changes to SOA are not easy. Domains are divided into services in the different systems and into business processes in orchestration. When a change to functionality also concerns services or the user interface, things get difficult. Changing the business processes is relatively simple, but changing the service is only possible by writing code and by deploying a new version of the application providing the service. The necessary code changes and the deployment can be very laborious. Thus, the flexibility of SOA, which was meant to arise from a simple orchestration of services, is lost. Modifications of the user interface cause changes to the portal or to the other user interface systems and also require a new deployment.

Technologies

SOA is an architectural approach and is independent of concrete technology. However, an SOA has to enforce common technology for communication between the services, like microservices do. In addition, a concrete technology needs to be enforced for the orchestration of services. Often, introducing an SOA leads to the introduction of complex technologies to enable the integration and orchestration of services. There are special products that support all aspects of SOA. However, they are typically complex, and their features are rarely ever used to full capacity.

This technology can rapidly turn into a bottleneck. Many problems with these technologies are attributed to SOA although SOA could be implemented with other technologies as well. One of the problems is the complexity of the web services protocols. SOA on its own is quite simple; however, in conjunction with the extensions from the WS-* environment, a complex protocol stack arises. WS-* is necessary for transactions, security, and other extensions. Complex protocols exacerbate the interoperability—however, interoperability is a prerequisite for an SOA.

An action on the user interface has to be processed by the orchestration and the different services. These are distributed calls within the network with associated overhead and latency. Worse still, this communication runs via the central integration and orchestration technology, which therefore has to cope with numerous calls.

6.2 Differences between SOA and Microservices

SOA and microservices are related: both aim at splitting applications into services. It is not easy to distinguish between SOA and microservices by just considering what is happening on the network. Both architectural approaches have services exchanging information over the network.

Communication

Like microservices, SOA can be based on asynchronous communication or synchronous communication. SOAs can be uncoupled by merely sending events such as "new order." In these situations, every SOA service can react to the event with different logic. One service can write a bill and another can initiate delivery. The services are strongly uncoupled since they only react to events without knowing the trigger for the events. New services can easily be integrated into the system by also reacting to such events.

Orchestration

However, at the integration level the differences between SOA and microservices appear. In SOA the integration solution is also responsible for orchestrating the services. A business process is built up from services. In a microservice-based architecture the integration solution does not possess any intelligence. The microservices are responsible for communicating with other services. SOA attempts to use orchestration to gain additional flexibility for the implementation of business processes. This will only work out when services and user interface are stable and do not have to be modified frequently.

Flexibility

For achieving the necessary flexibility microservices, on the other hand, exploit the fact that each microservice can be easily changed and brought into production. When the flexible business processes of SOA are not sufficient, SOA forces the change of services into deployment monolith or user interfaces in an additional deployment monolith.

Microservices place emphasis on isolation: Ideally a user interaction is completely processed within one microservice without the need to call another microservice. Therefore, changes required for new features are limited to individual microservices. SOA distributes the logic to the portal, the orchestration, and the individual services.

Microservices: Project Level

However, the most important difference between SOA and microservices is the level at which the architecture aims. SOA considers the entire enterprise. It defines how a multitude of systems interact within the enterprise IT. Microservices, on the other hand, represent an architecture for an individual system. They are an alternative to other modularization technologies. It would be possible to implement a microservice-based system with another modularization technology and then to bring the system into production as a deployment monolith without distributed services. An entire SOA spans the entire enterprise IT. It has to look at different systems. An alternative to a distributed approach is not possible. Therefore, the decision to use a microservice-based architecture can be limited to an individual project while the introduction and implementation of SOA relates to the entire enterprise.

The SOA scenario depicted in Figure 6.1 results in a fundamentally different architecture (see Figure 6.3) if implemented[2] using microservices:[3]

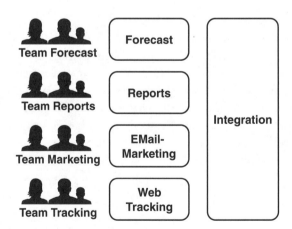

Figure 6.3 *CRM as a Collection of Microservices*

---

2. http://slideshare.net/ewolff/micro-services-neither-micro-nor-service

3. https://blogs.oracle.com/soacommunity/entry/podcast_show_notes_microservices_roundtable

- Since microservices refer to a single system, the architecture does not need to involve the entire IT with its different systems but can be limited to an individual system. In Figure 6.3 this system is the CRM. Thus, implementing microservices is relatively easy and not very costly as it is sufficient to implement one individual project rather than change the entire IT landscape of the enterprise.

- Accordingly, a microservice-based architecture does not require an integration technology to be introduced and used throughout the company. The use of a specific integration and communication technology is limited to the microservice system—it is even possible to use several approaches. For instance, high-performance access to large data sets can be implemented by replicating the data in the database. For access to other systems, again, other technologies can be used. In the case of SOA all services in the entire company need to be accessible via a uniform technology. This requires a uniform technology stack. Microservices focus on simpler technologies, which do not have to fulfill requirements as complex as those in SOA suites.

- In addition, communication between microservices is different: Microservices employ simple communication systems without any intelligence. Microservices call each other or send messages. The integration technology does not perform any orchestration. A microservice can call several other microservices and implement an orchestration on its own. In that situation, the logic for the orchestration resides in the microservice and not in an integration layer. In the case of microservices the integration solution contains no logic, because it would originate from different domains. This conflicts with the distribution according to domains, which microservice-based architectures aim at.

- The use of integration is also entirely different. Microservices avoid communication with other microservices by having the UI integrated into the microservice due to their domain-based distribution. SOA focuses on communication. SOA obtains its flexibility by orchestration—this is accompanied by communication between services. In the case of microservices the communication does not necessarily have to be implemented via messaging or REST: An integration at the UI level or via data replication is also possible.

- CRM as a complete system is not really present anymore in a microservice-based architecture. Instead there is a collection of microservices, each covering specific functionality like reports or forecasting transaction volume.

- While in SOA all functionality of the CRM system is collected in a single deployment unit, each service is an independent deployment unit and can be brought into production independently of the other services in the case of microservice-based approaches. Depending on the concrete technical infrastructure the services can be even smaller than the ones depicted in Figure 6.3.

- Finally, the handling of UI is different: For microservices the UI is part of the microservice, while SOA typically offers only services, which then can be used by a portal.

- The division into UI and service in SOA has far-reaching consequences: To implement a new piece of functionality including the UI in SOA, at minimum the service has to be changed and the UI adjusted. This means that at least two teams have to be coordinated. When other services in other applications are used, even more teams are involved, resulting in even greater coordination efforts. In addition, there are also orchestration changes, which are implemented by a separate team. Microservices, on the other hand, try to ensure that an individual team can bring new functionality into production with as little need for coordination with other teams as possible. Due to the microservice-based architecture, interfaces between layers, which are normally between teams, are now within a team. This facilitates the implementation of changes. The changes can be processed in one team. If another team were involved, the changes have to be prioritized in relation to other requirements.

- Each microservice can be developed and operated by one individual team. This team is responsible for a specific domain and can implement new requirements or changes to the domain completely independently of other teams.

- Also, the approach is different between SOA and microservices: SOA introduces only one new layer above the existing services in order to combine applications in new ways. It aims at a flexible integration of existing applications. Microservices serve to change the structure of the applications themselves—in pursuit of the goal of making changes to applications easier.

The communication relationships of microservices are depicted in Figure 6.4. The user interacts with the UI, which is implemented by the different microservices. In addition, the microservices communicate with each other. There is no central UI or orchestration.

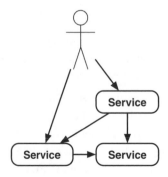

Figure 6.4 *Communication in the Case of Microservices*

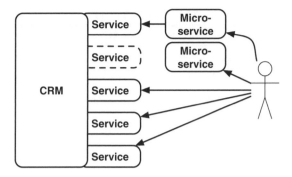

Figure 6.5 *SOA for Migrating to Microservices*

Synergies

There are definitely areas where microservices and SOA have synergies. In the end both approaches pursue the goal of separating applications into services. Such a step can be helpful when migrating an application to microservices: When the application is split into SOA services, individual services can be replaced or supplemented by microservices. Certain calls can be processed by a microservice while other calls are still processed by the application. This enables the migration of applications and the implementation of microservices in a step-by-step manner.

Figure 6.5 shows an example: The uppermost service of CRM is supplemented by a microservice. This microservice now takes all calls and can, if necessary, call the CRM. The second CRM service is completely replaced by a microservice. Using this approach, new functionality can be added to the CRM. At the same time, it is not necessary to reimplement the entire CRM; instead, microservices can complement it at selected places. Section 7.6 presents additional approaches to how legacy applications can be replaced by microservices.

6.3 Conclusion

Table 6.1 summarizes the differences between SOA and microservices.

At an organizational level the approaches are very different: SOAs place emphasis on the structure of the entire enterprise IT whereas microservices can be utilized in an individual project. SOAs focus on an organization where some teams develop backend services, while a different team implements the UI. In a microservice-based approach one team should implement everything in order to facilitate communication and speed up the implementation of features. That is not a goal of SOA. In SOA a new feature can involve changes to numerous services and therefore requires communication between a large number of teams. Microservices try to avoid this.

Table 6.1 *Differences between SOA and Microservices*

	SOA	Microservices
Scope	Enterprise-wide architecture	Architecture for one project
Flexibility	Flexibility by orchestration	Flexibility by fast deployment and rapid, independent development of Microservices
Organization	Services are implemented by different organizational units	Services are implemented by different organizational by teams in the same project
Deployment	Monolithic deployment of several services	Each microservice can be deployed individually
UI	Portal as universal UI for all services	Service contains UI

At a technical level there are similarities: Both concepts are based on services. The service granularity can be similar. Because of these technical similarities, it can be difficult to distinguish between SOA and microservices. However, from conceptual, architectural, and organizational viewpoints both approaches have very different features.

Essential Points

- SOA and microservices split applications into services that are available on the network. Similar technologies can be employed to this end.

- SOA aims at flexibility at the enterprise IT level through the orchestration of services. This is a complex undertaking and only works when the services don't need to be modified.

- Microservices focus on individual projects and aim at facilitating deployment and parallel work on different services.

Try and Experiment

- A new product feature is to be incorporated into the SOA landscape shown in Figure 6.1. The CRM does not have support for email campaigns. Therefore, a system for email campaigns has to be implemented. It is suggested that two services are created—one for the creation and execution of campaigns and a second service for evaluating the results of a campaign.

  An architect has to answer the following questions:

  - Is the SOA infrastructure needed to integrate the two new services? The service for campaign evaluation needs to handle a large amount of data.

  - Would it be better to use data replication, UI-level integration, or service calls for accessing large amounts of data?

  - Which of these integration options is typically offered by SOA?

  - Should the service integrate into the existing portal or have its own user interface? What are the arguments in favor of each option?

  - Should the new functionality be implemented by the CRM team?

PART III

Implementing Microservices

Part III demonstrates how microservices can be implemented. After studying the chapters in this part the reader should be able to not only design microservice-based architectures but also implement them and evaluate effects the microservices approach may have on his or her organization.

Chapter 7, "Architecture of Microservice-Based Systems," describes the architecture of microservice-based systems. It focuses on the interplay between individual microservices.

The domain architecture deals with domain-driven design as the basis of microservice-based architectures and shows metrics that allow you to measure the quality of the architecture. Architecture management is a challenge: It can be difficult to keep the overview of the numerous microservices. However, often it is sufficient to understand how a certain use case is implemented and which microservices interact in a specific scenario.

Practically all IT systems are subject to more or less profound change. Therefore, the architecture of a microservice system has to evolve, and the system has to undergo continuous development. To achieve this, several challenges have to be addressed, which do not arise in this form in the case of deployment monoliths—for instance, the overall distribution into microservices is difficult to change. However, changes to individual microservices are simple.

In addition, microservice systems need to integrate legacy systems. This is quite simple as microservices can treat legacy systems as a black box. A replacement of a deployment monolith by microservices can progressively transfer more functionalities into microservices without having to adjust the inner structure of the legacy system or having to understand the code in detail.

The technical architecture comprises typical challenges for the implementation of microservices. In most cases there is a central configuration and coordination for all microservices. Furthermore, a load balancer distributes the load between the individual instances of the microservices. The security architecture has to leave each microservice the freedom to implement its own authorizations in the system but also ensure that a user needs to log in only once. Finally, microservices should return information concerning themselves as documentation and as metadata.

Chapter 8, "Integration and Communication," shows the different possibilities for the integration and communication between microservices. There are three possible levels for integration:

- Microservices can integrate at the web level. In that case each microservice delivers a part of the web UI.

- At the logic level microservices can communicate via REST or messaging.

- Data replication is also possible.

Via these technologies the microservices have internal interfaces for other microservices. The complete system can have one interface to the outside. Changes to the different interfaces create different challenges. Accordingly, this chapter also deals with versioning of interfaces and the effects thereof.

Chapter 9, "Architecture of Individual Microservices," describes possibilities for the architecture of an individual microservice. There are different approaches for an individual microservice:

- CQRS divides read and write access into two separate services. This allows for smaller services and an independent scaling of both parts.

- Event Sourcing administrates the state of a microservice via a stream of events from which the current state can be deduced.

- In a hexagonal architecture the microservice possesses a core, which can be accessed via different adaptors and which communicates also via such adaptors with other microservices or the infrastructure.

Each Microservice can follow an independent architecture.

In the end all microservices have to handle technical challenges like resilience and stability—these issues have to be solved by their technical architecture.

Testing is the focus of **Chapter 10, "Testing Microservices and Microservice-Based Systems."** Also tests have to take the special challenges associated with microservices into consideration.

The chapter starts off by explaining why tests are necessary at all and how a system can be tested in principle.

Microservices are small deployment units. This decreases the risk associated with deployments. Accordingly, besides tests, optimization of deployment can also help to decrease the risk.

Testing the entire system represents a special problem in case of microservices since only one microservice at a time can pass through this phase. If the tests last one hour, only eight deployments will be feasible per working day. In the case of 50 microservices that is by far too few. Therefore, it is necessary to limit these tests as much as possible.

Often microservices replace legacy systems. The microservices and the legacy system both have to be tested—along with their interplay. Tests for the individual microservices differ in some respects greatly from tests for other software systems.

Consumer-driven contract tests are an essential component of microservice tests—They test the expectations of a microservice in regard to an interface. Thereby the correct interplay of microservices can be ensured without having to test the microservices together in an integration test. Instead a microservice defines its requirements for the interface in a test that the used microservice can execute.

Microservices have to adhere to certain standards in regard to monitoring or logging. The adherence to these standards can also be checked by tests.

Operation and continuous delivery are the focus of **Chapter 11, "Operation and Continuous Delivery of Microservices."** The infrastructure is especially an essential challenge when introducing microservices. Logging and monitoring have to be uniformly implemented across all microservices; otherwise, the associated expenditure gets too large. In addition, there should be a uniform deployment. Finally, starting and stopping of microservices should be possible in a uniform manner—in other words, via a simple control. For these areas the chapter introduces concrete technologies and approaches. Additionally, the chapter presents infrastructures that especially facilitate the operation of a microservices environment.

Finally, **Chapter 12, "Organizational Effects of a Microservice-Based Architecture,"** discusses how microservices influence the organization. Microservices enable a simpler distribution of tasks to independent teams and thus for parallel work on different features. To that end the tasks have to be distributed to the teams, which subsequently introduce the appropriate changes into their microservices. However, new features can also comprise several microservices. In that case one team has to put requirements to another team—this requires a lot of coordination and delays the implementation of new features. Therefore, it can be better that teams also change microservices of other teams.

Microservices divide the architecture into micro and macro architecture: In regards to micro architecture the teams can make their own decisions while the macro architecture has to be defined for and coordinated across all microservices. In areas like operation, architecture, and testing individual aspects can be assigned to micro or macro architecture.

DevOps as organizational form fits well with microservices since close cooperation between operation and development is very useful, especially for the infrastructure-intensive microservices.

The independent teams each need their own independent requirements, which in the end have to be derived from the domain. Consequently, microservices also have effects in these areas.

Code recycling is likewise an organizational problem: How do the teams coordinate the different requirements for shared components? A model that is inspired by open-source projects can help.

However, there is of course the question whether microservices are possible at all without organizational changes—after all, the independent teams constitute one of the essential reasons for introducing microservices.

Chapter 7

Architecture of Microservice-Based Systems

This chapter discusses how microservices should behave when viewed from the outside and how an entire microservice system can be developed. Chapter 8, "Integration and Communication," covers possible communication technologies that are an important technology component. Chapter 9, "Architecture of Individual Microservices," focuses on the architecture of individual microservices.

Section 7.1 describes what the domain architecture of a microservice system should look like. Section 7.2 presents appropriate tools to visualize and manage the architecture. Section 7.3 shows how the architecture can be adapted in a stepwise manner. Only a constant evolution of the software architecture will ensure that the system remains maintainable in the long run and can be developed further. Section 7.4 discusses the goals and approaches that are important to enable further development.

Next, a number of approaches for the architecture of a microservice-based system are explained. Section 7.6 discusses the special challenges that arise when a legacy application is to be enhanced or replaced by microservices. Section 7.8 introduces event-driven architecture. This approach makes possible architectures that are very loosely coupled.

Finally, Section 7.9 deals with the technical aspects relevant to the architecture of a microservice-based system. Some of these aspects are presented in depth in the following sections: mechanisms for coordination and configuration (section 7.10), Service Discovery (section 7.11), Load Balancing (section 7.12), scalability (section 7.13), security (section 7.14), and finally documentation and metadata (section 7.15).

7.1 Domain Architecture

The domain architecture of a microservice-based system determines which microservices within the system should implement which domain. It defines how the entire domain is split into different areas, each of which are implemented by one microservice and thus one team. Designing such an architecture is one of the primary challenges when introducing microservices. It is, after all, an important motivation for the use of microservices that changes to the domain can be implemented, ideally, by just one team changing just one microservice—minimizing coordination and communication across teams. Done correctly this ensures that microservices can support the scaling of software development since even large teams need little communication and therefore can work productively.

To achieve this, it is important that the design of the domain architecture for the microservices makes it possible for changes to be limited to single microservices and thus individual teams. When the distribution into microservices does not support this, changes will require additional coordination and communication, and the advantages that a microservice-based approach can bring will not be achieved.

Strategic Design and Domain-Driven Design

Section 3.3 discussed the distribution of microservices based on strategic design, a concept taken from domain-driven design. A key element is that the microservices are distributed into contexts—that is, areas that represent separate functionality.

Often architects develop a microservice architecture based on entities from a domain model. A certain microservice implements the logic for a certain type of entity. Using this approach might give, for instance, one microservice for customers, one for items, and one for deliveries. However, this approach conflicts with the idea of *Bounded Context*, which stipulates that uniform modeling of data is impossible. Furthermore, this approach isolates changes very badly. When a process is to be modified and entities have to be adapted, the change is distributed across different microservices. As a result, changing the order process will impact the entity modeling for customers, items, and deliveries. When that is the case, the three microservices for the different entities have to be changed in addition to the microservice for the order process. To avoid this, it can be sensible to keep certain parts of the data for customers, items, and deliveries in the microservice for the order process. With this approach when changes to the order process require the data model to be modified, then this change can be limited to a single microservice.

However, this does not prevent a system from having services dedicated to the administration of certain entities. It may be necessary to manage the most fundamental data of a certain business entity in a service. For example, a service can certainly administrate the client data but leave specific client data, such as a bonus program number, to other microservices—for example to the microservice for the order process, which likely has to know this number.

Example Otto Shop

An example—the architecture of the Otto shop[1]—illustrates this concept. Otto GmbH is one of the biggest e-commerce companies. In the architecture there are, on the one hand, services like user, order, and product, which are oriented toward data, and on the other hand, areas like tracking, search and navigation, and personalization, which are not geared to data but to functionality. This is exactly the type of domain design that should be aimed for in a microservice-based system.

A domain architecture requires a precise understanding of the domain. It comprises not only the division of the system into microservices but also the dependencies. A dependency arises when a dependent microservice uses another one—for instance, by calling the microservice, by using elements from the UI of the microservice, or by replicating its data. Such a dependency means that changes to a microservice can also influence the microservice that is dependent on it. If, for example, the microservice modifies its interface, the dependent microservice has to be adapted to these changes. Also new requirements affecting the dependent microservice might mean that the other microservice has to modify its interface. If the dependent microservice needs more data to implement the requirements, the other microservice has to offer this data and adjust its interface accordingly.

For microservices such dependencies cause problems beyond just software architecture: If the microservices involved in a change are implemented by different teams, then the change will require collaboration between those teams; this overhead can be time consuming and laborious.

Managing Dependencies

Managing dependencies between microservices is central to the architecture of a system. Having too many dependencies will prevent microservices from being changed in isolation—which goes against the objective of developing microservices

---

1. https://dev.otto.de/2016/03/20/why-microservices/

independently of each other. Here are two fundamental rules to apply for good architecture:

- There should be a **loose coupling** between components such as microservices. This means that each microservice should have few dependencies on other microservices. This makes it easier to modify them since changes will only affect individual microservices.

- Within a component such as a microservice, the constituent parts should work closely together. This is referred to as having **high cohesion**. This ensures that all constituent parts within a microservice really belong together.

When these two prerequisites are not met, it will be difficult to change an individual microservice in an isolated manner, and changes will have to be coordinated across multiple teams and microservices, which is just what microservice-based architectures are supposed to avoid. However, this is often a symptom: the fundamental problem is how the domain-based split of the functionality between the microservices was done. Obviously pieces of functionality that should have been placed together in one microservice have been distributed across different microservices. An order process, for instance, also needs to generate a bill. These two pieces of functionality are so different that they have to be distributed into at least two microservices. However, when each modification of the order process also affects the microservice that creates the bills, the domain-based modeling is not optimal and should be adjusted. The pieces of functionality have to be distributed differently to the microservices, as we will see.

Unintended Domain-Based Dependencies

It is not only the number of dependencies that can pose a problem. Certain domain-based dependencies can simply be nonsensical. For instance, it would be surprising in an e-commerce system if the team responsible for product search suddenly has an interface with the microservice for billing, because that should not be the case from a domain-based point of view. However, when it comes to domain modeling, there are always surprises for the unaware. When a dependency is not meaningful from a domain-based point of view, something regarding the functionality of the microservices has to be wrong. Maybe the microservice implements features that belong in other microservices from a domain-based perspective. Perhaps in the context of product search a scoring of the customer is required, which is implemented as part of billing. In that case one should consider whether this functionality is really implemented in the right microservice. To keep the system maintainable over the long term, such dependencies have to be questioned and, if necessary, removed

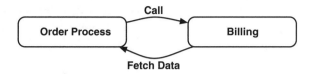

Figure 7.1 *Cyclic Dependency*

from the system. For instance, the scoring could be moved into a new, independent microservice or transferred into another existing microservice.

Cyclic Dependencies

Cyclic dependencies can present additional problems for a comprehensive architecture. Let us assume that the microservice for the order process calls the microservice for billing (see Figure 7.1). The microservice for billing fetches data from the order process microservice. When the microservice for the order process is changed, modifications to the microservice for billing might be necessary since this microservice fetches data from the microservice for the order process. Conversely, changes to the billing microservice require changes to the order microservice as this microservice calls the billing microservice. Cyclic dependencies are problematic: the components can no longer be changed in isolation, contrary to the underlying aim for a split into separate components. For microservices great emphasis is placed on independence, which is violated in this case. In addition to the coordination of changes that is needed, it may also be that the deployment has to be coordinated. When a new version of the one microservice is rolled out, a new version of the other microservice might have to be rolled out as well if they have a cyclic dependency.

The remainder of the chapter shows approaches to building microservice-based architectures in such a way that they have a sound structure from a domain-based perspective. Metrics like cohesion and loose coupling can verify that the architecture is really appropriate. In the context of approaches like event-driven architecture (section 7.8) microservices have hardly any direct technical dependencies since they only send messages. Who is sending the messages and who is processing them is difficult to determine from the code, meaning that the metrics may look very good. However, from a domain-based perspective the system can still be far too complicated, since the domain-based dependencies are not examined by the metrics. Domain-based dependencies arise when two microservices exchange messages. However, this is difficult to ascertain by code analysis, meaning that the metrics will always look quite good. Thus metrics can only suggest problems. By just optimizing the metrics, the symptoms are optimized, but the underlying problems remain unsolved. Even worse, even systems with good metrics can have architectural weaknesses. Therefore, the metric loses its value in determining the quality of a software system.

A special problem in the case of microservices is that dependencies between microservices can also influence their independent deployment. If a microservice requires a new version of another microservice because it uses, for instance, a new version of an interface, the deployment will also be dependent: The microservice has to be deployed before the dependent microservice can be deployed. In extreme cases this can result in a large number of microservices that have to be deployed in a coordinated manner—this is just what was supposed to be avoided. Microservices should be deployed independently of each other. Therefore, dependencies between microservices can present an even greater problem than would be the case for modules within a deployment monolith.

7.2 Architecture Management

For a domain architecture it is critical which microservices exist and what the communication relationships between the microservices look like. This is true in other systems as well where the relationships between the components are very important. When domain-based components are mapped on modules, classes, Java packages, JAR files, or DLLs, specific tools can determine the relationships between the components and control the adherence to certain rules. This is achieved by static code analysis.

Tools for Architecture Management

If an architecture is not properly managed, then unintended dependencies will quickly creep in. The architecture will get more and more complex and hard to understand. Only with the help of architecture management tools can developers and architects keep track of the system. Within a development environment developers view only individual classes. The dependencies between classes can only be found in the source code and are not readily discernible.

Figure 7.2 depicts the analysis of a Java project by the architecture management tool Structure 101. The image shows classes and Java packages, which contain classes. A levelized structure map (LSM) presents an overview of them. Classes and packages that are higher up the LSM use classes and packages that are depicted lower down the LSM. To simplify the diagram, these relationships are not indicated.

Cycle-Free Software

Architectures should be free of cycles. Cyclic dependencies mean that two artifacts are using each other reciprocally. In the screenshot such cycles are presented by dashed lines. They always run from bottom to top. The reciprocal relationship in the cycle would be running from top to bottom and is not depicted.

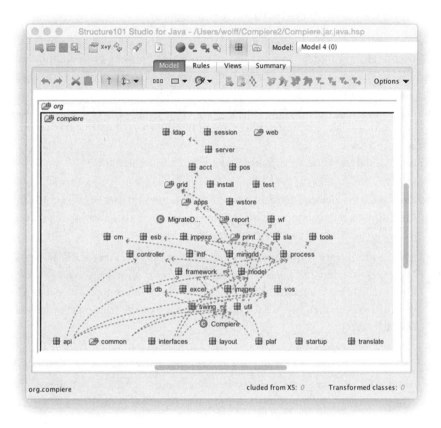

Figure 7.2 *Screenshot of the Architecture Management Tool Structure 101*

In addition to cycles, packages that are located in the wrong position are also relevant. There is, for instance, a package *util* whose name suggests it is supposed to contain helper classes. However, it is not located at the very bottom of the diagram. Thus, it has to have dependencies to packages or classes that are further down—which should not be the case. Helper classes should be independent from other system components and should therefore appear at the very bottom of an LSM.

Architecture management tools like Structure 101 don't just analyze architectures; they can also enable architects to define prohibited relationships between packages and classes. Developers who violate these rules will receive an error message and can modify the code.

With the help of tools like Structure 101 the architecture of a system can be easily visualized. The compiled code only has to be loaded into the tool for analysis.

Microservices and Architecture Management

For microservices the problem is much larger: relationships between microservices are not as easy to determine as the relationships between code components. After all, the microservices could even be implemented in different technologies. They communicate only via the network. Their relationships prevent management at a code level, because they appear only indirectly in the code. However, if the relationships between microservices are not known, architecture management becomes impossible.

There are different ways to visualize and manage the architecture:

- Each microservice can have associated documentation (see section 7.15) that lists all used microservices. This documentation has to adhere to a predetermined format, which enables visualization.

- The communication infrastructure can deliver the necessary data. If Service Discovery (section 7.11) is used, it will be aware of all microservices and will know which microservices have access to which other microservices. This information can then be used for the visualization of the relationships between the microservices.

- If access between microservices is safeguarded by a firewall, the rules of the firewall will at least detail which microservice can communicate with which other microservice. This can also be used as a basis for the visualization of relationships.

- Traffic within the network also reveals which microservices communicate with which other microservices. Tools like Packetbeat (see section 11.3) can be very helpful here. They visualize the relationships between microservices based on the recorded network traffic.

- The distribution into microservices should correspond to the distribution into teams. If two teams cannot work independently of each other anymore, this is likely due to a problem in the architecture: The microservices of the two teams depend so strongly on each other that they can now only be modified together. The teams involved probably know already which microservices are problematic due to the increased communication requirement. To verify the problem, an architecture management tool or a visualization can be used. However, manually collected information might be sufficient.

Tools

Different tools are useful to evaluate data about dependencies:

- There are versions of Structure 101[2] that can use custom data structures as input. One still has to write an appropriate importer. Structure 101 will then recognize cyclic dependencies and can depict the dependencies graphically.
- Gephi[3] can generate complex graphs, which are helpful for visualizing the dependencies between microservices. Again, a custom importer has to be written for importing the dependencies between the microservices from an appropriate source into Gephi.
- jQAssistant[4] is based on the graph database neo4j. It can be extended by a custom importer. Then the data model can be checked according to rules.

For all these tools custom development is necessary. It is not possible to analyze a microservice-based architecture immediately; there is always some extra effort required. Since communication between microservices cannot be standardized, it is likely that custom development will always be required.

Is Architecture Management Important?

The architecture management of microservices is important, as it is the only way to prevent chaos in the relationships between the microservices. Microservices are a special challenge in this respect: With modern tools, a deployment monolith can be quite easily and rapidly analyzed. For microservice-based architectures, there are no tools that can analyze the entire structure in a simple manner. The teams first have to create the necessary prerequisites for an analysis. Changing the relationships between microservices is difficult, as the next section will show. Therefore, it is even more important to continually review the architecture of the microservices in order to correct problems that arise as early as possible. It is a benefit of microservice-based architectures that the architecture is also reflected in the organization. Problems with communication will therefore point towards architectural problems. Even without formal architecture management, architectural problems often become obvious.

---

2. http://structure101.com
3. http://gephi.github.io/
4. http://jqassistant.org/

On the other hand, experiences with complex microservice-based systems teach us that in such systems, nobody understands the entire architecture. However, this is also not necessary since most changes are limited to individual microservices. If a certain use case involving multiple microservices is to be changed, it is sufficient to understand this interaction and the involved microservices. A global understanding is not absolutely necessary. This is a consequence of the independence of the individual microservices.

Context Map

Context Maps are a way to get an overview of the architecture of a microservice-based system.[5] They illustrate which domain models are used by which microservices and therefore visualize the different *Bounded Contexts* (see section 3.3). The *Bounded Contexts* not only influence the internal data presentation in the microservices but also impact the calls between microservices where data is exchanged. They have to be in line with some type of model. However, the data models underlying communication can be distinct from the internal representations. For example, if a microservice is supposed to identify recommendations for customers of an e-commerce shop, complex models can be employed internally for this that contain a lot of information about customers, products, and orders and correlate them in complex ways. On the outside, however, these models can be much simpler.

Figure 7.3 shows an example of a *Context Map*:

- The registration registers the basic data of each customer. The order process also uses this data format to communicate with registration.

- In the order process the customer's basic data is supplemented by data such as billing and delivery addresses to obtain the customer order data. This corresponds to a *Shared Kernel* (see section 3.3). The order process shares the kernel of the customer data with the registration process.

- The delivery and the billing microservices use customer order data for communication, and the delivery microservice uses it for the internal representation of the customer. This model is a kind of standard model for the communication of customer data.

---

5. Eric Evans. 2003. *Domain-Driven Design: Tackling Complexity in the Heart of Software*. Boston: Addison-Wesley.

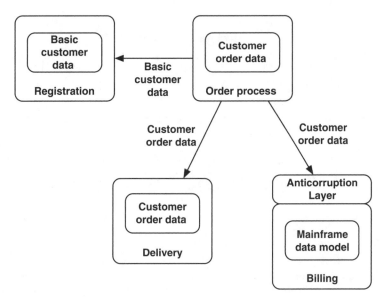

Figure 7.3 *An Example of a Context Map*

- Billing uses an old mainframe data model. Therefore, customer order data for outside communication is decoupled from the internal representation by an *anti-corruption layer*. The data model represents a very bad abstraction, which should not be allowed to affect other microservices.

In this model it is clear that the internal data representation in registration propagates to the order process. There, it serves as the basis for the customer order data. This model is used in delivery as an internal data model as well as in the communication with billing and delivery. This leads to the model being hard to change since it is used by so many services. If this model was to be changed, all these services would have to be modified.

However, there are also advantages associated with this. If all these services had to implement the same change to the data model, only a single change would be necessary to update all microservices at once. Nevertheless, this goes against the principle that changes should always only affect a single microservice. If the change remains limited to the model, the shared model is advantageous since all microservices automatically use the current modeling. However, when the change requires changes in the microservices, now multiple microservices have to be modified—and brought into production together. This conflicts with an independent deployment of microservices.

Try and Experiment

- Download a tool for the analysis of architectures. Candidates are Structure 101,[6] Gephi,[7] or jQAssistant.[8] Use the tool to get an overview of an existing code base. What options are there to insert your own dependency graphs into the tool? This would enable you to analyze the dependencies within a microservice-based architecture with this tool.

- spigo[9] is a simulation for the communication between microservices. It can be used to get an overview of more complex microservice-based architectures.

---

6. http://structure101.com
7. http://gephi.github.io/
8. http://jqassistant.org
9. https://github.com/adrianco/spigo

7.3 Techniques to Adjust the Architecture

Microservices are useful in situations where the software is subject to numerous changes. Due to the distribution into microservices the system separates into deployment units, which can be developed independently of each other. This means that each microservice can implement its own stream of stories or requirements. Consequently, multiple changes can be worked on in parallel without much need for coordination.

Experience teaches us that the architecture of a system is subject to change. A certain distribution into domain-based components might seem sensible at first. However, once architects get to know the domain better, they might come to the conclusion that another distribution would be better. New requirements are hard to implement with the old architecture since it was devised based on different premises. This is especially common for agile processes, which demand less planning and more flexibility.

Where Does Bad Architecture Come From?

A system with a bad architecture does not normally arise because the wrong architecture has been chosen at the outset. Based on the information available at the start of the project, the architecture is often good and consistent. The problem is frequently that the architecture is not modified when there are new insights that suggest changes to the architecture. The symptom of this was mentioned in the last section: New requirements cannot be rapidly and easily implemented anymore. To that end the architecture would have to be changed. When this pressure to introduce changes is ignored for too long, the architecture will, at some point, not fit at all. The continuous adjustment and modification of the architecture is essential in keeping the architecture in a really sustainable state.

This section describes some techniques that enable the interplay between microservices to be changed in order to adapt the overall system architecture.

Changes in Microservices

Within a microservice adjustments are easy. The microservices are small and manageable. It is no big deal to adjust structures. If the architecture of an individual microservice is completely insufficient, it can be rewritten since it is not very large. Within a microservice it is also easy to move components or to restructure the code in other ways. The term "refactoring"[10] describes techniques that serve to improve the structure of code. Many of these techniques can be automated using development tools. This enables an easy adjustment of the code of an individual microservice.

Changes to the Overall Architecture

However, when the division of functionality between the microservices is no longer in line with the requirements, changing just one microservice will not be sufficient. To achieve the necessary adjustment of the complete architecture, functionality has to be moved between microservices. There can be different reasons for this:

- The microservice is too large and has to be divided. Indications for this can be that the microservice is no longer intelligible anymore or so large that a single team is not sufficient to develop it further. Another indication can be that the microservice contains more than one *Bounded Context*.

- A piece of functionality really belongs in another microservice. An indication for that can be that certain parts of a microservice communicate a lot with another microservice. In this situation the microservices no longer have a loose coupling. Such intense communication can imply that the component belongs in another microservice. Likewise, a low cohesion in a microservice can suggest that the microservice should be divided. In that case there are areas in a microservice that depend little on each other. Consequently, they do not really have to be in one microservice.

---

10. Martin Fowler. 1999. *Refactoring: Improving the Design of Existing Code*, Boston: Addison-Wesley.

- A piece of functionality should be used by multiple microservices. For instance, this can become necessary when a microservice has to use logic from another microservice because of some new piece of functionality.

There are three main challenges: microservices have to be split, code has to be moved from one microservice into another, and multiple microservices are supposed to use the same code.

Shared Libraries

If two microservices are supposed to use code together, the code can be transferred into a shared library (see Figure 7.4). The code is removed from the microservice and packaged in a way that enables it to be used by the other microservices. A prerequisite for this is that the microservices are written in technologies that enable the use of a shared library. This is the case when they are written in the same language or at least use the same platform, such as JVM (Java Virtual Machine) or .NET Common Language Runtime (CLR).

A shared library means that the microservices become dependent on each other. Work on the library has to be coordinated. Features for both microservices have to be implemented in the library. Via the backdoor each microservice is affected by changes meant for the other microservice. This can result in errors, meaning that the teams have to coordinate the development of the library. Under certain conditions changes to a library can mean that a microservice has to be newly deployed—for instance because a security gap has been closed in the library.

It is also possible that through the shared library the microservices might obtain additional code dependencies to third-party libraries. In a Java JVM, third-party libraries can only be present in one version. If the shared library requires a certain version of a third-party library, the microservice also has to use this specific version and cannot use a different one. Additionally, libraries often have a certain programming model. In that way libraries can provide code, which

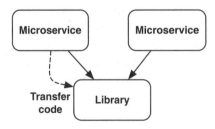

Figure 7.4 *Shared Library*

can be called, or a framework into which custom code can be integrated, which is then called by the framework. The library might pursue an asynchronous model or a synchronous model. Such approaches can fit more or less well to a respective microservice.

Microservices do not focus on the reuse of code since this leads to new dependencies between the microservices. An important aim of microservices is independence—so code reuse often causes more problems than it solves. This is a rejection of the ideal of code recycling. Developers in the nineties still pinned their hopes on code reuse in order to increase productivity. Moving code into a library also has advantages. Errors and security gaps have to be corrected only once. The microservices use always the current library version and thus automatically get fixes for errors.

Another problem associated with code reuse is that it requires a detailed understanding of the code—especially in the case of frameworks into which the custom code has to embed itself. This kind of reuse is known as white-box reuse: The internal code structures have to be known, not only the interface. This type of reuse requires a detailed understanding of the code that is to be reused, which sets a high hurdle for the reuse.

An example would be a library that makes it easier to generate metrics for system monitoring. It will be used in the billing microservice. Other teams also want to use the code. Therefore, the code is extracted into a library. Since it is technical code, it does not need to modified if domain-based changes are made. Therefore, the library does not influence the independent deployment and the independent development of domain-based features. The library was supposed to be turned into an internal open-source project (see section 12.8).

However, to transfer domain code into a shared library is problematic, as it might introduce deployment dependencies into microservices. When, for instance, the modeling of a customer is implemented in a library, then each change to the data structure has to be passed on to all microservices, and they all have to be newly deployed. Besides, a uniform modeling of a data structure like customer is difficult due to *Bounded Context*.

Transfer Code

Another way to change the architecture is to transfer code from one microservice to another (see Figure 7.5). This is sensible when doing so ensures a loose coupling and a high cohesion of the entire system. When two microservices communicate a lot, they are not loosely coupled. When the part of the microservice that communicates a lot with the other microservice is transferred, this problem can be solved.

This approach is similar to the removal into a shared library. However, the code is not a common dependency, which solves the problem of coupling between the

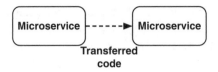

Figure 7.5 *Transferring Code*

microservices. However, it is possible that the microservices have to have a common interface in order to be able to use the functionality after the code transfer. This is a black-box dependency: Only the interface has to be known, not the internal code structures.

In addition, it is possible to transfer the code into another microservice while keeping it in the original microservice. This causes redundancy. Errors will then have to be corrected in both versions, and the two versions can develop in different directions. However, this will ensure that the microservices are independent, especially with regard to deployment.

The technological limitations are the same as for a shared library—the two microservices have to use similar technologies; otherwise, the code cannot be transferred. However, in a pinch the code can also be rewritten in a new programming language or with a different programming model. Microservices are not very large. The code that has to be rewritten is only a part of a microservice. Consequently, the required effort is manageable.

However, there is the problem that the size of that microservice into which the code is transferred increases. Thus, the danger increases that the microservice turns into a monolith over time.

One example: The microservice for the order process frequently calls the billing microservice in order to calculate the price for the delivery. Both services are written in the same programming language. The code is transferred from one microservice into the other. From a domain perspective it turns out that the calculation of delivery costs belongs in the order-process microservice. The code transfer is only possible when both services use the same platform and programming language. This also means that the communication between microservices has been replaced by local communication.

Reuse or Redundancy?

Instead of attributing shared code to one or the other microservices, the code can also be maintained in both microservices. At first this sounds dangerous—after all, the code will then be redundant in two places, and bug fixes will have to be performed in both places. Most of the time developers try to avoid such situations. An established best practice is "Don't Repeat Yourself" (DRY). Each decision and consequently all code should only be stored at exactly one place in the system. In a microservice-based architectures redundancy has a key advantage: the two microservices stay independent of each other and can be independently deployed and independently developed further. In this way the central characteristic of microservices is preserved.

It is questionable whether a system can be built without any redundancies at all. Especially in the beginning of object-orientation, many projects invested significant effort to transfer shared code into shared frameworks and libraries. This was meant to reduce the expenditure associated with the creation of the individual projects. In reality the code to be reused was often difficult to understand and thus hard to use. A redundant implementation in the different projects might have been a better alternative. It can be easier to implement code several times than to design it in a reusable manner and then to actually reuse it.

There are, of course, cases of successful reuse of code: hardly any project can get along nowadays without open-source libraries. At this level code reuse is taking place all the time. This approach can be a good template for the reuse of code between microservices. However, this has effects on the organization. Section 12.8 discusses organization and also code reuse using an open-source model.

Shared Service

Instead of transferring the code into a library, it can also be moved into a new microservice (see Figure 7.6). Here the typical benefits of a microservice-based architecture can be achieved; the technology of the new microservice does not matter, as long as it uses the universally defined communication technologies and can be operated like the other microservices. Its internal structure can be arbitrary, even to the point of programming language.

The use of a microservice is simpler than the use of a library. Only the interface of the microservice has to be known—the internal structure does not matter. Moving code into a new service reduces the average size of a microservice and therefore improves the intelligibility and replaceability of the microservices. However, the

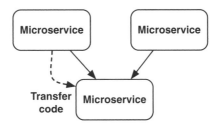

Figure 7.6 *Shared Microservice*

transfer replaces local calls with calls via the network, and changes for new features might no longer be limited to one microservice.

In software development big modules are often a problem. Therefore, transferring code into new microservices can be a good option for keeping modules small. The new microservice can be developed further by the team that was already responsible for the original microservice. This will facilitate the close coordination of new and old microservices since the required communication happens within only one team.

The split into two microservices also has the consequence that a call to the microservice-based system is not processed by just one single microservice but by several microservices. These microservices call each other. Some of those microservices will not have a UI but are pure backend services.

To illustrate this, let us turn again to the order process, which frequently calls the billing microservice for calculating the delivery costs. The calculation of delivery costs can be separated into a microservice by itself. This is even possible when the billing service and the order process microservice use different platforms and technologies. However, a new interface will have to be established that enables the new delivery cost microservice to communicate with the remainder of the billing service.

Spawn a New Microservice

In addition, it is possible to use part of the code of a certain microservice to generate a new microservice (see Figure 7.7). The advantages and disadvantages are identical to the scenario in which code is transferred into a shared microservice. However, the motivation is different in this case: The size of the microservices is meant to be reduced to increase their maintainability or maybe to transfer the responsibility for a certain functionality to another team. Here, the new microservice is not supposed to be shared by multiple other microservices.

For instance, the service for registration might have become too complex. Therefore, it is split into multiple services, each handling certain user groups. A separation along technical lines would also be possible—for instance according to CQRS (see section 9.2), event sourcing (section 9.3) or hexagonal architecture (section 9.4).

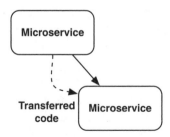

Figure 7.7 *Spawning a New Microservice*

Rewriting

Finally, an additional way to handle microservices whose structure does not fit anymore is to rewrite them. This is more easily done with microservices-based architectures than with other architectural approaches due to the small size of microservices and their use via defined interfaces. This means that the entire system does not have be rewritten—just a part. It is also possible to implement the new microservice in a different programming language, which may be better suited for this purpose. Rewriting microservices can also be beneficial since new insights about the domain can leave their mark on the new implementation.

A Growing Number of Microservices

Experience with microservice-based systems teaches us that during the time a project is running, new microservices will be generated continuously. This involves greater effort around infrastructure and the operation of the system. The number of deployed services will increase all the time. For more traditional projects, such a development is unusual and may therefore appear problematic. However, as this section demonstrates, the generation of new microservices is the best alternative for the shared use of logic and for the ongoing development of a system. In any case the growing number of microservices ensures that the average size of individual microservices stays constant. Consequently, the positive characteristics of microservices are preserved.

Generating new microservices should be made as easy as possible as this enables the properties of the microservice system to be preserved. Potential for optimization is mainly present when it comes to establishing continuous delivery pipelines and build infrastructure and the required server for the new microservice. Once these things are automated, new microservices can be generated comparably easily.

Microservice-Based Systems Are Hard to Modify

This section has shown that it is difficult to adjust the overall architecture of a microservice-based system. New microservices have to be generated. This entails changes to the infrastructure and the need for additional continuous delivery pipelines. Shared code in libraries is rarely a sensible option.

In a deployment monolith such changes would be easy to introduce: Often the integrated development environments automate the transfer of code or other structural changes. Due to automation the changes are easier and less prone to errors. There are no effects whatsoever on the infrastructure or continuous delivery pipelines in the case of deployment monoliths.

Thus, changes are difficult at the level of the entire system—because it is hard to transfer functionality between different microservices. Ultimately, this is exactly the effect that was termed "strong modularization" and listed as an advantage in section 1.2: To cross the boundaries between microservices is difficult so that the architecture at the level between the microservices will remain intact in the long run. However, this means that the architecture is hard to adjust at this level.

Try and Experiment

- A developer has written a helper class, which facilitates the interaction with a logging framework that is also used by other teams. It is not very large and complex.

  - Should it be used by other teams?

  - Should the helper class be turned into a library or an independent microservice, or should the code simply be copied?

7.4 Growing Microservice-Based Systems

The benefits of microservices are seen most clearly in very dynamic environments. Due to the independent deployment of individual microservices, teams can work in parallel on different features without the need for significant coordination. This is especially advantageous when it is unclear which features are really meaningful and experiments on the market are necessary to identify promising approaches.

Planning Architecture?

In this sort of environment, it is difficult to plan a good split of the domain logic into microservices right from the start. The architecture has to adjust to the evidence.

- The separation of a system into its domain aspects is even more important for microservices than in the context of a traditional architectural approach. This is because the domain-based distribution also influences the distribution into teams and therefore the independent working of the teams—the primary benefit of microservices (section 7.1).

- Section 7.2 demonstrated that tools for architecture management cannot readily be used in microservice-based architectures.

- As section 7.3 discussed, it is difficult to modify the architecture of microservices—especially in comparison to deployment monoliths.

- Microservices are especially beneficial in dynamic environments—where it is even more difficult to determine a meaningful architecture right from the start.

The architecture has to be changeable; however, this is difficult due to the technical limitations. This section shows how the architecture of a microservice-based system can nevertheless be modified and developed further in a step-by-step manner.

Start Big

One way to handle this inherent problem is to start out with several big systems that are subsequently split step by step into microservices (see Figure 7.8). Section 3.1 defined an upper limit for the size of a microservice as the amount of code that an individual team can still handle. At the start of a project it is hard to violate this upper limit. The same is true for the other upper limits: modularization and replaceability.

When the entire project consists of only one or a few microservices, pieces of functionality are still easy to move, because the transfer will mostly occur within one service rather than between services. Step by step, more people can be moved into the project so that additional teams can be assembled. In parallel, the system can be divided into progressively more microservices to enable the teams to work independently of each other. Such a ramp-up is also a good approach from an organizational perspective since the teams can be assembled in a stepwise manner.

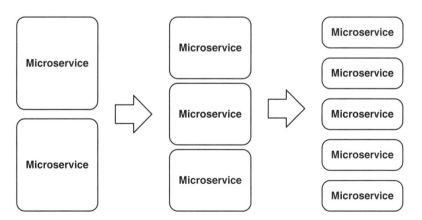

Figure 7.8 *Start Big: A Few Microservices Develop into Progressively More Microservices*

Of course, it would also be possible to start off with a deployment monolith. However, starting with a monolith has a key disadvantage: There is the danger that dependencies and problems creep into the architecture, which make a later separation into microservices difficult. Also there will be only one continuous delivery pipeline. When the monolith gets distributed into microservices, the teams will have to generate new continuous delivery pipelines. This can be very onerous, especially when the continuous delivery pipeline for the deployment monolith had been generated manually. In that situation all the additional continuous delivery pipelines would most likely have to be manually generated in a laborious manner.

When projects start out with multiple microservices, this problem is avoided. There is no monolith that later would have to be divided, and there has to be an approach for the generation of new continuous delivery pipelines. Thus the teams can work independently from the start on their own microservices. Over the course of the project the initial microservices are split into additional smaller microservices.

"Start big" assumes that the number of microservices will increase over the course of the project. It is therefore sensible to start with a few big microservices and spawn new microservices in a stepwise manner. The most recent insights can always be integrated into the distribution of microservices. It is just not possible to define the perfect architecture right from the start. Instead, the teams should adapt the architecture step by step to new circumstances and insights and have the courage to implement the necessary changes.

This approach results in a uniform technology stack—this will facilitate operation and deployment. For developers it is also easier to work on other microservices.

Start Small?

It is also possible to start with a system split into a large number of microservices and use this structure as the basis for further development. However, the distribution of the services is very difficult. *Building Microservices* [11] provides an example where a team was tasked with developing a tool to support continuous delivery of a microservice-based system. The team was very familiar with the domain, had already created products in this area, and thus chose an architecture that distributed the system early on into numerous microservices. However, as the new product was supposed to be offered in the cloud, the architecture was, for subtle reasons, not suitable in some respects. To implement changes got difficult because modifications to features had to be introduced in multiple microservices. To solve

---

11. Sam Newman. 2015. *Building Microservices: Designing Fine-Grained Systems*. Sebastopol, CA: O'Reilly Media.

this problem and make it easier to change the software, the microservices were united again into a monolith. One year later the team decided on the final architecture and split the monolith back into microservices. This example demonstrates that a splitting into microservices too early can be problematic—even if a team knows the domain very well.

Limits of Technology

However, this is in the end a limitation of the technology. If it were easier to move functionality between microservices (see section 7.4), the split into microservices could be corrected. In that case it would be much less risky to start off with a split into small microservices. When all microservices use the same technology, it is easier to transfer functionality between them. Chapter 14, "Technologies for Nanoservices," discusses technologies for nanoservices, which are based on a number of compromises but in exchange enable smaller services and an easier transfer of functionality.

Replaceability as a Quality Criterion

An advantage of the microservice approach is the replaceability of the microservices. This is only possible when the microservices do not grow beyond a certain size and internal complexity. One objective during the continued development of microservices is to maintain the replaceability of microservices. Then a microservice can be replaced by a different implementation—for instance, if its further development is no longer feasible due to bad structure. In addition, replaceability is a meaningful aim to preserve the intelligibility and maintainability of the microservice. If the microservice is not replaceable anymore, it is probably also not intelligible anymore and therefore hard to develop any further.

The Gravity of Monoliths

One problem is that large microservices attract modifications and new features. They already cover several features; therefore, it seems a good idea to also implement new features in this service. This is true in the case of microservices that are too large but even more so for deployment monoliths. A microservices-based architecture can be aimed at replacing a monolith. However, in that case the monolith contains so much functionality that care is needed not to introduce too many changes into the monolith. For this purpose, microservices can be created, even if they contain hardly any functionality at the beginning. To introduce changes and extensions to the monolith is exactly the course of action that has rendered the maintenance of the deployment monolith impossible and led to its replacement by microservices.

Keep Splitting

As mentioned, most architectures do not have the problem that they were originally planned in a way that did not fit the task. In most cases the problem is more that the architecture did not keep up with the changes in the environment. A microservice-based architecture also has to be continuously adjusted; otherwise, at some point it will no longer be able to support the requirements. These adjustments include the management of the domain-based split as well as of the size of the individual microservices. This is the only way to ensure that the benefits of the microservice-based architecture are maintained over time. Since the amount of code in a system usually increases, the number of microservices should also grow in order to keep the average size constant. Thus an increase in the number of microservices is not a problem but rather a good sign.

Global Architecture?

However, the size of microservices is not the only problem. The dependencies of the microservices can also cause problems (see section 7.1). Such problems can be solved most of the time by adjusting a number of microservices—that is, those that have problematic dependencies. This requires contributions only from the teams that work on these microservices. These teams are also the ones to spot the problems, because they will be affected by the bad architecture and the greater need for coordination. By modifying the architecture, they are able to solve these issues. In that case there is no need for a global management of dependencies. Metrics like a high number of dependencies or cyclic dependencies are only an indication of a problem. Whether such metrics actually show a problem can only be solved by evaluating them together with the involved teams. If the problematic components are, for instance, not going to be developed any further in the future, it does not matter if the metrics indicate a problem. Even if there is global architecture management, it can only work effectively in close cooperation with the different teams.

7.5 Don't Miss the Exit Point or How to Avoid the Erosion of a Microservice (Lars Gentsch)

by Lars Gentsch, E-Post Development GmbH

Practically, it is not too difficult to develop a microservice. But how can you ensure that the microservice remains a microservice and does not secretly become a monolith? An example shall illustrate at which point a service starts to develop in the wrong direction and which measures are necessary to ensure that the microservice remains a microservice.

Let's envision a small web application for customer registration. This scenario can be found in nearly every web application. A customer wants to buy a product in an Internet shop (Amazon, Otto, etc.) or to register for a video-on-demand portal (Amazon Prime, Netflix, etc.). As a first step the customer is led through a small registration workflow. He/she is asked for his/her username, a password, the email address, and the street address. This is a small self-contained functionality, which is very well suited for a microservice.

Technologically this service has probably a very simple structure. It consists of two or three HTML pages or an AngularJS-Single Page App, a bit of CSS, some Spring Boot and a MySQL database. Maven is used to build the application.

When data are entered, they are concomitantly validated, transferred into the domain model, and put into the database for persistence. How can the microservice grow step by step into a monolith?

Incorporation of New Functionality

Via the shop or the video-on-demand, portal items and content are supposed to be delivered, which are only allowed to be accessed by people who are of age. For this purpose, the age of the customer has to be verified. One possibility to do this is to store the birth date of the client together with other data and to incorporate an external service for the age verification.

Thus, the data model of our service has to be extended by the birth date. More interesting is the incorporation of the external service. To achieve this, a client for an external API has to be written, which should also be able to handle error situations like the nonavailability of the provider.

It is highly probable that the initiation of the age verification is an asynchronous process so that our service might be forced to implement a callback interface. So the microservice must store data about the state of the process. When was the age verification process initiated? Is it necessary to remind the customer via email? Was the verification process successfully completed?

What Is Happening to the Microservice Here?

The following things are going on:

1. The customer data is extended by the birthdate. That is not problematic.

2. In addition to customer data, there is now process data. Attention: here process data is mixed with domain data.

3. In addition to the original CRUD functionality of the service, some kind of workflow is now required. Synchronous processing is mixed with asynchronous processing.

4. An external system is incorporated. The testing effort for the registration microservice increases. An additional system and its behavior have to be simulated during test.

5. The asynchronous communication with the external system has other demands with regard to scaling. While the registration microservice requires an estimated ten instances due to load and failover, the incorporation of the age verification can be operated in a fail-safe and stable manner with just two instances. Thus, different run time requirements are mixed here.

As the example demonstrates, an apparently small requirement like the incorporation of age verification can have tremendous consequences for the size of the microservice.

Criteria Arguing for a New Microservice Instead of Extending an Existing One

The criteria for deciding on when to start a new microservice include the following:

1. Introduction of different data models and data (domain versus process data)

2. Mixing of synchronous and asynchronous data processing

3. Incorporation of additional services

4. Different load scenarios for different aspects within one service

The example of the registration service could be further extended: the verification of the customer's street address could also be performed by an external provider. This is common in order to ensure the existence of the denoted address. Another scenario is the manual clearance of a customer in case of double registration. The incorporation of a solvency check or customer scoring upon registration likewise are frequent scenarios.

All these domain-based aspects belong in principle to the customer registration and tempt developers and architects to integrate the corresponding requirements into the existing microservice. As a result the microservice grows into more than just one microservice.

How to Recognize Whether the Creation of a New Microservice Should Have Occurred Already

If your situation exhibits the following characteristics, then you probably already needed another microservice:

- The service can only be sensibly developed further as a Maven multimodule project or a Gradle multimodule project.

- Tests have to be divided into test groups and have to be parallelized for execution since the runtime of the tests surpasses five minutes (a violation of the "fast feedback" principle).

- The configuration of the service is grouped by domain within the configuration file, or the file is divided into single configuration files to improve the overview.

- A complete build of the service takes long enough to have a coffee break. Fast feedback cycles are not possible anymore (a violation of the "fast feedback" principle).

Conclusion

As the example of the registration microservice illustrates, it is a significant challenge to let a microservice remain a microservice and not give in to the temptation of integrating new functionality into an existing microservice due to time pressure. This holds true even when the functionality clearly belongs, as in the example, to the same domain.

What defensive steps can be taken to prevent the erosion of a microservice? In principle, it has to be as simple as possible to create new services, including their own data storage. Frameworks like Spring Boot, Grails, and Play make a relevant contribution to this. The allocation of project templates like Maven archetypes and the use of container deployments with Docker are additional measures to simplify the generation and configuration of new microservices as well as their passage into the production environment as much as possible. By reducing the "expenditure" required to set up of a new service, the barriers to introducing a new microservice clearly decrease as does the temptation to implement new functionality into existing services.

7.6 Microservices and Legacy Applications

The transformation of a legacy application into a microservice-based architecture is a scenario that is frequently met with in practice. Completely new developments are rather rare, and microservices, first of all, promise advantages for long-term maintenance. This is especially interesting for applications that are already on the brink of not being maintainable anymore. Besides, the distribution into microservices makes possible easier handling of continuous delivery: Instead of deploying and testing a monolith in an automated fashion, small microservices can be deployed and tested. The expenditure for this is by far lower. A continuous delivery pipeline for a microservice is not very complex; however, for a deployment monolith the expenditure can be very large. This advantage is sufficient for many companies to justify the effort of migrating to microservices.

In comparison to building up completely new systems, there are some important differences when migrating from a deployment monolith to microservices:

- For a legacy system the functionality is clear from the domain perspective. This can be a good basis for generating a clean domain architecture for the microservices. Such a clean domain-based division is especially important for microservices.

- However, there is already a large amount of code in existence. The code is often of bad quality. There are few tests for the code, and deployment times are often much too long. Microservices should remove these problems. Accordingly, the challenges in this area are often significant.

- Likewise, it is well possible that the module boundaries in the legacy application do not answer to the *Bounded Context* idea (see section 3.3). In that case migrating to a microservice-based architecture is a challenge because the domain-based design of the application has to be changed.

Breaking Up Code?

In a simple approach the code of the legacy application can be split into several microservices. This can be problematic when the legacy application does not have a good domain architecture, which is often the case. The code can be easily split into microservices when the microservices are geared to the existing modules of the legacy application. However, when those have a bad domain-based split, this bad division will be passed on to the microservice-based architecture. Additionally, the consequences of a bad domain-based design are even more profound in a microservice-based architecture: The design also influences the communication between teams. Besides, the initial design is hard to change later on in a microservice-based architecture.

Supplementing Legacy Applications

However, it is also possible to get by without a division of the legacy application. An essential advantage of microservices is that the modules are distributed systems. Because of that, the module boundaries are at the same time the boundaries of processes that communicate via the network. This has advantages for the distribution of a legacy application: It is not at all necessary to know the internal structures of the legacy application or, based on that, to perform a split into microservices. Instead microservices can supplement or modify the legacy application at the interface. For this it is very helpful when the system to be replaced is already built in an SOA (section 6.2). If there are individual services, they can be supplemented by microservices.

Enterprise Integration Patterns

Enterprise Integration Patterns [12, 13] offer an inspiration for possible integrations of legacy applications and microservices:

- *Message Router* describes that certain messages go to another service. For example, a microservice can select some messages that are processed then by the microservice instead of by the legacy application. In this way, the microservice-based architecture does not have to newly implement the entire logic at once but can at first select some parts.

- A special router is the *Content Based Router*. It determines based on the content of a message where the message is supposed to be sent. This enables the sending of specific messages to a specific microservice—even if the message differs only in one field.

- The *Message Filter* avoids uninteresting messages that a microservice receives. For that it just filters out all messages the microservice is not supposed to get.

- A *Message Translator* translates a message into another format. Therefore, the microservices architecture can use other data formats and does not necessarily have to employ the formats used by the legacy application.

---

12. http://www.eaipatterns.com/toc.html
13. Gregor Hohpe, Bobby Woolf. 2003. *Enterprise Integration Patterns: Designing, Building, and Deploying Messaging Solutions*. Boston: Addison-Wesley.

- The *Content Enricher* can supplement data in the messages. If a microservice requires supplementary information in addition to the data of the legacy application, the *Content Enricher* can add this information without the legacy application or the microservice noticing anything.

- The *Content Filter* achieves the opposite: Certain data are removed from the messages so that the microservice obtains only the information relevant for it.

Figure 7.9 shows a simple example. A Message Router takes calls and sends them to a microservice or the legacy system. This enables implementation of certain functionalities in microservices. These functionalities are also still present in the legacy system but are not used there anymore. In this way the microservices are largely independent of the structures within the legacy system. For instance, microservices can start off with processing orders for certain customers or certain items. Because their scope is limited, they do not have to implement all special cases.

The patterns can serve as inspiration for how a legacy application can be supplemented by microservices. There are numerous additional patterns—the list provides only a glimpse of the entire catalog. As in other cases the patterns can be implemented in different ways: actually, they focus on messaging systems. However, it is possible to implement them with synchronous communication mechanisms, though less elegant. For instance, a REST service can take a POST message, supplement it with additional data, and finally send it to another microservice. That would then be a *Content Enricher*.

To implement such patterns, the sender has to be uncoupled from the recipient. This enables the integration of additional steps into the processing of requests without the sender noticing anything. In case of a messaging approach, this is easily possible, as the sender knows only one queue in which he/she places the messages. The sender does not know who fetches the messages. However, in the case of synchronous communication via REST or SOAP, the message is sent directly to the

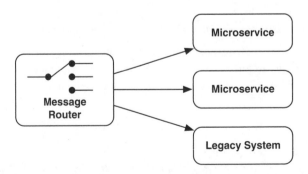

Figure 7.9 *Supplementing Legacy Applications by a* Message Router

recipient. Only by Service Discovery (see section 7.11) the sender gets uncoupled from the recipient. Then one service can be replaced by another service without need to change the senders. This enables an easier implementation of the patterns. When the legacy application is supplemented by a *Content Enricher*, this *Content Enricher*, instead of the legacy application, is registered in the Service Discovery, but no sender has to be modified. To introduce Service Discovery can therefore be a first step towards a microservices architecture since it enables supplementation or replacement of individual services of the legacy application without having to modify the users of the legacy application.

Limiting Integration

Especially for legacy applications, it is important that the microservices are not too dependent on the legacy application. Often the bad structure of the old application is the specific reason why the application is supposed to be replaced in the first place. Therefore, certain dependencies should not be allowed at all. When microservices directly access the database of the legacy application, the microservices are dependent on the internal data representation of the legacy application. Besides neither the legacy application nor the microservices can still change the schema, because such changes have to be implemented in microservices and legacy application. The shared use of a database in legacy application and microservices has to be avoided on all accounts. However, to replicate the data of the legacy application into a separate database schema is, of course, still an option.

Advantages

It is an essential advantage of such an approach that the microservices are largely independent of the architecture of the legacy application. And the replacement of a legacy application is mostly initiated because its architecture is not sustainable any more. This also enables supplementation of systems by microservices that are actually not at all meant to be extended. Though, for instance, standard solutions in the area of CRM, e-commerce, or ERP are internally extensible, their extension by external interfaces can be a welcome alternative since such a supplement is often easier. Moreover, such systems often attract functionalities that do not really belong there. A distribution into a different deployment unit via a microservice ensures a permanent and clear delimitation.

Integration via UI and Data Replication

However, this approach only tackles the problem on the level of logic integration. Chapter 8 describes another level of integration, namely data replication. This allows a microservice to access comprehensive datasets of a legacy application also with good performance. It is important that the replication does not happen based on the data model of the legacy application. In that case the data model of the legacy application would practically not be changeable anymore since it is also used by the microservice. An integration based on the use of the same database would be even worse. Also at the level of UI integrations are possible. Links in web applications are especially attractive since they cause only few changes in the legacy application.

Content Management Systems

In this manner content management systems (CMS), for instance, which often contain many functionalities, can be supplemented by microservices. CMS contain the data of a website and administrate the content so that editors can modify it. The microservices take over the handling of certain URLs. Similar to a *Message Router*, an HTTP request can be sent to a microservice instead of to the CMS. Or the microservice changes elements of the CMS as in the case of a *Content Enricher* or modifies the request as in the case of a *Message Translator*. Last, the microservices could store data in the CMS and thereby use it as a kind of database. Besides JavaScript representing the UI of a microservice can be delivered into the CMS. In that case the CMS turns into a tool for the delivery of code in a browser.

Some examples could be:

- A microservice can import content from certain sources. Each source can have its own microservice.

- The functionality that enables a visitor of the web page—for example, to follow an author—can be implemented in a separate microservice. The microservice can either have its own URL and be integrated via links, or it modifies the pages that the CMS delivers.

- While an author is still known in the CMS, there is other logic that is completely separate from the CMS. This could be vouchers or e-commerce functionalities. Also in this case a microservice can appropriately supplement the system.

Especially in the case of CMS systems, which create static HTML, microservices-based approaches can be useful for dynamic content. The CMS moves into the background and is only necessary for certain content. There is a monolithic deployment of the CMS content, while the microservices can be deployed much more rapidly and in an independent manner. In this context the CMS is like a legacy application.

Conclusion

The integrations all have the advantage that the microservices are not bound to the architecture or the technology decisions of the legacy application. This provides the microservices with a decisive advantage compared to a modifications of the legacy application. However, the migration away from the legacy application using this approach poses a challenge at the level of architecture; in effect, microservice-based systems have to have a well-structured domain-based design to enable the implementation of features within one microservice and by an individual team. In case of a migration, which follows the outlined approach, this cannot always be put into effect since the migration is influenced by the interfaces of the legacy application. Therefore, the design cannot always be as clear-cut as desirable. Besides, domain-based features will still be also implemented in the legacy application until a large part of the migration has been completed. During this time the legacy application cannot be finally removed. When the microservices confine themselves to transforming the messages, the migration can take a very long time.

No Big Bang

The outlined approaches suggest that the existing legacy application is supplemented in a stepwise manner by microservices or that individual parts of the legacy application are replaced by microservices. This type of approach has the advantage that the risk is minimized. Replacing the entire legacy application in one single step entails high risk due to the size of the legacy application. In the end, all functionalities have to be represented in the microservices. In this process numerous mistakes can creep in. In addition, the deployment of microservices is complex as they all have to be brought into production in a concerted manner in order to replace the legacy application in one step. A stepwise replacement nearly imposes itself in the case of microservices since they can be deployed independently and supplement the legacy application. Therefore, the legacy application can be replaced by microservices in a stepwise manner.

Legacy = Infrastructure

Part of a legacy application can also simply be continued to be used as infrastructure for the microservices. For example, the database of the legacy application can also be used for the microservices. It is important that the schemas of the microservices are separate from each other and also from the legacy application. After all, the microservices should not be closely coupled.

The use of the database of the legacy application does not have to be mandatory for the microservices. Microservices can definitely also use other solutions. However, the existing database is established with regard to operation or backup. Using this database can also present an advantage for the microservices. The same is true for other infrastructure components. A CMS, for instance, can likewise serve as common infrastructure, to which functionalities are added from the different microservices and into which the microservices can also deliver content.

Other Qualities

The migration approaches introduced so far focus on enabling the domain-based division into microservices in order to facilitate the long-term maintenance and continued development of the system. However, microservices have many additional advantages. When migrating it is important to understand which advantage motivates the migration to microservices because, depending on this motivation, an entirely different strategy might be adopted. Microservices also offer, for instance, increased robustness and resilience since the communication with other services is taken care of accordingly (see section 9.5). If the legacy application currently has a deficit in this area or a distributed architecture already exists that has to be optimized with respect to these points, appropriate technology and architecture approaches can be defined without necessarily requiring that the application be divided into microservices.

Try and Experiment

- Do research on the remaining Enterprise Integration Patterns:

  - Can they be meaningfully employed when dealing with microservices? In which context?

  - Can they really only be implemented with messaging systems?

7.7 Hidden Dependencies (Oliver Wehrens)

by Oliver Wehrens, E-Post Development GmbH

In the beginning there is the monolith. Often it is sensible and happens naturally that software is created as a monolith. The code is clearly arranged, and the business domain is just coming into being. In that case it is better when everything has a common base. There is a UI, business logic, and a database. Refactoring is simple, deployment is easy, and everybody can still understand the entire code.

Over time the amount of code grows, and it gets hard to see through. Not everybody knows all parts of the code anymore. The compiling takes longer, and the unit and integration tests invite developers to take a coffee break. In case of a relatively stable business domain and a very large code basis, many projects will consider at this point the option to distribute the functionality into multiple microservices.

Depending on the status of the business and the understanding of the business/ product owners, the necessary tasks will be completed. Source code is distributed, continuous delivery pipelines are created, and server provisioned. During this step no new features are developed. The not-negligible effort is justified just by the hope that in the future, features will be faster and more independently created by other teams. While developers are going to be very assured of this, other stakeholders often have to be convinced first.

In principle everything has been done to reach a better architecture. There are different teams that have independent source code. They can bring their software at any time into production and independent of other teams.

Almost.

The Database

Every developer has a more or less pronounced affinity to the database. In my experience many developers view the database as necessary evil that is somewhat cumbersome to refactor. Often tools are being used that generate the database structure for the developers (e.g., Liquibase or Flyway in the JVM area). Tools and libraries (Object-relation mapping) renders it very easy to make objects persistent. A few annotations later and the domain is saved in the database.

All these tools remove the database from the typical developers, who "only" want to write their code. This has sometimes the consequence that there is not much attention given to the database during the development process. For instance, indices that were not created will slow down searches on the database. This will not show up in a typical test, which does not work with large data amounts, and thus go like that into production.

Let's take the fictional case of an online shoe shop. The company requires a service that enables users to log in. A user service is created containing the typical fields like ID, first name, family name, address, and password. To now offer fitting shoes to the users, only a selection of shoes in their actual size is supposed to be displayed. The size is registered in the welcome mask. What could be more sensible than to store this data in the already existing user service? Everybody is sure this is the right decision: these are user-associated data, and this is the right location.

Now the shoe shop expands and starts to sell additional types of clothing. Dress size, collar size, and all other related data are now also stored in the user service.

Several teams are employed in the company. The code gets progressively more complex. It is this point in time where the monolith is split into domain-based services. The refactoring in the source code works well, and a soon the monolith is split apart into many microservices.

Unfortunately, it turns out that it is still not easy to introduce changes. The team in charge of shoes wants to accept different currencies because of international expansion and has to modify the structure of the billing data to include the address format. During the upgrade the database is blocked. Meanwhile no dress size or favorite color can be changed. Moreover, the address data are used in different standard forms of other services and thus cannot be changed without coordination and effort. Therefore, the feature cannot be implemented promptly.

Even though the code is well separated, the teams are indirectly coupled via the database. To rename columns in the user service database is nearly impossible because nobody knows anymore in detail who is using which columns. Consequently, the teams do workarounds. Either fields with the name 'Userattribute1' are created, which then are mapped onto the right description in the code, or separations are introduced into the data like '#Color: Blue#Size:10.' Nobody except the involved team knows what is meant by 'Userattribute1,' and it is difficult to generate an index on '#Color: #Size.' Database structure and code are progressively harder to read and maintain.

It has to be essential for every software developer to think about how to make the data persistent, not only about the database structures but also about where which data is stored. Is the table respective database the place where these data should be located? From a business domain perspective, does this data have connections to other data? In order to remain flexible in the long term, it is worthwhile to carefully consider these questions every time. Typically, databases and tables are not created very often. However, they are a component that is very hard to modify later. Besides, databases and tables are often the origin of a hidden interdependence between services. In general, it has to be that data can only be used by exactly one service via direct database access. All other services that want to use the data may only access it via the public interfaces of the service.

7.8 Event-Driven Architecture

Microservices can call each other in order to implement shared logic. For example, at the end of the order process the microservice for billing as well as the microservice for the order execution can be called to create the bill and make sure that the ordered items are indeed delivered (see Figure 7.10).

This requires that the order process knows the service for the billing and for the delivery. If a completed orders necessitates additional steps, the order service also has to call the services responsible for these steps.

Event-driven architecture (EDA) enables a different modeling: When the order processing has been successfully finished, the order process will send an event. It is an event emitter. This event signals all interested microservices (event consumers) that there is a new successful order. Thus, one microservice can now print a bill, and another microservice can initiate a delivery (see Figure 7.11).

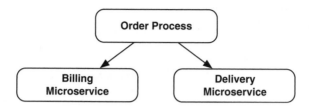

Figure 7.10 *Calls between Microservices*

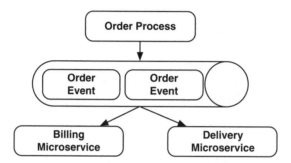

Figure 7.11 *Event-Driven Architecture*

This procedure has a number of advantages:

- When other microservices are also interested in orders, they can easily register. Modifying the order process is not necessary anymore.

- Likewise, it is imaginable that other microservices also trigger identical events—again without changes to the order process.

- The processing of events is temporally unlinked. It can be linked later on.

At the architectural level, event-driven architectures have the advantage that they enable a very loose coupling and thus facilitate changes. The microservices need to know very little about each other. However, the coupling requires that logic is integrated and therefore implemented in different microservices. Thereby a split into microservice with UI and microservices with logic can arise. That is not desirable. Changes to the business logic entail often changes to logic and UI. These are then separate microservices. The change cannot readily take place in only one microservice anymore and thus gets more complex.

Technically, such architectures can be implemented without a lot of effort via messaging (see section 8.4). Microservices within such an architecture can very easily implement CQRS (section 9.2) or event sourcing (section 9.3).

7.9 Technical Architecture

To define a technology stack with which the system can be built is one of the main parts of an architecture. For individual microservices this is likewise a very important task. However, the focus of this chapter is the microservice-based system in its entirety. Of course, a certain technology can bindingly be defined for all microservices. This has advantages: In that case the teams can exchange knowledge about the technology. Refactorings are simpler because members of one team can easily help out on other teams.

However, defining standard technologies is not mandatory: if they are not defined, there will be a plethora of different technologies and frameworks. However, since typically only one team is in contact with each technology, such an approach can be acceptable. Generally, microservice-based architectures aim for the largest possible independence. With respect to the technology stack, this independence translates into the ability to use different technology stacks and to independently make technology decisions. However, this freedom can also be restricted.

Technical Decisions for the Entire System

Nevertheless, at the level of the entire system there are some technical decisions to make. However, other aspects are more important for the technical architecture of the microservice-based system than the technology stack for the implementation:

- As discussed in the last section, there might be technologies that can be used by all microservices—for instance, databases for data storage. Using these technologies does not necessarily have to be mandatory. However, especially in the case of persistence technologies, like databases, backups, and disaster recovery concepts have to exist so that at least these technical solutions have to be obligatory. The same is true for other basic systems such as CMS, for instance, which likewise have to be used by all microservices.

- The microservices have to adhere to certain standards with respect to monitoring, logging and deployment. Thereby, it can be ensured that the plethora of microservices can still be operated in a uniform manner. Without such standards this is hardly possible anymore in the case of a larger number of microservices.

- Additional aspects relate to configuration (section 7.10), Service Discovery (section 7.11) and security (section 7.14).

- Resilience (section 9.5) and Load Balancing (section 7.12) are concepts that have to be implemented in a microservice. Still, the overall architecture can demand that each microservice takes precautions in this area.

- An additional aspect is the communication of the microservices with each other (see Chapter 8). For the system in its entirety a communication infrastructure has to be defined which the microservices adhere to also.

The overall architecture does not necessarily restrict the choice of technologies. For logging, monitoring, and deployment an interface could be defined so there can be a standard according to which all microservices log messages in the same manner and hand them over to a common log infrastructure. However, the microservices do not necessarily have to use the same technologies for this. Similarly, how data can be handed to the monitoring system and which data are relevant for the monitoring can be defined. A microservice has to hand over the data to the monitoring, but a technology does not necessarily have to be prescribed. For deployment a completely automated continuous delivery pipeline can be demanded that deploys software or deposits it into a repository in a certain manner. Which specific technology is used is, again, a question for the developers of the respective microservice to decide. Practically, there are advantages when all microservices employ the same technology. This reduces complexity, and there will also be more experience in how to deal with the employed technology. However, in case of specific requirements, it is still possible to use a different technical solution when, for this special case, the advantages of such a solution predominate. This is an essential advantage of the technology freedom of microservice-based architectures.

Sidecar

Even if certain technologies for implementing the demands on microservices are rigidly defined, it will still be possible to integrate other technologies. Therefore, the concept of a sidecar can be very useful. This is a process that integrates into the microservices-based architecture via standard technologies and offers an interface that enables another process to use these features. This process can be implemented in an entirely different technology so that the technology freedom is preserved. Figure 7.12 illustrates this concept: The sidecar uses standard technologies and renders them accessible for another microservice in an optional technology. The sidecar is an independent process and therefore can be called for instance via REST so that microservices in arbitrary technologies can use the sidecar. Section 13.12 shows a concrete example for a sidecar.

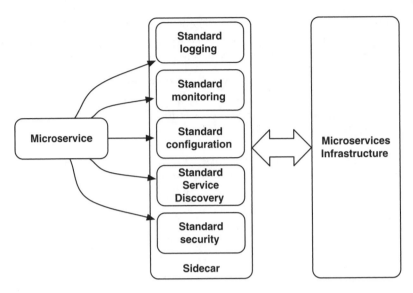

Figure 7.12 *A Sidecar Renders All Standard Technologies Accessible via a Simple Interface*

Also, with this approach such microservices can be integrated into the architecture whose technological approach otherwise would exclude the use of the general technical basis for configuration, Service Discovery and security, as the client component is not available for the entire technology.

In some regards the definition of the technology stack also affects other fields. The definition of technologies across all microservices also affects the organization or can be the product of a certain organization (see Chapter 12, "Organizational Effects of a Microservices-Based Architecture").

Try and Experiment

- A microservices-based architecture is supposed to be defined.

  - Which technical aspects could it comprise?

  - Which aspects would you prescribe to the teams? Why?

  - Which aspects should the teams decide on their own? Why?

In the end, the question is how much freedom you allow the teams to have. There are numerous possibilities, ranging from complete freedom up to the prescription of practically all aspects. However, some areas can only be centrally defined—the communication protocols, for example. Section 12.3 discusses in more detail who should make which decisions in a microservice-based project.

7.10 Configuration and Coordination

Configuring microservice-based systems is laborious. They comprise a plethora of microservices, which all have to be provided with the appropriate configuration parameters.

Some tools can store the configuration values and make them available to all microservices. Ultimately, these are solutions in key/value stores, which save a certain value under a certain key:

- *Zookeeper*[14] is a simple hierarchical system that can be replicated onto multiple servers in a cluster. Updates arrive in an orderly fashion at the clients. This can also be used in a distributed environment, for instance for synchronization. Zookeeper has a consistent data model: all nodes have always the same data. The project is implemented in Java and is available under the Apache license.

- *etcd*[15] originates from the Docker/CoreOS environment. It offers an HTTP interface with JSON as data format. etcd is implemented in Go and also is available under the Apache license. Similar to Zookeeper, etcd also has a consistent data model and can be used for distributed coordination. For instance, etcd enables implementation of locking in a distributed system.

- *Spring Cloud Config*[16] likewise has a REST-API. The configuration data can be provided by a Git backend. Therefore Spring Cloud Config directly supports data versioning. The data can also be encrypted to protect passwords. The system is well integrated into the Java framework Spring and can be used without additional effort in Spring systems for Spring itself provides already configuration mechanisms. Spring Cloud Config is written in Java and is available under the Apache license. Spring Cloud Config does not offer support for synchronizing different distributed components.

Consistency as Problem

Some of the configuration solutions offer consistent data. This means that all nodes return the same data in case of a call. This is in a sense an advantage. However, according to the CAP theorem a node can only return an inconsistent response in case of a network failure—or none at all. In the end, without a network connection the node cannot know whether other nodes have already received other values. If the system allows only consistent responses, there can be no response at all in this situation. For certain scenarios this is highly sensible.

---

14. https://zookeeper.apache.org/

15. https://github.com/coreos/etcd

16. http://cloud.spring.io/spring-cloud-config/

For instance, only one client should execute a certain code at a given time—for example, to initiate a payment exactly once. The necessary locking can be done by the configuration system: within the configuration system there is a variable that, upon entering this code, has to be set. Only in that case may the code be executed. In the end, it is better when the configuration system does not return a response two clients will not execute the code in parallel by chance.

However, for configurations such strict requirements regarding consistency are often not necessary. Maybe it is better when a system gets an old value rather than when it does not get any value at all. However, in the case of CAP different compromises are possible. For instance, etcd returns an incorrect response rather than no response at all under certain conditions.

Immutable Server

Another problem associated with the centralized storage of configuration data is that the microservices do not only depend on the state of their own file system and the contained files but also on the state of the configuration server. Therefore, a microservice now cannot be exactly replicated anymore—for this the state of the configuration server is relevant also. This makes the reproduction of errors and the search for errors in general more difficult.

In addition, the configuration server is in opposition to the concept of an immutable server. In this approach every software change leads to a new installation of the software. Ultimately, the old server is terminated upon an update, and a new server with an entirely new installation of the software is started. However, in case of an external configuration server, a part of the configuration will not be present on the server, and therefore the server is after all changeable in the end by adjusting the configuration. However, this is exactly what is not supposed to happen. To prevent it, a configuration can be made in the server itself instead of the configuration server. In that case configuration changes can only be implemented by rolling out a new server.

Alternative: Installation Tools

The installation tools (discussed in section 11.4) represent a completely different approach for the configuration of individual microservices. These tools support not only the installation of software, but also the configuration. The configuration files, for instance, can be generated, which can subsequently be read by microservices. The microservice itself does not notice the central configuration since it reads only a configuration file. Still, these approaches support all scenarios, which typically occur in a microservices-based architecture. Thus, this approach allows a central configuration and is not in opposition to the immutable server as the configuration is completely transferred to the server.

7.11 Service Discovery

Service Discovery ensures that microservices can find each other. This is, in a sense, a very simple task: For instance, a configuration file detailing the IP address and the port of the microservice can be delivered on all computers. Typical configuration management systems enable the rollout of such files. However, this approach is not sufficient:

- Microservices can come and go. This does not only happen due to server failures but also because of new deployments or the scaling of the environment by the start of new servers. Service Discovery has to be dynamic. A fixed configuration is not sufficient.

- Due to Service Discovery, the calling microservices are not so closely coupled anymore to the called microservice. This has positive effects for scaling: A client is not bound to a concrete server, instance, anymore but can contact different instances—depending on the current load of the different servers.

- When all microservices have a common approach for Service Discovery, a central registry of all microservices arises. This can be helpful for an architecture overview (see section 7.2). Or monitoring information can be retrieved by all systems.

In systems that employ messaging, Service Discovery can be dispensable. Messaging systems already decouple sender and recipient. Both know only the shared channel by which they communicate. However, they do not know the identity of their communication partner. The flexibility that Service Discovery offers is then provided by the decoupling via the channels.

Service Discovery = Configuration?

In principle it is conceivable to implement Service Discovery by configuration solutions (see section 7.10). In the end, only the information that service is reachable at which location is supposed to be transferred. However, configuration mechanisms are, in effect, the wrong tools for this. For Service Discovery, high availability is more important than for a configuration server. In the worst case a failure of Service Discovery can have the consequence that communication between microservices becomes impossible. Consequently, the trade-off between consistency and availability is different compared to configuration systems. Therefore, configuration systems should be used for Service Discovery only when they offer an appropriate availability. This can have consequences for the necessary architecture of the Service Discovery system.

Technologies

There are many different technologies for Service Discovery:

- One example is *DNS*[17] (Domain Name System). This protocol ensures that a host name like *www.ewolff.com* can be resolved to an IP address. DNS is an essential component of the Internet and has clearly proven its scalability and availability. DNS is hierarchically organized: There is a DNS server that administrates the *.com* domain. This DNS server knows which DNS server administrates the subdomain *ewolff.com*, and the DNS server of this subdomain finally knows the IP address of *www.ewolff.com*. In this way a namespace can be hierarchically organized, and different organizations can administrate different parts of the namespace. If a server named *server.ewolff.com* is supposed to be created, this can be easily done by a change in the DNS server of the domain *ewolff.com*. This independence fits well to the concept of microservices, which especially focus on independence with regard to their architecture. To ensure reliability there are always several servers, which administrate a domain. In order to reach scalability DNS supports caching so that calls do not have to implement the entire resolution of a name via multiple DNS servers, but can be served by a cache. This does not only promote performance, but also reliability.

- For Service Discovery it is not sufficient to resolve the name of a server into an IP address. In addition, there has to be a network port for each service. Therefore, the DNS has SRV records. These contain the information on which computer and port the service is reachable. In addition, a priority and a weight can be set for a certain server. These values can be used to select one of the servers and thereby to prefer powerful servers. Via this approach, DNS offers reliability and Load Balancing onto multiple servers. Advantages of DNS are apart from scalability also the availability of many different implementations and the broad support in different programming languages.

- A frequently used implementation for a DNS server is *BIND (Berkeley Internet Name Domain Server)*.[18] BIND runs on different operating systems (Linux,

---

17. http://www.zytrax.com/books/dns/
18. https://www.isc.org/downloads/bind/

BSD, Windows, Mac OS X), is written in the programming language C and is under an open-source license.

- *Eureka*[19] is part of the Netflix stack. It is written in Java and is available under the Apache license. The example application in this book uses Eureka for Service Discovery (see section 13.8). For every service Eureka stores under the service name a host and a port, under which the service is available. Eureka can replicate the information about the services onto multiple Eureka servers in order to increase the availability. Eureka is a REST service. A Java library for the clients belongs to Eureka. Via the sidecar concept (section 7.9) this library can also be used by systems, which are not written in Java. The sidecar takes over the communication with the Eureka server, which then offers Service Discovery to the microservice. On the clients the information from the server can be held in a cache so that calls are possible without communication with the server. The server regularly contacts the registered services to determine which services failed. Eureka can be used as basis for Load Balancing since several instances can be registered for one service. The load can then be distributed onto these instances. Eureka was originally designed for the Amazon Cloud.

- *Consul*[20] is a key/value store and therefore fits also into the area of configuration servers (section 7.10). Apart from consistency it can also optimize availability.[21] Clients can register with the server and react to certain events. In addition to a DNS interface it also has a HTTP/JSON interface. It can check whether services are still available by executing health checks. Consul is written in Go and is available under the Mozilla open-source license. Besides, Consul can create configuration files from templates. Therefore, a system expecting services in a configuration file can likewise be configured by Consul.

Every microservice-based architecture should use a Service Discovery system. It forms the basis for the administration of a large number of microservices and for additional features like Load Balancing. If there is only a small number of microservices, it is still imaginable to get along without Service Discovery. However, for a large system Service Discovery is indispensable. Since the number of microservices increases over time, Service Discovery should be integrated into the architecture right from the start. Besides, practically each system uses at least the name resolution of hosts, which is already a simple Service Discovery.

---

19. https://github.com/Netflix/eureka
20. http://www.consul.io
21. https://aphyr.com/posts/316-call-me-maybe-etcd-and-consul

7.12 Load Balancing

It is one of the advantages of microservices that each individual service can be independently scaled. To distribute the load between the instances, multiple instances, which share the load, can simply be registered in a messaging solution (see section 8.4). The actual distribution of the individual messages is then performed by the messaging solution. Messages can either be distributed to one of the receivers (point-to-point) or to all receivers (publish/subscribe).

REST/HTTP

In case of REST and HTTP a load balancer has to be used. The load balancer has the function to behave to the outside like a single instance, but to distribute requests to multiple instances. Besides, a load balancer can be useful during deployment: Instances of the new version of the microservice can initially start without getting a lot of load. Afterwards the load balancer can be reconfigured in a way that the new microservices are put into operation. In doing so the load can also be increased in a stepwise manner. This decreases the risk of a system failure.

Figure 7.13 illustrates the principle of a proxy-based load balancer: the client sends its requests to a load balancer running on another server. This load balancer is responsible for sending each request to one of the known instances. There the request is processed.

This approach is common for websites and relatively easy to implement. The load balancer retrieves information from the service instances to determine the load of the different instances. In addition, the load balancer can remove a server from the Load Balancing when the node does not react to requests anymore.

On the other hand, this approach has the disadvantage that the entire traffic for one kind of service has to be directed via a load balancer. Therefore, the load

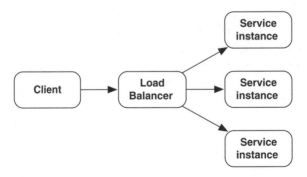

Figure 7.13 *Proxy-Based Load Balancer*

balancer can turn into a bottleneck. Besides, a failure of the load balancer results in the failure of a microservice.

Central Load Balancer

A central load balancer for all microservices is not only not recommended for these reasons but also because of the configuration. The configuration of the load balancer gets very complex when only one load balancer is responsible for many microservices. Besides, the configuration has to be coordinated between all microservices. Especially when a new version of a microservice is being deployed, a modification of the load balancer can be sensible in order to put the new microservice only after a comprehensive test under load. The need for coordination between microservices should especially be avoided with regard to deployment to ensure the independent deployment of microservices. In case of such a reconfiguration, one has to make sure that the load balancer supports a dynamic reconfiguration and, for instance, does not lose information regarding sessions if the microservice uses sessions. Also for this reason it is not recommended that stateful microservices should be implemented.

A Load Balancer per Microservice

There should be one load balancer per microservice, which distributes the load between the instances of the microservice. This enables the individual microservices to independently distribute load, and different configurations per microservice are possible. Likewise, it is simple to appropriately reconfigure the load balancer upon the deployment of a new version. However, in case of a failure of the load balancers, the microservice will not be available anymore.

Technologies

For Load Balancing there are different approaches:

- The Apache httpd web server supports Load Balancing with the extension mod_proxy_balancer.[22]
- The web server nginx[23] can likewise be configured in a way that it supports Load Balancing. To use a web server as load balancer has the advantage that it can also deliver static websites, CSS, and images. Besides, the number of technologies will be reduced.

---

22. http://httpd.apache.org/docs/2.2/mod/mod_proxy_balancer.html
23. http://nginx.org/en/docs/http/load_balancing.html

- HAProxy[24] is a solution for Load Balancing and high availability. It does not support HTTP, but all TCP-based protocols.

- Cloud providers frequently also offer Load Balancing. Amazon, for instance, offers Elastic Load Balancing.[25] This can be combined with auto scaling so that higher loads automatically trigger the start of new instances, and thereby the application automatically scales with load.

Service Discovery

Another possibility for Load Balancing is Service Discovery (see Figure 7.14; see section 7.11). When the Service Discovery returns different nodes for a service, the load can be distributed across several nodes. However, this approach allows redirecting to another node only in the case that a new Service Discovery is performed. This makes it difficult to achieve a fine granular Load Balancing. For a new node it will therefore take some time until it gets a sufficient share of load. Finally, the failure of a node is hard to correct because a new Service Discovery would be necessary for that. It is useful that in case of DNS it can be stated for a set of data how long the data is valid (time-to-live). Afterwards the Service Discovery has to be run again. This enables a simple Load Balancing via DNS solutions and also with Consul. However, unfortunately this time-to-live is often not completely correctly implemented.

Load Balancing with Service Discovery is simple because Service Discovery has to be present in a microservice-based system anyhow. Therefore, the Load Balancing

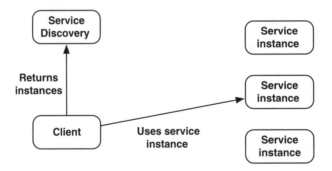

Figure 7.14 *Load Balancing with Service Discovery*

---

24. http://www.haproxy.org/

25. http://aws.amazon.com/de/elasticloadbalancing/

does not introduce additional software components. Besides, avoiding a central load balancer has the positive effect that there is no bottle neck and no central component whose failure would have tremendous consequences.

Client-Based Load Balancing

The client itself can also use a load balancer (see Figure 7.15). The load balancer can be implemented as a part of the code of the microservice or it can come as a proxy-based load balancer such as nginx or Apache httpd, which runs on the same computer as the microservice. In that case there is no bottleneck because each client has its own load balancer, and the failure of an individual load balancer has hardly any consequences. However, configuration changes have to be passed on to all load balancers, which can cause quite a lot of network traffic and load.

Ribbon[26] is an implementation of client-based Load Balancing. It is a library that is written in Java and can use Eureka to find service instances. Alternately, a list of servers can be handed over to Ribbon. Ribbon implements different algorithms for Load Balancing. Especially when using it in combination with Eureka, the individual load balancer does not need to be configured anymore. Because of the sidecar concept Ribbon can also be used by microservices that are not implemented in Java. The example system uses Ribbon (see section 13.11).

Consul offers the possibility to define a template for configuration files of load balancers. This enables feeding the load balancer configuration with data from Service Discovery. Client-based Load Balancing can be implemented by defining a template for each client, into which Consul writes all service instances. This process can

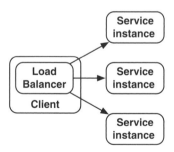

Figure 7.15 *Client-Based Load Balancing*

---

26. https://github.com/Netflix/ribbon

be regularly repeated. In this manner a central system configuration is again possible, and client-based Load Balancing is relatively simple to implement.

Load Balancing and Architecture

It is hardly sensible to use more than one kind of Load Balancing within a single microservice-based system. Therefore, this decision should be made once for the entire system. Load Balancing and Service Discovery have a number of contact points. Service Discovery knows all service instances; Load Balancing distributes the loads between the instances. Both technologies have to work together. Thus, the technology decisions in this area will influence each other.

7.13 Scalability

To be able to cope with high loads, microservices have to scale. Scalability means that a system can process more load when it gets more resources.

There are two different kinds of scalability as represented in Figure 7.16:

- **Horizontal scalability**—This means that more resources are used, which each process part of the load, that is, the number of resources increases.

- **Vertical scalability**—This means that more powerful resources are employed to handle a higher load. Here, an individual resource will process more load, while the number of resources stays constant.

Horizontal scalability is often the better choice since the limit for the possible number of resources and therefore the limit for the scalability is very high. Besides,

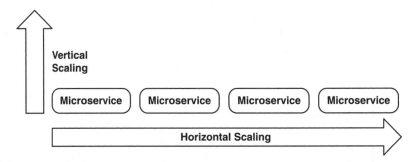

Figure 7.16 *Horizontal and Vertical Scaling*

it is cheaper to buy more resources than more powerful ones. One fast computer is often more expensive than many slow ones.

Scaling, Microservices, and Load Balancing

Microservices employ mostly horizontal scaling, where the load is distributed across several microservice instances via Load Balancing. The microservices themselves have to be stateless for this. More precisely, they should not have any state, which is specific for an individual user, because then the load can only be distributed to nodes, which have the respective state. The state for a user can be stored in a database or alternatively be put into an external storage (for example, In-Memory-Store), which can be accessed by all microservices.

Dynamic Scaling

Scalability means only that the load can be distributed to multiple nodes. How the system really reacts to the load is not defined. In the end it is more important that the system really adapts to an increasing load. For that it is necessary that, depending on the load, a microservice starts new instances onto which the load can be distributed. This enables the microservice to also cope with high loads. This process has to be automated, as manual processes would be too laborious.

There are different places in the continuous deployment pipeline (Chapter 11, "Operations and Continuous Delivery of Microservices") where it is necessary to start a microservice to test the services. For that a suitable deployment system such as Chef or Puppet can be used. Alternatively, a new virtual machine or a new Docker container with the microservice is simply started. This mechanism can also be used for dynamic scaling. It only has to additionally register the new instances with the Load Balancing. However, the instance should be able to handle the production load right from the start. Therefore, the caches should, for instance, already be filled with data.

Dynamic scaling is especially simple with Service Discovery: The microservice has to register with the Service Discovery. The Service Discovery can configure the load balancer in a way that it distributes load to the new instance.

The dynamic scaling has to be performed based on a metric. When the response time of a microservice is too long or the number of requests is very high, new instances have to be started. The dynamic scaling can be part of a monitoring (see section 11.3) since the monitoring should enable the reaction to extraordinary metric values. Most monitoring infrastructures offer the possibility to react to metric values by calling a script. The script can start additional instances of the microservice. This is fairly easy to do with most cloud and virtualization environments. Environments like the Amazon Cloud offer suitable solutions for automatic scaling, which work in a similar manner. However, a home-grown solution is not very complicated since the scripts run anyhow, only every few minutes, so that failures are tolerable, at least for a limited time. Since the scripts are part of the monitoring, they will have a similar availability like the monitoring and should therefore be sufficiently available.

Especially in the case of cloud infrastructures, it is important to shut the instances down again in case of low load because every running instance costs money in a cloud. Also in this case scripts can be used to provide automated responses when values reach predefined levels.

Microservices: Advantages for Scaling

With regard to scaling, microservices have, first of all, the advantage that they can be scaled independently of each other. In case of a deployment monolith, starting each instance requires starting the entire monolith. The fine granular scaling does not appear to be an especially striking advantage at first glance. However, to run an entire e-commerce shop, in many instances just to speed up the search, causes high expenditures: A lot of hardware is needed, a complex infrastructure has to be built up, and system parts are held available, not all of which are used. These system parts render the deployment and monitoring more complex. The possibilities for dynamic scaling depend critically on the size of the services and on the speed with which new instances can be started. In this area microservices possess clear advantages.

In most cases microservices have already an automated deployment, which is also very easy to implement. In addition, there is already monitoring. Without automated deployment and monitoring, a microservice-based system can hardly be operated. If there is in addition Load Balancing, then it is only a script that is still missing for automated scaling. Therefore, microservices represent an excellent basis for dynamic scaling.

Sharding

Sharding means that the administrated data amount is divided and that each instance gets the responsibility for part of the data. For example, an instance can be responsible for the customers A–E or for all customers whose customer number ends with the number 9. Sharding is a variation of horizontal scaling: more servers are used. However, not all servers are equal, but every server is responsible for a different subset of the dataset. In case of microservices this type of scaling is easy to implement since the domain is anyhow distributed across multiple microservices. Every microservice can then shard its data and scale horizontally via this sharding. A deployment monolith is hardly scalable in this manner because it handles all the data. When the deployment monolith administrates customers and items, it can hardly be sharded for both types of data. In order to really implement sharding, the load balancer has to distribute the load appropriately to the shards, of course.

Scalability, Throughput, and Response Times

Scalability means that more load can be processed by more resources. The throughput increases—that is, the number of processed requests per unit of time increase. However, the response time stays constant in the best case—depending on circumstances it might rise, but not to such an extent that the system causes errors or gets too slow for the user.

When faster response times are required, horizontal scaling does not help. However, there are some approaches to optimize the response time of microservices:

- The microservices can be deployed on faster computers. This is vertical scaling. Then the microservices can process the individual requests more rapidly. Because of the automated deployment, vertical scaling is relatively simple to implement. The service has only to be deployed on faster hardware.

- Calls via the network have a long latency. Therefore, a possible optimization can be to avoid such calls. Instead caches can be used, or the data can be replicated. Caches can often very easily be integrated into the existing communication. For REST, for instance, a simple HTTP cache is sufficient.

- If the domain architecture of microservices is well designed, a request should only be processed in one microservice so that no communication via the network is necessary. In case of a good domain architecture the logic for processing a request is implemented in one microservice so that changes to the logic only require changes to one microservice. In that case microservices do not have longer response times than deployment monoliths. With regard to an optimization of response times microservices have the disadvantage that their communication via the network causes rather longer response times. However, there are means to counteract this effect.

7.14 Security

In a microservice-based architecture, each microservice has to know which user triggered the current call and wants to use the system. Therefore, a uniform security architecture has to exist: After all, microservices can work together for a request, and for each part of the processing of the request, another microservice might be responsible. Thus, the security structure has to be defined at the level of the entire system. This is the only way to ensure that the access of a user is uniformly treated in the entire system with regard to security.

Security comprises two essential aspects: authentication and authorization. Authentication is the process that validates the identity of the user. Authorization denotes the decision whether a certain user is allowed to execute a certain action. Both processes are independent of each other: The validation of the user identity in the context of authentication is not directly related to authorization.

Security and Microservices

In a microservice-based architecture the individual microservices should not perform authentication. It does not make much sense for each microservice to validate user name and password. For authentication a central server has to be used. For authorization an interplay is necessary: often there are user groups or roles that have to be centrally administered. However, whether a certain user group or role is allowed to use certain features of a microservice should be decided by the concerned microservice. Therefore changes to the authorization of a certain microservice can be limited to the implementation of this microservice.

OAuth2

One possible solution for this challenge is OAuth2. This protocol is also widely used in the Internet. Google, Microsoft, Twitter, XING, and Yahoo all offer support for this protocol.

Figure 7.17 shows the workflow of the OAuth2 protocol as defined by the standard:[27]

1. The client inquires of the resource owner whether it might execute a certain action. For example, the application can request access to the profile or certain data in a social network that the resource owner stored there. The resource owner is usually the user of the system.

2. If the resource owner grants the client access, the client receives a respective response from the resource owner.

3. The client uses the response of the resource owner to put a request to the authorization server. In the example the authorization server would be located in the social network.

---

27. http://tools.ietf.org/html/rfc6749

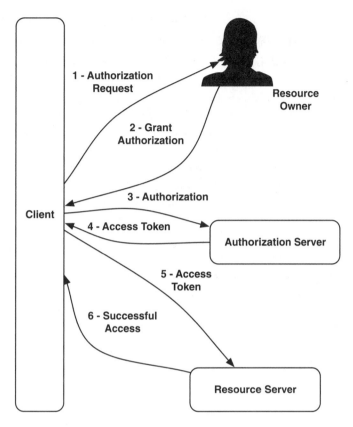

Figure 7.17 *The OAuth2 Protocol*

4. The authorization server returns an access token.

5. With this access token the client can now call a Resource Server and there obtain the necessary information. For the call the token can for instance be put into an HTTP header.

6. The resource server answers the requests.

Possible Authorization Grants

The interaction with the authorization server can work in different ways:

* In case of the password grant the client shows an HTML form to the user in step 1. The resource owner can enter user name and password. In step 3 this information is used by the client to obtain the access token from the authorization server via an HTTP POST. This approach has the disadvantage that the

client processes user name and password. The client can be insecurely implemented, and then these data are endangered.

- In case of the authorization grant the client directs the user in step 1 to a web page that the authorization server displays. There the user can choose whether he/she permits the access. If that is the case, in step 2 the client will obtain an authorization code via an HTTP-URL. In this way the authorization server can be sure that the correct client obtains the code since the server chooses the URL. In step 3 the client can then generate the access token with this authorization code via an HTTP POST. The approach is mainly implemented by the authorization server and thus very easy to use by a client. In this scenario the client would be a web application on the server: It will obtain the code from the authorization server and is the only one able to turn it via the HTTP POST into an access token.

- In case of an implicit grant, the procedure resembles the authorization grant. After the redirect to the authorization server in step 1 the client directly gets an access token via an HTTP redirect. This enables the browser or a mobile application to immediately read out the access token. Steps 3 and 4 are omitted. However, here the access token is not as well protected against attacks since the authorization server does not directly send it to the client. This approach is sensible when JavaScript code on the client or a mobile application is supposed to use the access token.

- In case of client credentials, the client uses a credential in step 1 that the client knows to obtain the access token from the authorization server. Therefore, the client can access the data without additional information from the resource owner. For example, a statistics software could read out and analyze customer data in this manner.

Via the access token the client can access resources. The access token has to be protected: When unauthorized people obtain access to the access token, they can thereby trigger all actions that the resource owner can also trigger. Within the token itself some information can be encoded. For instance, in addition to the real name of the resource owner the token can also contain information that assigns certain rights to the user or the membership to certain user groups.

JSON Web Token (JWT)

JSON Web Token (JWT) is a standard for the information that is contained in an access token. JSON serves as data structure. For the validation of the access token a digital signature with JWS (JSON Web Signature) can be used. Likewise, the access token can be encrypted with JSON Web Encryption (JWE). The access token can contain information about the issuer of the access token, the resource owner, the validity inter-val, or the addressee of the access token. Individual data can also be contained in the access token. The access token is optimized for use as HTTP header by an encoding of the JSON with BASE64. These headers are normally subject to size restrictions.

OAuth2, JWT, and Microservices

In a microservice-based architecture the user can initially authenticate via one of the OAuth2 approaches. Afterwards the user can use the web page of a microservice or call a microservice via REST. With each further call every microservice can hand over the access token to other microservices. Based on the access token the microservices can decide whether a certain access is granted or not. For that the validity of the token can first be checked. In case of JWT the token only has to be decrypted, and the signature of the authorization server has to be checked. Subsequently, whether the user may use the microservice as he/she intends can be decided based on the informa-tion of the token. Information from the token can be used for that. For instance, it is possible to store the affiliation with certain user groups directly in the token.

It is important that it is not defined in the access token which access to which microservice is allowed. The access token is issued by the authorization server. If the information about the access was available in the authorization server, every modifi-cation of the access rights would have to occur in the authorization server—and not in the microservices. This limits the changeability of the microservices since modi-fications to the access rights would require changes of the authorization server as central component. The authorization server should only administer the assignment to user groups, and the microservices should then allow or prohibit access based on such information from the token.

Technologies

In principle, other technical approaches than OAuth2 could also be used as long as they employ a central server for authorization and use a token for regulating the access to individual microservices. One example is Kerberos,[28] which has a relatively long history. However, it is not well tuned to REST like OAuth2. Other alternatives are SAML and SAML 2.0.[29] They define a protocol that uses XML and HTTP to perform authorization and authentication.

Finally, signed cookies can be created by a home-grown security service. Via a cryptographic signature, it can be determined whether the cookie has really been

---

28. http://tools.ietf.org/html/rfc4556
29. https://www.oasis-open.org/committees/security/

issued by the system. The cookie can then contain the rights or groups of the user. Microservices can examine the cookie and restrict the access if necessary. There is the risk that the cookie is stolen. However, for that to occur the browser has to be compromised, or the cookie has to be transferred via a unencrypted connection. This is often acceptable as risk.

With a token approach it is possible that microservices do not have to handle the authorization of the caller but still can restrict the access to certain user groups or roles.

There are good reasons for the use of OAuth2:

- There are numerous libraries for practically all established programming languages that implement OAuth2 or an OAuth2 server.[30] The decision for OAuth2 hardly restricts the technology choice for microservices.

- Between the microservices only the access token still has to be transferred. This can occur in a standardized manner via an HTTP header when REST is used. In case of different communication protocols similar mechanisms can be exploited. Also in this area OAuth2 hardly limits the technology choice.

- Via JWT information can be placed into the token that the authorization server communicates to the microservices in order for them to allow or prohibit access. Therefore, also in this area the interplay between the individual microservice and the shared infrastructure is simple to implement—with standards that are widely supported.

Spring Cloud Security[31] offers a good basis for implementing OAuth2 systems, especially for Java-based microservices.

Additional Security Measures

OAuth2 solves, first of all, the problem of authentication and authorization—primarily for human users. There are additional measures for securing a microservice-based system:

- The communication between the microservices can be protected by SSL/TLS against wiretapping. All communication is then encrypted. Infrastructures like REST or messaging systems mostly support such protocols.

---

30. http://oauth.net/2/
31. http://cloud.spring.io/spring-cloud-security/

- Apart from authentication with OAuth2 certificates can be used to authenticate clients. A certificate authority creates the certificates. They can be used to verify digital signatures. This makes it possible to authenticate a client based on its digital signature. Since SSL/TLS supports certificates, at least at this level the use of certificates and authentication via certificates is possible.

- API keys represent a similar concept. They are given to external clients to enable them to use the system. Via the API key the external clients authenticate themselves and can obtain the appropriate rights. In case of OAuth2 this can be implemented with Client Credential.

- Firewalls can be used to protect the communication between microservices. Normally firewalls secure a system against unauthorized access from outside. A firewall for the communication between the microservices prevents that all microservices are endangered if an individual microservice has been successfully taken over. In this way the intrusion can be restricted to one microservice.

- Finally, there should be an intrusion detection to detect unauthorized access to the system. This topic is closely related to monitoring. The monitoring system can also be used to trigger an appropriate alarm in case of an intrusion.

- Datensparsamkeit[32] is also an interesting concept. It is derived from the data security field and states that only data that is absolutely necessary to be saved. Form a security perspective this results in the advantage that collecting lots of data is avoided. This makes the system less attractive for attacks, and in addition the consequences of a security breach will not be as bad.

Hashicorp Vault

Hashicorp Vault[33] is a tool that solves many problems in the area of microservice security. It offers the following features:

- Secrets like passwords, API keys, keys for encryption, or certificates can be saved. This can be useful for enabling users to administrate their secrets. In addition, microservices can be equipped with certificates in such a manner as to protect their communication with each other or with external servers.

---

32. http://martinfowler.com/bliki/Datensparsamkeit.html
33. https://www.vaultproject.io/

- Secrets are given via a lease to services. Besides, they can be equipped with an access control. This helps to limit the problem in case of a compromised service. Secrets can, for instance, also be declared invalid.

- Data can be immediately encrypted or decrypted with the keys without the microservices themselves having to save these keys.

- Access is made traceable by an audit. This enables tracing of who got which secret and at what time.

- In the background Vault can use HSMs, SQL databases, or Amazon IAM to store secrets. In addition, it can for instance also generate new access keys for the Amazon Cloud by itself.

In this manner Vault takes care of handling keys and thereby relieves microservices of this task. It is a big challenge to really handle keys securely. It is difficult to implement something like that in a really secure manner.

Additional Security Goals

With regard to a software architecture security comes in very different shapes. Approaches like OAuth2 only help to achieve confidentiality. They prevent data access to unauthorized users. However, even this confidentiality is not entirely safeguarded by OAuth2 on its own: The communication in the network likewise has to be protected against wiretapping—for instance via HTTPS or other kinds of encryption.

Additional security aspects include the following:

- **Integrity**—Integrity means that there are no unnoticed changes to the data. Every microservice has to solve this problem. For instance, data can be signed to ensure that they have not been manipulated in some way. The concrete implementation has to be performed by each microservice.

- **Confidentiality**—The concept of confidentiality means ensuring that modifications made by someone cannot be denied. This can be achieved by signing the changes introduced by different users by keys that are specific for the individual user. Then it is clear that exactly one specific user has modified the data. The overall security architecture has to provide the keys; the signing is then the task of each individual service.

- **Data security**—Data security is ensured as long as no data are lost. This issue can be handled by backup solutions and highly available storage solutions. This problem has to be addressed by the microservices since it is within their responsibility as part of their data storage. However, the shared infrastructure can offer certain databases that are equipped with appropriate backup and disaster recovery mechanisms.

- **Availability**—Availability means that a system is available. Also here the microservices have to contribute individually. However, since one has to deal with the possibility of failures of individual microservices, especially in the case of microservice-based architectures, microservice-based systems are often well prepared in this area. Resilience (section 9.5) is, for instance, useful for this.

These aspects are often not considered when devising security measures; however, the failure of a service has often even more dramatic consequences than the unauthorized access to data. One danger is denial-of-service attacks, which result in such an overloading of servers that they cannot perform any sensible work anymore. The technical hurdles for this are often shockingly low, and the defense against such attacks is frequently very difficult.

7.15 Documentation and Metadata

To keep the overview in a microservice-based architecture certain information about each microservice has to be available. Therefore, the microservice-based architecture has to define how microservices can provide such information. Only when all microservices provide this information in a uniform way, the information can be easily collected. Possible information of interest is, for instance:

- Fundamental information like the name of the service and the responsible contact person.

- Information about the source code: where the code can be found in the version control and which libraries have been used. The used libraries can be interesting in order to compare open-source licenses of the libraries with the company policies or to identify in case of a security gap in a library the affected microservices. For such purposes the information has to be available even if the decision about the use of a certain library rather concerns only one microservice. The decision itself can be made largely independently by the responsible team.

- Another interesting information is with which other microservices the microservice works. This information is central for the architecture management (see section 7.2).

- In addition, information about configuration parameters or about feature toggles might be interesting. Feature toggles can switch features on or off. This is useful for activating new features only in production when their implementation is really finished, or for avoiding the failure of a service by deactivating certain features.

It is not sensible to document all components of the microservices or to unify the entire documentation. A unification only makes sense for information that is relevant outside of the team implementing the microservice. Whenever it is necessary to manage the interplay of microservices or to check licenses, the relevant information has to be available outside of the responsible team. These questions have to be solved across microservices. Each team can create additional documentation about their own microservices. However, this documentation is only relevant for this one team and therefore does not have to be standardized.

Outdated Documentation

A common problem concerning the documentation of any software is that the documentation gets easily outdated and then documents a state that is not up to date anymore. Therefore, the documentation should be versioned together with the code. Besides, the documentation should be created from information that is present in the system anyhow. For instance, the list of all used libraries can be taken from the build system since exactly this information is needed during the compilation of the system. Which other microservices are used can be obtained from Service Discovery. This information can, for instance, be used to create firewall rules when a firewall is supposed to be used to protect the communication between the microservices. In summary, the documentation does not have to be maintained separately, but documentation should be generated from information present in the system anyhow.

Access to Documentation

The documentation can be part of the artifacts that are created during the build. In addition, there can be a run-time interface that enables reading out of metadata. Such an interface can correspond to the otherwise common interfaces for monitoring and, for instance, provide JSON documents via HTTP. In this way, the metadata are only an additional information microservices provide at run-time.

A service template can show how the documentation is created. The service template can then form the basis for the implementation of new microservices. When the service template already contains this aspect, it facilitates the implementation of a standard-conform documentation. In addition, at least the formal characteristics of the documentation can be checked by a test.

7.16 Conclusion

The domain architecture of a microservice-based system is essential because it influences not only the structure of the system, but also the organization (section 7.1). Unfortunately, tools for dependency management are rare, especially for microservices, so that teams have to develop home-made solutions. However, often an understanding of the implementation of the individual business processes will be sufficient, and an overview of the entire architecture is not really necessary (section 7.2).

For an architecture to be successful it has to be permanently adjusted to the changing requirements. For deployment monoliths there are numerous refactoring techniques to achieve this. Such possibilities also exist for microservices; however without the support of tools and with much higher hurdles (section 7.3). Still, microservice-based systems can be sensibly developed further—for instance, by starting initially with a few large microservices and creating more and more microservices over time (section 7.4). An early distribution into many microservices entails the risk to end up with a wrong distribution.

A special case is the migration of a legacy application to a microservice-based architecture (section 7.6). In this case, the code base of the legacy application can be divided into microservices; however this can lead to a bad architecture due to the often bad structure of the legacy application. Alternatively, the legacy application can be supplemented by microservices, which replace functionalities of the legacy application in a stepwise manner.

Event-driven architecture (section 7.8) can serve to uncouple the logic in the microservices. This enables easy extensibility of the system.

Defining the technological basis is one of the tasks of an architecture (section 7.9). In case of microservice-based systems this does not relate to the definition of a shared technology stack for implementation but to the definition of shared communication protocols, interfaces, monitoring, and logging. Additional technical functions of the entire system are coordination and configuration (section 7.10). In this area tools can be selected that all microservices have to employ. Alternatively, one can do without a central configuration and instead leave each microservice to bring along its own configuration.

Likewise, for Service Discovery (section 7.11) a certain technology can be chosen. A solution for Service Discovery is in any case sensible for a microservice-based system—except messaging is used for communication. Based on Service Discovery,

Load Balancing can be introduced (section 7.12) to distribute the load across the instances of the microservices. Service Discovery knows all instances; the Load Balancing distributes the load to these instances. Load Balancing can be implemented via a central load balancer, via Service Discovery or via one load balancer per client. This provides the basis for scalability (section 7.13). This enables a microservice to process more load by scaling up.

Microservices have a significantly higher technical complexity than deployment monoliths. Operating systems, networks, load balancer, Service Discovery, and communication protocols all become part of the architecture. Developers and architects of deployment monoliths are largely spared from these aspects. Thus architects have to deal with entirely different technologies and have to carry out architecture at an entirely different level.

In the area of security, a central component has to take over at least authentication and parts of authorization. The microservices should then settle the details of access (section 7.14). In order to obtain certain information from a system, which is composed of many microservices, the microservices have to possess a standardized documentation (section 7.15). This documentation can, for instance, provide information about the used libraries—to compare them with open-source license regulations or to remove security issues when a library has a security gap.

The architecture of a microservice-based system is different from classical applications. Many decisions are only made in the microservices, while topics like monitoring, logging or continuous delivery are standardized for the entire system.

Essential Points

- Refactoring between microservices is laborious. Therefore, it is hard to change the architecture at this level. Accordingly, the continued development of the architecture is a central point.

- An essential part of the architecture is the definition of overarching technologies for configuration and coordination, Service Discovery, Load Balancing, security, documentation, and metadata.

Chapter 8

Integration and Communication

Microservices have to be integrated, and they need to communicate. This can be achieved at different levels (see Figure 8.1). Each approach has certain advantages and disadvantages, and at each level different technical implementations of integration are possible.

- Microservices contain a graphical user interface. This means that microservices can be integrated at the UI level. This type of integration is introduced in section 8.1.

- Microservices can also be integrated at the logic level. They can use REST (section 8.2), SOAP, remote-procedure call (RPC); (section 8.3), or messaging (section 8.4) to achieve this.

- Finally, integration can be performed at the database level using data replication (section 8.5).

General rules for the design of interfaces are provided in section 8.6.

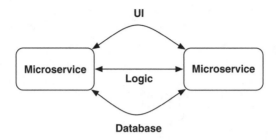

Figure 8.1 *Different Levels of Integration*

8.1 Web and UI

Microservices should bring their own UI along with them. By having the UI included with the relevant microservice, changes to that microservice that affect the UI can be done in one place. It is then necessary to integrate the UIs of the microservices together to form the system as a whole. This can be achieved using different approaches, which are reviewed in the innoQ Blog.[1, 2]

Multiple Single-Page-Apps

Single-page-apps (SPA)[3] implement the entire UI with just one HTML page. The logic is implemented in JavaScript, which dynamically changes parts of the page. The logic can also manipulate the URL displayed in the browser so that bookmarks and other typical browser features can be used. However, SPAs do not conform to the way the web was originally designed; they demote HTML from being the central web technology and have most of their logic implemented in JavaScript. Traditional web architectures implement logic almost exclusively on the server.

SPAs are particularly useful when complex interactions or offline capability are required. Google's Gmail is an example that helped to shape the meaning of the term SPA. Traditionally, mail clients have been native applications; however, Gmail as a SPA is able to offer nearly the same user experience.

There are different technologies for the implementation of single-page-apps:

- AngularJS[4] is very popular. Among other features, AngularJS has bidirectional UI data-binding: if the JavaScript code assigns a new value to an attribute of

---

1. https://www.innoq.com/blog/st/2014/11/web-based-frontend-integration/
2. https://www.innoq.com/en/blog/transclusion/
3. http://en.wikipedia.org/wiki/Single-page_application
4. https://angularjs.org/

a bound model, the view components displaying the value are automatically changed. The binding also works from UI to the code: AngularJS can bind a user input to a JavaScript variable. Furthermore, AngularJS can render HTML templates in the browser. This enables JavaScript code to generate complex DOM structures. The entire front-end logic can be implemented in JavaScript code running on the browser. AngularJS was created by Google, which released the framework under the very liberal MIT license.

- Ember.js[5] follows the "convention over configuration" principle and represents essentially the same feature set as AngularJS. Through the supplementary module Ember Data, it offers a model-driven approach for accessing REST resources. Ember.js is made available under the MIT license and is maintained by developers from the open-source community.

- Ext JS[6] offers an MVC approach and also components which developers can compose to build a UI similar to the way they would for rich client applications. Ext JS is available as open source under GPL v3.0. However, for commercial development a license has to be bought from the creators Sencha.

SPA per Microservice

When using microservices with single-page apps each microservice can bring along its own SPA (see Figure 8.2). The SPA can, for instance, call the microservice via JSON/REST. This is particularly easy to implement with JavaScript. Links can then be used to join the different SPAs together.

This enables the SPAs to be completely separate and independent. New versions of a SPA and of the associated microservice can be rolled out with ease. However,

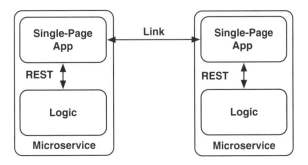

Figure 8.2 *Microservices with Single-Page Apps*

---

5. http://emberjs.com/

6. http://www.sencha.com/products/extjs/

a tighter integration of SPAs is difficult. When the user switches from one SPA to another, the browser loads a new web page and starts a different JavaScript application. Even modern browsers need time to do this, and therefore this approach is only sensible when switching between SPAs is rare.

Asset Server for Uniformity

SPAs can be heterogeneous, and each can bring along its own individually designed UI. This can be a problem as it can lead to a UI that is not uniform across the system as a whole. This issue can be resolved by using an asset server. This type of server is used to provide JavaScript files and CSS files for the applications. When the SPAs of the microservices are only allowed to access these kinds of resources via the asset server, a uniform user interface can be achieved. To accomplish this, a proxy server can distribute requests to the asset server and the microservices. From the web browser's perspective, it looks as if all resources, as well as the microservices, have a shared URL. This approach avoids security rules that prohibit the use of content that originates from different URLs. Caching can then reduce the time for loading the applications. When only JavaScript libraries, which are stored on the asset server, can be used, the choice of technologies for the microservices is reduced. Uniformity and free technology choice are competing aims.

The shared assets will create code dependencies between the asset server and all microservices. A new version of an asset requires the modification of all microservices that use this asset—they have to modified in order to use the new version. Such code dependencies endanger independent deployment and should therefore be avoided. Code dependencies in the back end are often a problem (see section 7.3). In fact, such dependencies should also be reduced in the front-end. This can mean that an asset server causes more problems than it solves.

UI guidelines, which describe the design of the application in more detail and help to establish a uniform approach at different levels, can be helpful. This enables the implementation of a uniform UI without a shared asset server and the related code dependencies.

In addition, SPAs need to have a uniform authentication and authorization scheme so that the users do not have to log in multiple times. An OAuth2 or a shared signed cookie can be a solution to this (see also section 7.14).

JavaScript can only access data that is available under the domain from which the JavaScript code originates. This "same-origin policy" prevents JavaScript code from reading data from other domains. When a proxy makes all microservices accessible to the outside world under the same domain, this is no longer a limitation. Otherwise the policy has to be deactivated when the UI of a microservice needs to access data from another microservice. This problem can be solved with CORS (cross-origin resource sharing) where the server delivering the data allows JavaScript from other domains. Another option is to offer all SPA and REST services to the outside via a single domain so that cross-domain access is not required. This also allows access to shared JavaScript code on an asset server to be implemented.

A Single-Page App for All Microservices

The division into multiple SPAs results in a strict separation of the front-ends of the microservices. For instance, if an SPA is responsible for registering orders and another one for a fundamentally different use case like reports, the load time needed to change between SPAs is still acceptable. Potentially, the different SPAs might be used by different sets of users who never need to switch between them at all.

However, there are situations when a tighter integration of the microservices user interfaces is necessary. For example, when viewing an order, details about the items may need to be displayed. Displaying the order is the responsibility of one microservice, displaying the items is performed by another. To tackle this problem, the SPA can be distributed into modules (see Figure 8.3). Each module belongs to another microservice and therefore to another team. The modules should be deployed separately. They can be stored on the server in individual JavaScript files and use separate Continuous Delivery pipelines, for instance. There needs to be suitable conventions for the interfaces. For example, only the sending of events might be allowed. Events uncouple the modules because the modules only communicate changes in state, but not how other modules have to react to them.

AngularJS has a module concept that enables the implementation of individual parts of the SPA in separate units. A microservice could provide an AngularJS

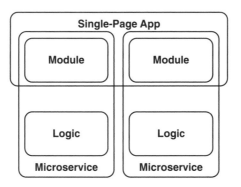

Figure 8.3 *Close Integration of Microservices Sharing One Single-Page App*

module for displaying the user interface of the microservice. The model can then integrate, if necessary, AngularJS modules from other microservices.

However, such an approach has disadvantages:

- Deploying the SPA is often only possible as a complete application. When a module is modified, the entire SPA has to be rebuilt and deployed. This has to be coordinated between the microservices that provide the modules for the application. In addition, the deployment of the microservices on the server has to be coordinated with the deployment of the modules since the modules call the microservices. This requirement to coordinate the deployment of modules of an application should be avoided.

- The modules can call each other. Depending on the way calls are implemented, changes to a module can mean that other modules also have to be changed, for instance, because an interface has been modified. When the modules belong to separate microservices, this again requires a coordination across microservices, which should be avoided.

For SPA modules a much closer coordination is necessary than for links between applications. On the other hand, SPA modules offer the benefit that UI elements from different microservices can be simultaneously displayed to the user. However, this approach closely couples the microservices at the UI level. The SPA modules correspond to the module concepts that exist in other programming languages and cause a simultaneous deployment. This leads to the microservices, which really should be independent of each other, being combined at the UI level in one shared deployment artifact. Therefore, this approach undoes one of the most important benefits of a microservice-based architecture—independent deployment.

HTML Applications

Another way to implement the UI is with HTML-based user interfaces. Every microservice has one or more web pages that are generated on the server. These web pages can also use JavaScript. Here, unlike SPAs, only a new HTML web page and not necessarily an application, is loaded by the server when changing between web pages.

ROCA

ROCA (resource-oriented client architecture)[7] proposes a way to arrange the handling of JavaScript and dynamic elements in HTML user interfaces. ROCA views itself as

---

7. http://roca-style.org/

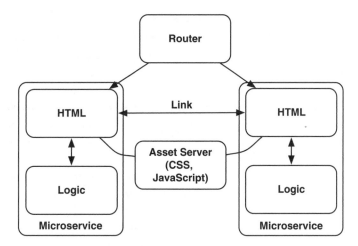

Figure 8.4 *HTML User Interface with an Asset Server*

an alternative to SPAs. In ROCA the role of JavaScript is limited to optimizing the usability of the web pages. JavaScript can facilitate their use or can add effects to the HTML web pages. However, the application has to remain usable without JavaScript. It is not the purpose of ROCA that users really use web pages without JavaScript. The applications are only supposed to use the architecture of the web, which is based on HTML and HTTP. Also ROCA makes sure that all logic is actually implemented on the server instead of JavaScript on the client. That way other clients can use the very same logic.

When a web application is divided into microservices, ROCA reduces the dependencies and simplifies the division. Between microservices the coupling of the UI can be achieved by links. For HTML applications links are the usual tool for navigating between web pages and represent a natural integration. There are no foreign bodies as in the case of SPAs.

To help with the uniformity of the HTML user interfaces, the microservices can use a shared asset server the same was as SPAs can (see Figure 8.4). It contains all the CSS and JavaScript libraries. If the teams create design guidelines for the HTML web pages and look after the assets on the asset server, the user interfaces of the different microservices will be largely identical. However, as discussed previously, this will lead to code dependencies between the UIs of the microservices.

Easy Routing

To the outside world the microservices should appear like a single web application—ideally with one URL. This also helps with the shared use of assets since the same-origin-policy is not violated. However, user requests from the outside have to be directed to the right microservice. This is the function of the router. It can receive HTTP requests and forward them to one of the microservices. This can be done based on the URL. How individual URLs are mapped to microservices can be decided by rules that can be complex. The example application uses Zuul for this task (see section 13.9). Reverse proxies are an alternative. These can be web servers, like Apache httpd or nginx, that can direct requests to other servers. In the process the requests can be modified, URLs can, for instance, be rewritten. However, these mechanisms are not as flexible as Zuul, which is very easy to extend with home-grown code.

When the logic in the router is very complex, this can cause problems. If this logic has to be changed because a new version of a microservice is brought into production, an isolated deployment is no longer straightforward. This endangers the philosophy of independent development and deployment of the microservices.

Arrange HTML with JavaScript

In some cases, a closer integration is necessary. It might be that information originating from different microservices needs to be displayed on a single HTML web page. For example, a web page might display order data from one microservice and data concerning the ordered items from another microservice. In this situation one router is no longer sufficient. A router can only enable a single microservice to generate a complete HTML web page.

A simple solution that employs the architecture presented in Figure 8.4 is based on links. AJAX (Asynchronous JavaScript and XML) enables content from a link to be loaded from another microservice. JavaScript code calls the microservice. Once the HTML is received from the microservice the link is replaced with it. In the example a link to an item could be transformed into an HTML description of this item. This enables the logic for the presentation of a product to be implemented in one microservice, while the design of the entire web page is implemented in another microservice. The entire web page would be the responsibility of the order microservice, while the presentation of the products would be the responsibility of the product microservice. This enables the continued independent development of both microservices and for content to be displayed from both components. If the presentation of the items has to be changed or new products necessitate a revised presentation, these modifications can be implemented in the product microservice. The entire logic of the order microservice remains unchanged.

Another example for this approach is Facebook's BigPipe.[8] It optimizes not only the load time, but also enables the composition of web pages from pagelets.

---

8. https://www.facebook.com/notes/facebook-engineering/bigpipe-pipelining-web-pages-for-high-performance/389414033919

A custom implementation can use JavaScript to replace certain elements of the web page by other HTML. This can be links or **div**-elements like the ones commonly used for structuring web pages that can be replaced by HTML code.

However, this approach causes relatively long load times. It is mainly beneficial when the web UI already uses a lot of JavaScript and when there are not many transitions between web pages.

Front-End Server

Figure 8.5 shows an alternative way to achieve tight integration. A front-end server composes the HTML web page from HTML snippets, each of which are generated by a microservice. Assets like CSS and JavaScript libraries are also stored in the front-end server. Edge Side Includes (ESI) is a mechanism to implement this concept. ESI offers a relatively simple language for combining HTML from different sources. With ESI, caches can supplement static content—for instance, the skeleton of a web page—with dynamic content. This means that caches can help with the delivery of web pages, even ones that contain dynamic content. Proxies and caches like Varnish[9] or Squid[10] implement ESI. Another alternative is Server Side Includes (SSI). They are very similar to ESIs; however, they are not implemented in caches, but in web servers. With SSIs web servers can integrate HTML snippets from other servers into HTML web pages. The microservices can deliver components for the web page that are then

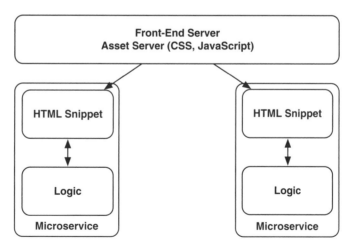

Figure 8.5 *Integration Using a Front-End Server*

---

9. https://www.varnish-cache.org/
10. http://www.squid-cache.org/

assembled on the server. Apache httpd supports SSIs with mod_include.[11] nginx uses the ngx_http_ssi_module[12] for the support of SSIs.

Portals also consolidate information from different sources on one web page. Most products use Java portlets that adhere to the Java standard JSR 168 (Portlet 1.0) or JSR 286 (Portlet 2.0). Portlets can be brought into production independently of each other and therefore solve one of the major challenges surrounding microservice-based architectures. In practice these technologies frequently result in complex solutions. Portlets behave very differently to normal Java web applications technically making the use of many technologies from the Java environment either difficult or impossible. Portlets enable the user to compose a web page from previously defined portlets. In this way the user can assemble, for instance, their most important information sources on one web page. However, this is not really necessary for creating a UI for microservices. The additional features result in additional complexity. Therefore, portal servers that are based on portlets are not a very good solution for the web user interfaces of microservices. In addition, they restrict the available web technologies to the Java field.

Mobile Clients and Rich Clients

Web user interfaces do not need any software to be installed on the client. The web browser is the universal client for all web applications. On the server side the deployment of the web user interface can easily be coordinated with the deployment of the microservice. The microservice implements a part of the UI and can deliver the code of the web user interface via HTTP. This makes possible a relatively easy coordinated deployment of client and server.

For mobile apps, rich clients, and desktop applications the situation is different: software has to be installed on the client. This client application is a deployment monolith that has to offer an interface for all microservices. If the client application delivers functionality from different microservices to the user, it would technically have to be modularized, and the individual modules, like the associated microservices, would have to be brought into production independently of each other. However, this is not possible since the client application is a deployment monolith. A SPA can also easily turn into a deployment monolith. Sometimes an SPA is used to separate the development of client and server. In a microservices context such a use of SPAs is undesirable.

When a new feature is implemented in a microservice, that also requires modifications of the client application. This change cannot be rolled out solely via a

---

11. http://httpd.apache.org/docs/2.2/mod/mod_include.html
12. http://nginx.org/en/docs/http/ngx_http_ssi_module.html

new version of the microservice. A new version of the client application also has to be delivered. However, it is unrealistic to deliver the client application over and over again for each small change of a feature. If the client application is being made available in the app store of a mobile platform, an extensive review of each version is necessary. If multiple changes are supposed to be delivered together, the change has to be coordinated. Additionally, the new version of the client application has to be coordinated with the microservices so that the new versions of the microservices are ready in time. This results in deployment dependencies between the microservices, which should ideally be avoided.

Organizational Level

At an organizational level there is often a designated team for developing the client application. In this manner the division into an individual module is also implemented at the organizational level. Especially when different platforms are supported, it is unrealistic to have one developer in each microservice team for each platform. The developers are going to form one team for each platform. This team has to communicate with all the microservice teams that offer microservices for mobile applications. This can necessitate a lot of communication, which microservices-based architecture sets out to avoid. Therefore, the deployment monolith poses a challenge for client applications at the organizational level (see Figure 8.6).

One possible solution is to develop new features initially for the web. Each microservice can directly bring functionality onto the web. With each release of the client application these new features can then be included. However, this means that each microservice needs to support a certain set of features for the web application and, where required, another set for the client application. In exchange this approach can keep the web application and the mobile application uniform. It supports an approach where the domain-based teams provide features of the microservices to mobile users as well as to web users. Mobile applications and web applications are simply two channels to offer the same functionality.

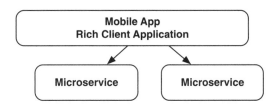

Figure 8.6 *Mobile Apps and Rich Client are Deployment Monoliths that Integrate Multiple Microservices*

Back-End for Each Front-End

However, the requirements can also be entirely different. For instance, the mobile application can be a largely independent application which is supposed to be developed further as independently of the microservices and the web user interface as possible. Often the use cases of the mobile application are so different from the use cases of the web application that a separate development is required due to the differences in features.

In this situation, the approach depicted in Figure 8.7 can be sensible: the team responsible for the mobile app or the rich client application has a number of developers who implement a special back-end. This enables functionality for the mobile app to be developed independently to the back-end, because at least a part of the requirements for the microservices can be implemented by developers from the same team. This should avoid logic for the mobile app being implemented in the microservice, when it really belongs in a back-end microservice. The back-end for a mobile application may differ from other APIs. Mobile clients have little bandwidth and a high latency. Therefore, APIs for mobile devices are optimized to operate with as few calls as possible and to only transfer really essential data. This is also true for rich clients—however not to the same extent. The adaption of an API to the specific requirements of a mobile application can be implemented in a microservice, which is built by the front-end team.

A mobile app should be highly responsive to user interaction. This can be difficult to achieve when the user interaction means a microservice call, with its associated latency, is required. If there are multiple calls, the latency will increase further. Therefore, the API for a mobile app should be optimized to deliver the required data with as few calls as possible. These optimizations can also be implemented by a back-end for the mobile app.

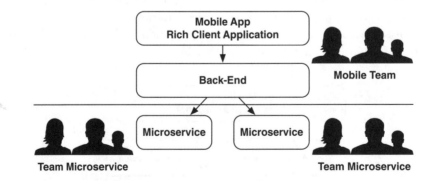

Figure 8.7 *Mobile Apps or Rich Clients with Their Own Back-End*

The optimizations can be implemented by the team that is responsible for the mobile app. Doing this enables the microservices to offer universally valid interfaces while the teams responsible for the mobile apps can assemble their own special APIs by themselves. This leads to the mobile app teams not being so dependent on the teams that are responsible for the implementation of the microservices.

Modularizing web applications is simpler than modularizing mobile apps, especially when the web applications are based on HTML and not on SPAs. For mobile apps or rich client apps it is much more difficult since they form an individual deployment unit and cannot be easily divided.

The architecture shown in Figure 8.7 has a number of advantages and disadvantages. It makes it possible to reuse microservices for different clients and at the same time acts as an entry point into the layered architecture. However, the UI layer is now separated from the microservices and is implemented by another team. This leads to a situation where requirements have to be implemented by multiple teams. Microservices were meant to avoid exactly this situation. This architecture also risks logic being implemented in the services for the client application, when it really belongs in the microservices.

Try and Experiment

- This section presented alternative ways to implement web applications: an SPA per microservice, an SPA with modules per microservice, an HTML application per microservice, and a front-end server with HTML snippets. Which of these approaches would you choose? Why?

- How would you deal with mobile apps? One option would be a mobile app team with back-end developers—or would you rather choose a team without back-end developers?

8.2 REST

Microservices have to be able to call each other in order to implement logic together. This can be supported by different technologies.

REST (representational state transfer) is one way to enable communication between microservices. REST is the term for the fundamental approaches of the World Wide Web (WWW):

- There are a large number of resources which can be identified via URIs. URI stands for uniform resource identifier. It unambiguously and globally identifies resources. URLs are practically the same as URIs.

- The resources can be manipulated via a fixed set of methods. For instance, in the case of HTTP these are GET for requesting a resource, PUT for storing a resource and DELETE for deleting a resource. The methods' semantics are rigidly defined.

- There can be different representations for resources—for instance as a PDF or HTML. HTTP supports the so-called content negotiation via the Accept header. This means that the client can determine which data representation it can process. The content negotiation enables resources to be made available in a way that is readable to humans and to provide them at the same time under the same URL in a machine-readable manner. The client can communicate via an Accept header whether it only accepts human-readable HTML or only JSON.

- Relationships between resources can be represented by links. Links can point to other microservices enabling the logic of different microservices to be integrated.

- The servers in a REST system are supposed to be stateless. Therefore, HTTP implements a stateless protocol.

The limited vocabulary represents the exact opposite of what object-oriented systems employ. Object-orientation focuses on a specific vocabulary with specific methods for each class. The REST vocabulary can also execute complex logic. When data validations are necessary, this can be checked at the POST or PUT of new data. If complex processes need to be represented, a POST can start the process, and subsequently the state can be updated. The current state of the process can be fetched by the client under a known URL via GET. Likewise, POST or PUT can be used to initiate the next state.

Cache and Load Balancer

A RESTful HTTP interface can be very easily supplemented with a cache. Because RESTful HTTP uses the same HTTP protocol as the web, a simple web cache is sufficient. Similarly, a standard HTTP load balancer can also be used for RESTful HTTP. The power of these concepts is impressively illustrated by the size of the WWW. This size is only possible due to the properties of HTTP. HTTP, for instance, possesses simple and useful mechanisms for security—not only encryption via HTTPS but also authentication with HTTP Headers.

HATEOAS

HATEOAS (Hypermedia as the Engine of Application State) is another important component of REST. It enables the relationships between resources to be modeled with links. Therefore, a client only has to know an entry point, and from there it can go on navigating at will and locate all data in a step-by-step manner. In the WWW it is, for instance, possible to start from Google and from there to reach practically the entire web via links.

REST describes the architecture of the WWW and therefore the world's largest integrated computer system. However, REST could also be implemented with other protocols. It is an architecture that can be implemented with different technologies. The implementation of REST with HTTP is called RESTful HTTP. When RESTful HTTP services exchange data using JSON or XML instead as HTML, they can exchange data and not just access web pages.

Microservices can also benefit from HATEOAS. HATEOAS does not have central coordination, just links. This fits very well with the concept that microservices should have as little central coordination as possible. REST clients need know only entry points based on which they can discover the entire system. Therefore, in a REST-based architecture, services can be moved in a way that is transparent for the client. The client simply gets new links. Central coordination is not necessary for this—the REST service just has to return different links. In the ideal case the client only has to understand the fundamentals of HATEOAS and can then navigate via links to any data in the microservice system. The microservice-based systems, on the other hand, can modify their links and therefore change the distribution of functionality between microservices. Even extensive architecture changes can be kept transparent.

HAL

HATEOAS is a concept, and HAL[13] (Hypertext Application Language) is a way to implement it. It is a standard for describing how the links to other documents should be contained in a JSON document. HATEOAS is particularly easy to implement in JSON/RESTful HTTP services. The links are separate from the actual document, enabling links to details or to independent data sets.

XML

XML has a long history as a data format. It is easy to use with RESTful HTTP. There are different types of systems for XML that can determine whether an XML

---

13. http://stateless.co/hal_specification.html

document is valid. This is very useful for the definition of an interface. Among the languages for the definition of valid data is XML Schema (XSD)[14] or RelaxNG.[15] Some frameworks make possible the generation of code in order to administer XML data that corresponds to such a schema. Via XLink[16] XML documents can contain links to other documents. This enables the implementation of HATEOAS.

HTML

XML was designed to transfer data and documents. To display the information is the task of different software. HTML has a similar approach to XML: HTML defines only the structures, with display occurring via CSS. For communication between processes HTML documents can be sufficient because in modern web applications, HTML documents contain only data—just like XML. In a microservices world this approach has the advantage that the communication to the user and between the microservices employs the same format. This reduces effort and makes it even easier to implement microservices that contain a UI and a communication mechanism for other microservices.

JSON

JSON (JavaScript Object Notation) is a representation of data that is well suited to JavaScript. Like JavaScript, the data is dynamically typed. There are suitable JSON libraries for all programming languages. In addition, there are type systems, such as JSON Schema,[17] that supplement JSON with validation concepts. With this addition JSON is no longer inferior to data formats like XML.

Protocol Buffer

Binary protocols such as Protocol Buffer[18] can be used instead of text-based data representations. This technology has been designed by Google to represent data more efficiently and to achieve higher performance. There are implementations for many different programming languages so Protocol Buffer can be used universally, similar to JSON and XML.

---

14. http://www.w3.org/XML/Schema

15. http://relaxng.org/

16. http://www.w3.org/TR/xlink11/

17. http://json-schema.org/

18. https://developers.google.com/protocol-buffers/

RESTful HTTP Is Synchronous

RESTful HTTP is synchronous: typically, a service sends out a request and waits for a response, which is then analyzed in order to continue with the program sequence. This can cause problems if there are long latency times within the network. It can lengthen the processing of a request since responses from other services have to be waited for. After waiting for a certain period of time the request has to be aborted because it is likely that the request is not going to be answered at all. Possible reasons for a failure are that the server is not available at the moment or that the network has a problem. Correctly handled timeouts increase the stability of the system (section 9.5).

The timeout should be used to ensure that the calling service does not fail simply because it does not get a response from the system it is calling. This ensures that a failure does not propagate through the system as a whole.

8.3 SOAP and RPC

It is possible to build a microservices-based architecture using SOAP. Like REST, SOAP uses HTTP, but it only uses POST messages to transfer data to a server. Ultimately, a SOAP call runs a method on a certain object on the server and is therefore an RPC mechanism (remote-procedure call).

SOAP lacks concepts such as HATEOAS that enable relationships between microservices to be handled flexibly. The interfaces have to be completely defined by the server and known on the client.

Flexible Transport

SOAP can convey messages using different transport mechanisms. For instance, it's possible to receive a message via HTTP and to then send it on via JMS or as an email via SMTP/POP. SOAP-based technologies also support forwarding of requests. For example, the security standard WS-Security can encrypt or sign parts of a message. After this has been done, the parts can be sent on to different services without having to be decrypted. The sender can send a message in which some parts are encrypted. This message can be processed via different stations. Each station can process a part of the message or send it to other recipients. Finally, the encrypted parts will arrive at their final recipients—and only there do they have to be decrypted and processed.

SOAP has many extensions for special use contexts. For instance, the different extensions from the WS-*-environment cater for transactions and the coordination of web services. This enables a complex protocol stack to arise. The interoperability between the different services and solutions can suffer due to this complexity. Also, some technologies are not well suited for microservices. For example, a coordination of different microservices is problematic as this will result in a coordination layer, and modifications of a business process will probably impact the coordination of the microservices and also the microservices themselves. When the coordination layer consists of all microservices, a monolith is created that needs to be changed upon each modification. This contradicts the microservices concept of independent deployment. WS-* is better suited to concepts such as SOA.

Thrift

Another communication option is Apache Thrift.[19] It uses very efficient binary encodings such as Protocol Buffer. Thrift can also forward requests from a process via the network to other processes. The interface is described in an interface definition specific to Thrift. Based on this definition different client and server technologies can communicate with each other.

8.4 Messaging

Another way for microservices to communicate is using messages and messaging systems. As the name suggests, these systems are based on the sending of messages. A message may result in a response that is sent as a message again. Messages can go to one or multiple recipients.

The use of messaging solutions is particularly advantageous in distributed systems:

- Message transfer is resilient to network failures. The messaging system buffers them and delivers them when the network is available again.

- Guarantees can be strengthened further: the messaging system can guarantee not only the correct transfer of the messages but also their processing. If there was a problem during the processing of the message, the message can be transferred again. The system can attempt to handle the message a number of times until either the message is correctly processed or discarded because it cannot be processed successfully.

- In a messaging architecture responses are transferred and processed asynchronously. This approach is well suited to the high latency times that can occur in the network. Waiting a period of time for a response is normal with messaging

---

19. https://thrift.apache.org/

systems and therefore the programming model works on the assumption of high latency.

- A call to another service does not block further processing. Even if the response has not been received yet, the service can continue working and potentially call other services.

- The sender does not know the recipient of the message. The sender sends the message to a queue or a topic. There the recipient registers. This means that the sender and recipient are decoupled. There can even be multiple recipients without the sender being aware of this. Also, the messages can be modified on their way—for instance, data can be supplemented or removed. Messages can also be forwarded to entirely different recipients.

Messaging works well with certain architectures of microservice-based systems such as Event Sourcing (see section 9.3) or event-driven architecture (section 7.8).

Messages and Transactions

Messaging is an approach that can be implemented in transactional systems that use microservices. It can be difficult to guarantee transactions when microservices call each other in a microservice-based system. When multiple microservices have to participate in a transaction, they can only be allowed to write changes when all microservices in the transaction have processed the logic without errors. This means that changes have to be held back for a long time. That is bad for performance since no new transactions can change the data in the meantime. Also, in a network it is always possible that a participant fails. When this happens the transaction could remain open for a long time or might not be closed at all. This will potentially block changes to the data for a long period of time. Such problems arise, for instance, when the calling system crashes.

In a messaging system, transactions can be treated differently. The sending and receiving of messages is part of a transaction—just as, for instance, the writing to and reading from the database (see Figure 8.8). When an error occurs during the processing of the message, all outgoing messages are canceled, and the database changes are rolled back. In the case of success all these actions take place. The recipients of the messages can be similarly safeguarded transactionally. To achieve this the processing of the outgoing messages is subject to the same transactional guarantees.

The important point is that the sending and receiving of messages and the associated transactions on the database can be combined in one transaction. The

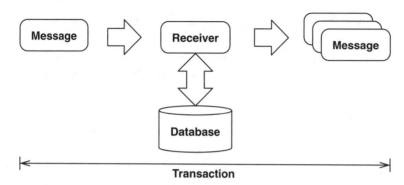

Figure 8.8 *Transactions and Messaging*

coordination is then taken care of by the infrastructure—no extra code needs to be written. For the coordination of messaging and databases the two-phase commit (2PC) protocol can be employed. This protocol is the normal method for coordinating transactional systems like databases and messaging systems with each other. Alternatives are products like Oracle AQ or ActiveMQ, which store messages in a database. By storing messages in a database, the coordination between database and messaging can be achieved simply by writing the messages as well as the data modifications in the same database transaction. Ultimately, messaging and database are the same systems in this setup.

Messaging enables the implementation of transactions without the need for a global coordination. Each microservice is transactional. The transactional sending of messages is ensured by the messaging technology. However, when a message cannot be processed, for instance because it contains invalid values, there is no way to roll back the messages that have already been processed. Therefore, the correct processing of transactions is not guaranteed in all circumstances.

Messaging Technology

In order to implement messaging a technology has to selected:

- AMQP (Advanced Message Queuing Protocol)[20] is a standard. It defines a protocol with which messaging solutions can communicate on the wire with each other and with clients. An implementation of this standard is RabbitMQ,[21] which is written in Erlang and is made available under the Mozilla license. Another implementation is Apache Qpid.

---

20. https://www.amqp.org/
21. https://www.rabbitmq.com/

- Apache Kafka[22] focuses on high throughput, replication, and fault-tolerance. Therefore, it is well suited for distributed systems like microservices, especially the fault-tolerance, which is very helpful in this context.

- 0MQ[23] (also called ZeroMQ or ZMQ) operates without a server and is therefore very lightweight. It has some primitives that can be assembled into complex systems. 0MQ is released under the LGPL license and written in C++.

- JMS (Java Messaging Service)[24] defines an API that a Java application can use to receive messages and send them. In contrast to AMQP the specification does not define how the technology transfers messages on the wire. Since it is a standard, Java-EE server implements this API. Well-known implementations are ActiveMQ[25] and HornetQ.[26]

- Azure Service Bus[27] is Microsoft's hosted messaging system. SDKs are provided for Java, Node.js, and also .NET.

- It is also possible to use ATOM[28] Feeds[29] for messaging. This technology is normally used to transfer blog content enabling clients a relatively easily way to request new entries on a blog. In the same way a client can use ATOM to request new messages. ATOM is based on HTTP and therefore fits well in a REST environment. However, ATOM only has functionality for delivering new information. It does not support more complex techniques like transactions.

For many messaging solutions a messaging server and therefore additional infrastructure is required. This infrastructure has to be operated in a way that prevents failures because these would cause communication in the entire microservice-based system to fail. However, messaging solutions are normally designed to achieve high availability via clustering or other techniques.

For many developers messaging is a somewhat unfamiliar concept since it requires asynchronous communication, making it appear rather complex. In most cases the calling of a method in a different process is easier to understand. With approaches like Reactive (see section 9.6) asynchronous development is introduced into the microservices themselves. Also the AJAX model from JavaScript development

---

22. http://kafka.apache.org/

23. http://zeromq.org/

24. https://jcp.org/en/jsr/detail?id=343

25. http://activemq.apache.org/

26. http://hornetq.jboss.org/

27. https://azure.microsoft.com/services/service-bus

28. http://tools.ietf.org/html/rfc4287

29. http://tools.ietf.org/html/rfc5023

resembles the asynchronous treatment of messages. More and more developers are therefore becoming familiar with the asynchronous model.

Try and Experiment

- REST, SOAP/RPC, and messaging each have advantages and disadvantages. List the advantages and disadvantages and make up your mind which of the alternatives to use.

- In a microservice-based system there can be different types of communication; however, there should be one predominant communication type. Which would you choose? Which others would be allowed in addition? In which situations?

8.5 Data Replication

At the database level microservices could share a database and all access the same data. This type of integration is something that has been used in practice for a long time: it is not unusual that a database is used by several applications. Often databases last longer than applications, leading to a focus on the database rather than the applications that sit on top of it. Although integration via a shared database is widespread, it has major disadvantages:

- The data representation cannot be modified easily since several applications access the data. A change could cause one of the applications to break. This means that changes have to be coordinated across all applications.

- This makes it impossible to rapidly modify applications in situations where database changes are involved. However, the ability to rapidly change an application is exactly the benefit that microservices should bring.

- Finally, it is very difficult to tidy up the schema—for example, to remove columns that are no longer needed—because it is unclear whether any system is still using these columns. In the long run the database will get more and more complex and harder to maintain.

Ultimately, the shared use of a database is a violation of an important architectural rule. Components should be able to change their internal data representation without other components being affected. The database schema is an example of an internal data representation. When multiple components share the database, it is no longer possible to change the data representation. Therefore, microservices should have strictly separate data storage and not share a database schema.

A database instance can be used by multiple microservices when the data sets of the individual microservices are completely separate. For instance, each microservice can use its own schema within a shared database. However, in that situation there shouldn't be any relationships between the schemas.

Replication

Replicating data is an alternative method for integrating microservices. But care should be taken that the data replication does not introduce a dependency on the database schemas by the back door. When the data is just replicated and the same schema is used, the same problem occurs as with a shared use of the database. A schema change will affect other microservices, and the microservices become coupled again. This has to be avoided.

The data should be transferred into another schema to ensure the independence of the schemas and therefore the microservices. In most cases, *Bounded Context* means that different representations or subsets of data are relevant for different microservices. Therefore, when replicating data between microservices it will often be necessary to transform the data or to replicate just subsets of the data anyway.

A typical example for the use of replication in traditional IT is data warehouses. They replicate data but store it differently. This is because the data access requirement for a data warehouse is different: the aim is to analyze lots of data. The data is optimized for read access and often also combined, as not every single data set is relevant for statistics.

Problems: Redundancy and Consistency

Replication causes a redundant storage of the data. This means that the data is not immediately consistent: it takes time until changes are replicated to all locations.

However, immediate consistency is often not essential. For analysis tasks such as those carried out by a data warehouse, an analysis that does not include orders from the last few minutes can be sufficient. There are also cases in which consistency is not that important. When an order takes a little bit of time until it is visible in the delivery microservice, this can be acceptable because nobody will request the data in the meanwhile.

High consistency requirements make replication difficult. When system requirements are determined, it is often not clear how consistent the data really has to be. This limits the options when it comes to data replication.

When designing a replication mechanism there should ideally be a leading system that contains the current data. All other replicas should obtain the data from this system. This makes it clear which data is really up-to-date. Data modifications should not be stored in different systems as this easily causes conflicts and makes for a very complex implementation. Such conflicts are not a problem when there is just one source for changes.

Implementation

Some databases offer replication as a feature. However, this is often not helpful with the replication of data between microservices because the schemas of the microservices should be different. The replication has to be self-implemented. For this purpose, a custom interface can be created. This interface should enable high performance access even to large data sets. To achieve the necessary performance, one can also directly write into the target schema. The interface does not necessarily have to use a protocol like REST, but can employ faster alternative protocols. To achieves this, it may be necessary to use another communication mechanism than the one normally used by the microservices.

Batch

The replication can be activated in a batch. In this situation the entire data set—or at least changes from the last run—can be transferred. For the first replication run the volume of data can be large, meaning that the replication takes a long time. However, it can still be sensible to transfer all the data each time. This makes possible the correction of mistakes that occurred during the last replication run.

A simple implementation can assign a version to each data set. Based on the version, data sets that have changed can specifically be selected and replicated. This approach means that the process can be easily restarted if it is interrupted for some reason, as the process itself does not hold a state. Instead the state is stored with the data itself.

Event

An alternative method is to start the replication on certain events. For instance, when a data set is newly generated, the data can be immediately copied into the replicas. This approach is particularly easy to implement with messaging (section 8.4).

Data replication is an especially good choice where high-performance access is required to large amounts of data. Many microservice-based systems get along without replicating data. Even those systems that use data replication can also employ other integration mechanisms.

Try and Experiment

Would you use data replication in a microservice-based system? In which areas? How would you implement it?

8.6 Interfaces: Internal and External

Microservice-based systems have different types of interfaces:

- Each microservice can have one or more interfaces to other microservices. A change to the interface can require coordination with other microservice teams.

- The interfaces between microservices that are developed by the same team are a special case. Team members can closely work together so that these interfaces are easier to change.

- The microservice-based system can offer interfaces to the outside world, making the system accessible beyond just the organization. In extreme cases this can potentially be every Internet user if the system offers a public interface on the Internet.

These interfaces vary in how easy they are to change. It is very easy to ask a colleague in the same team for a change. This colleague is potentially in the same room, so it is very easy to communicate with him.

A change to an interface of a microservice belonging to another team is more difficult. The change has to compete against other changes and new features that team may be implementing. When the change has to be coordinated with other teams, additional effort arises.

Interface changes between microservices can be safeguarded by appropriate tests (consumer-driven contract tests, section 10.7). These tests examine whether the interface still meets the expectations of the interface users.

External Interfaces

When considering interfaces to the outside, coordination with users is more complicated. There may be very many users, and for public interfaces the users might even be unknown. This makes techniques like consumer-driven contract tests hard to implement. However, for interfaces to the outside, rules can be defined that determine, for instance, how long a certain version of the interface will be supported. A stronger focus on backwards compatibility can make sense for public interfaces.

For interfaces to the outside it can be necessary to support several versions of the interface in order to not force all users to perform changes. Between microservices it should be an aim to accept multiple versions only for uncoupling deployments. When a microservice changes an interface, it should still support the old interface. In that case the microservices that depend on the old interface do not have to be instantly deployed anew. However, the next deployment should use the new interface. Afterwards the old interface can be removed. This reduces the number of interfaces that have to be supported and therefore the complexity of the system.

Separating Interfaces

Since interfaces vary in how easy they are to change, they should be implemented separately. When the interface of a microservice is to be used externally, it can subsequently only be changed when this change is coordinated with the external users. However, a new interface for internal use can be split off. In this situation the interface that is exposed to the outside is the starting point for a separate internal interface that can be more easily changed.

Also several versions of the same interface can be implemented together internally. New parameters on a new version of the interface can be set to default values when the old interface is called so that internally both interfaces use the same implementation.

Implementing External Interfaces

Microservice-based systems can offer interfaces to the outside in different ways. On top of a web interface for users there can also be an API, which can be accessed from outside. For the web interface section 8.1 described how the microservices can be integrated in a way that enables all microservices to implement part of the UI.

When the system offers a REST interface to the outside world, the calls from outside can be forwarded to a microservice with the help of a router. In the example application the router Zuul is used for this (section 13.9). Zuul is highly flexible and can forward requests to different microservices based on very detailed rules. However, HATEOAS gives the freedom to move resources and makes routing dispensable.

The microservices are accessible from the outside via URLs, but they can be moved at any time. In the end the URLs are dynamically determined by HATEOAS.

It would also be possible to offer an adaptor for the external interface that modifies the external calls before they reach the microservices. However, in that case a change to the logic cannot always be limited to a single microservice because it could also affect the adaptor.

Semantic Versioning

To denote changes to an interface a version number can be used. Semantic Versioning[30] defines possible version number semantics. The version number is split into MAJOR, MINOR, and PATCH. The components have the following meaning:

- A change in MAJOR indicates that the new version breaks backwards compatibility. The clients have to adjust to the new version.

- The MINOR version is changed when the interface offers new features. However, the changes should be backwards compatible. A change of the clients is only necessary if they want to use the new features.

- PATCH is increased in the case of bug fixes. Such changes should be completely backwards compatible and should not require any modifications to the clients.

When using REST one should keep in mind that it is not wise to encode the version in the URL. The URL should represent a resource—independent of which version of the API version is called. The version can be defined, for instance, in an Accept header of the request.

Postel's Law or the Robustness Principle

Another important principle for the definition of interfaces is Postel's Law,[31] which is also known as the Robustness Principle. It states that components should be strict with regard to what they are passing on and liberal with regard to what they are accepting from others. Put differently, each component should adhere as closely as possible to the defined interface when using other components but should, whenever possible, compensate for errors that arise during the use of its own interface.

---

30. http://semver.org/
31. http://tools.ietf.org/html/rfc793#section-2.10

When each component behaves according to the Robustness Principle interoperability will improve: in fact, if each component adheres exactly to the defined interfaces, interoperability should already be guaranteed. If a deviation does happen, then the component being used will try to compensate for it and thereby attempt to "save" the interoperability. This concept is also known as Tolerant Reader.[32]

In practice a called service should accept the calls as long as this is at all possible. One way to achieve this is to only read out those parameters from a call that are really necessary. On no account should a call be rejected just because it does not formally conform to the interface specification. However, the incoming calls should be validated. Such an approach makes it easier to ensure smooth communication in distributed systems like microservices.

8.7 Conclusion

The integration of microservices can occur at different levels.

Client

One possible level for the integration is the web interface (section 8.1):

- Each microservice can bring along its own single-page-app (SPA). The SPAs can be developed independently. The transition between the microservices, however, starts a completely new SPA.

- There can be one SPA for the entire system. Each microservice supplies one module for the SPA. This makes the transitions between the microservices very simple in the SPA. However, the microservices get very tightly integrated, meaning that coordination of deployments can become necessary.

- Each microservice can bring along an HTML application, and integration can occur via links. This approach is easy to implement and enables a modularization of the web application.

- JavaScript can load HTML. The HTML can be supplied by different microservices so that each microservice can contribute a representation of its data. Using this technique an order can, for example, load the presentation of a product from another microservice.

---

32. http://martinfowler.com/bliki/TolerantReader.html

- A skeleton can assemble individual HTML snippets. This would enable, say, an e-commerce landing page to display the last order from one microservice and recommendations from another microservice. ESI (Edge Side Includes) or SSI (Server Side Includes) can be useful for this.

In the case of a rich client or a mobile app the integration is difficult because the client application is a deployment monolith. Therefore, changes to different microservices can only be deployed together. The teams can modify the microservices and then deliver a certain amount of matching UI changes together for a new release of the client application. There can also be a team for each client application that adopts new functionality of the microservices into the client application. From an organizational perspective there can even be developers in the team of the client application that develop a custom service that can, for instance, implement an interface that enables the client application to use it in a high-performance way.

Logic Layer

REST can be used for communication at the logic layer (section 8.2). REST uses the mechanisms of the WWW to enable communication between services. HATEOAS means that the relationships between systems are represented as links. The client only needs to know an entry URL. All the other URLs can be changed because they are not directly contacted by the clients but are found by them via links starting at the entry URL. HAL defines how links can be expressed and supports the implementation of REST. Other possible data formats for REST are XML, JSON, HTML, and Protocol Buffer.

Classical protocols like SOAP or RPC (section 8.3) can also be used for the communication between microservices. SOAP offers ways for messages to be forwarded to other microservices. Thrift has an efficient binary protocol and can also forward calls between processes.

Messaging (section 8.4) has the benefit that it can handle network problems and high latency times very well. In addition, transactions are also very well supported by messaging.

Data Replication

At the database level a shared schema is not recommended (section 8.5). This would couple microservices too tightly since they would have a shared internal data representation. The data has to be replicated into another schema. The schema should meet the requirements of the respective microservice. As microservices are *Bounded Contexts*, it is very unlikely that the microservices will use the same data model.

Interfaces and Versions

Finally, interfaces are an important foundation for communication and integration (section 8.6). Not all interfaces are equally easy to change. Public interfaces can be practically impossible to change because too many systems depend on them. Internal interfaces can be changed more easily. In the simplest case public interfaces just route certain functionality to suitable microservices. Semantic Versioning is useful for giving a meaning to version numbers. To ensure a high level of compatibility the Robustness Principle is helpful.

This section has hopefully shown that microservices are not just services that use RESTful HTTP. This is just one way for microservices to communicate.

Essential Points

- At the UI level the integration of HTML user interfaces is particularly straightforward. SPAs, desktop applications, and mobile apps are deployment monoliths where changes to the user interface for a microservice have to be closely coordinated with other changes.

- Though REST and RPC approaches offer a simple programming model at the logic level, messaging makes a looser coupling possible and can cope better with the challenges of distributed communication via the network.

- Data replication enables high-performance access to large amounts of data. However, microservices should never use the same schema for their data since this means the internal data representation can no longer be changed.

Chapter 9

Architecture of Individual Microservices

When microservices are implemented, close attention must be paid to a number of key points. First, this chapter addresses the domain architecture of microservices (section 9.1). Next up is CQRS (Command Query Responsibility Segregation) (section 9.2), which can be interesting when implementing a microservice-based system. This approach separates data writes from data reads. Event Sourcing (section 9.3) places events at the center of the modeling. The structure of a microservice can correspond to a hexagonal architecture (section 9.4), which subdivides functionality into a logic kernel and adapters. Section 9.5 focuses on resilience and stability—essential requirements for microservices. Finally, technical approaches for the implementation of microservices, such as Reactive, are discussed in section 9.6.

9.1 Domain Architecture

The domain architecture of a microservice defines how the microservice implements its domain-based functionality. A microservice-based architecture should not aim to predetermine this decision for all microservices. The internal structure of each microservice should be decided independently. This enables the teams to act largely autonomously of each other. It is sensible to adhere to established rules in order to keep the microservice easy to understand, simple to maintain, and also replaceable. However, there is no strict need for regulations at this level.

This section details how to identify potential problems with the domain architecture of a microservice. Once a potential issue has been discovered, the team responsible for the microservice will need to determine whether it constitutes a real problem and how it can be solved.

Cohesion

The domain architecture of the overall system influences the domain architecture of the individual microservices. As presented in section 7.1, microservices should be loosely coupled to each other and have high cohesion internally. This means that a microservice should have only one responsibility with regard to the domain. If microservices are not highly cohesive, then most likely the microservice has more than one responsibility. If the cohesion within the microservice is not high enough, the microservice can be split into several microservices. The split ensures that the microservices remain small and thus are easier to understand, maintain, and replace.

Encapsulation

Encapsulation means that part of the architecture hides internal information from the outside—particularly internal data structures. Access should instead occur only through an interface. This makes sure that the software remains easy to modify, because internal structures can be changed without influencing other parts of the system. For this reason, microservices should never allow other microservices access to their internal data structures. If they do, then these data structures can no longer be modified. In order to use another microservice, only the interface for that microservice needs to be understood. This improves the structure and intelligibility of the system.

Domain-Driven Design

Domain-driven design (DDD) is one way to internally structure microservices. Each microservice can have a DDD domain model. The patterns required from domain-driven design were introduced in section 3.3. When domain-driven design and strategic design define the structure of the overall system (section 7.1), the microservices should also use these approaches. During the development of the overall system strategic design is concerned with the domain models that exist and how these are distributed across the microservices.

Transactions

Transactions bundle multiple actions that should only be executed together or not at all. It is difficult for a transaction to span more than one microservice. Only messaging is able to support transactions across microservices (see section 8.4). The domain-based design within a microservice ensures that each operation at the interface only corresponds to one transaction. By doing this it is possible to avoid having multiple microservices participating in one transaction. This would be very hard to implement technically.

9.2 CQRS

Systems usually save a state. Operations can change data or read it. These two types of operations can be separated: Operations that change data and therefore have side effects (commands) can be distinguished from operations that just read data (queries). It is also possible to stipulate that an operation should not simultaneously change the state and return data. This distinction makes the system easier to understand: When an operation returns a value, it is a query and does not change any values. This leads to additional benefits. For example, queries can be provided by a cache. If read operations can also change data, then the addition of a cache becomes more difficult since operations with side effects still have to be executed. The separation between queries and commands is called CQS (Command Query Separation). This principle is not limited to microservices, but can be applied more generally. For example, classes in an object-oriented system can divide operations in the same manner.

CQRS

CQRS (Command Query Responsibility Segregation)[1] is more extreme than CQS and completely separates the processing of queries and commands.

Figure 9.1 shows the structure of a CQRS system. Each command is stored in the command store. In addition, there can be command handlers. The command handler in the example uses the commands for storing the current state of the data in a database. A query handler uses this database to process queries. The database can be adjusted to the needs of the query handler. For example, a database for the analysis of order processes can look completely different from a database that customers use for displaying their own order processes. Entirely different technologies can be employed for the query database. For instance, it is possible to use an in-memory

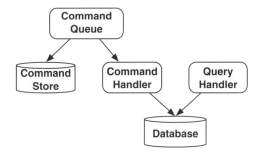

Figure 9.1 *Overview of CQRS*

---

1. https://speakerdeck.com/owolf/cqrs-for-great-good-2

cache, which loses data if there is a server failure. Information persistency is ensured by the command store. In an emergency the contents of the cache can be reconstructed by the command store.

Microservices and CQRS

CQRS can be implemented with microservices:

- The communication infrastructure can implement the command queue when a messaging solution is used. With approaches such as REST a microservice has to forward the commands to all interested command handlers and implement the command queue that way.

- Each command handler can be a separate microservice and can handle the commands with its own logic. This enables logic to be very easily distributed to multiple microservices.

- A query handler can also be a separate microservice. The changes to the data which the query handler uses can be introduced by a command handler in the same microservice. However, the command handler can also be a separate microservice. In that situation the query handler has to offer a suitable interface for accessing the database so that the command handler can change the data.

Advantages

CQRS has a number of benefits particularly when it comes to the interplay between microservices:

- Reading and writing of data can be separated into individual microservices. This makes possible even smaller microservices. When the writing and reading is so complex that a single microservice for both would get too large and too hard to understand, a split might make sense.

- Also a different model can be used for writing and reading. Microservices can each represent a *Bounded Context* and therefore use different data models. For instance, in an e-commerce shop a lot of data may be written for an online purchase while statistical evaluations read only a small part of that data for each purchase. From a technical perspective the data can be optimized for reading operations via denormalization or via other means for certain queries.

- Writing and reading can be scaled differently by starting a different number of query handler microservices and command handler microservices. This supports the fine-grained scalability of microservices.

- The command queue helps to handle any load peaks that occur during writing. The queue buffers the changes that are then processed later on. However, this does mean that a change to the data will not immediately be taken into consideration by the queries.

- It is easy to run different versions of the command handlers in parallel. This facilitates the deployment of new versions of the microservices.

CQRS can serve to make microservices even smaller, even when operations and data are very closely connected. Each microservice can independently decide for or against CQRS.

There are different ways to implement an interface that offers operations for changing and reading data. CQRS is only one option. Both aspects can also be implemented without CQRS in just one microservice. The freedom to be able to use different approaches is one of the main benefits of microservice-based architectures.

Challenges

CQRS also brings some challenges:

- Transactions that contain both read and write operations are hard to implement. The read and write operations may be implemented in different microservices. This may mean it is very difficult to combine the operations into one transaction since transactions across microservices are usually impossible.

- It is hard to ensure data consistency across different systems. The processing of events is asynchronous, meaning that different nodes can finish processing at different points in time.

- The cost for development and infrastructure is higher. More system components and more complex communication technologies are required.

It is not wise to implement CQRS in every microservice. However, the approach can be valuable for microservice-based architectures in many circumstances.

9.3 Event Sourcing

Event Sourcing[2] has a similar approach to CQRS. However, the events from Event Sourcing differ from the commands from CQRS. Commands are specific: They define exactly what is to be changed in an object. Events contain information about

---

2. http://slideshare.net/mploed/event-sourcing-introduction-challenges

something that has happened. Both approaches can be combined: A command can change data. This will result in events that other components of the system can react to.

Instead of the maintaining state itself Event Sourcing stores the events that have led to the current state. While the state itself is not saved, it can be reconstructed from the events.

Figure 9.2 gives an overview of Event Sourcing:

- The event queue sends all events to the different recipients. It can, for instance, be implemented with messaging middleware.

- The event store saves all events. This makes it possible to reconstruct the chain of events and the events themselves.

- An event handler reacts to the events. It can contain business logic that reacts to events.

- In such a system it is only the events that are easy to trace. The current state of the system is not easy to follow up on. Therefore, it can be sensible to maintain a snapshot that contains the current state. At each event or after a certain period of time the data in the snapshot will be changed to bring it up-to-date with the new events. The snapshot is optional. It is also possible to reconstruct the state from the events in an ad hoc manner.

Events may not be changed afterwards. Erroneous events have to be corrected by new events.

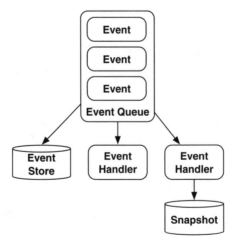

Figure 9.2 *Overview of Event Sourcing*

Event Sourcing is based on domain-driven design (see section 3.3). To adhere to the concept of *Ubiquitous Language*, the events should have names that also make sense in the business context. In some cases, an event-based model makes particular sense from a domain perspective. For instance, bookings to an account can be considered as events. Requirements like auditing are very easy to implement with Event Sourcing. Because the booking is modeled as an event, it is very easy to trace who has performed which booking. In addition, it is relatively easy to reconstruct a historical state of the system and old versions of the data. So Event Sourcing can be a good choice from a domain perspective. Generally, approaches like Event Sourcing make sense in complex domains which also benefit from domain-driven design.

Event Sourcing has similar advantages and disadvantages to CQRS, and both approaches can easily be combined. Event Sourcing makes particular sense when the overall system works with an event-driven architecture (section 7.8). In this type of system, the microservices already send events relating to changes of state, and it is logical to also use this approach in the microservices.

Try and Experiment

Choose a project you know.

- In which places would Event Sourcing make sense? Why? Would Event Sourcing be usable in an isolated manner in some places, or would the entire system have to be changed to events?

- Where could CQRS be helpful? Why?

- Do the interfaces adhere to the CQR rule? If they do, then the read and write operations would have to be separate in all interfaces.

9.4 Hexagonal Architecture

A hexagonal architecture[3] focuses on the logic of the application (see Figure 9.3). The logic contains only business functionality. It has different interfaces, each of which are represented by an edge of the hexagon. In the example shown, these are the interfaces for the interaction with users and the interface for administrators.

---

3. http://alistair.cockburn.us/Hexagonal+architecture

Users can utilize these interfaces via a web interface implemented by HTTP adapters. For tests there are special adapters enabling the tests to simulate users. Finally, there is an adapter that makes the logic accessible via REST. This enables other microservices to call the logic.

Interfaces don't just take requests from other systems; they are also used to initiate contact with other systems. In the example the database is accessed via the DB adapter—an alternative adapter is provided for test data. Another application can be contacted via the REST adapter. Instead of these adapters a test adapter can be used to simulate the external application.

Another name for hexagonal architecture is "ports and adapters." Each facet of the application like user, admin, data, or event is a port. The adapters implement the ports based on technologies like REST or web user interfaces. Through the ports on the right side of the hexagon the application fetches data, while the ports on the left side offer the system's functionality to users and other systems.

The hexagonal architecture divides a system into a logic kernel and adapter. Only the adapters can communicate with the outside.

Hexagons or Layers?

A hexagonal architecture is an alternative to a layered architecture. In a layered architecture there is a layer in which the UI is implemented and a layer in which the persistence is implemented. In a hexagonal architecture there are adapters that are connected to the logic via ports. A hexagonal architecture enables more ports than just persistence and UI. The term "adapter" illustrates that the logic and the ports are supposed to be separate from the concrete protocols and implementations of the adapter.

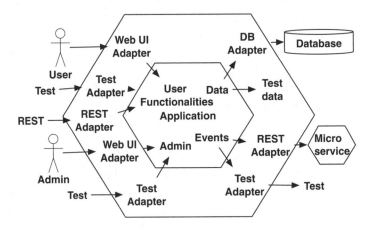

Figure 9.3 *Overview of Hexagonal Architecture*

Hexagonal Architectures and Microservices

It is very natural for hexagonal architectures to offer logic not only to other microservices via a REST interface but also to users via a web UI. This concept is also the basis of microservices. They are supposed to not only provide logic for other microservices but should also support direct interaction by users through a UI.

Since individual test implementations can be implemented for all ports, the isolated testing of a microservice is easier with a hexagonal architecture. For this purpose, test adapters just have to be used instead of the actual implementation. The independent testing of individual microservices is an important prerequisite for the independent implementation and the independent deployment of microservices.

The logic required for resilience and stability (see section 9.5) or Load Balancing (section 7.12) can also be implemented in the adapter.

It is also possible to distribute the adapters and the actual logic into individual microservices. This will result in more distributed communication with its associated overhead. However, this does mean that the implementation of the adapter and kernel can be distributed to different teams. For instance, a team developing a mobile client can implement a specific adapter that is adapted to the bandwidth restrictions of mobile applications (see also section 8.1).

An Example

As an example of a hexagonal architecture, consider the order microservice shown in Figure 9.4. The user can make use of the microservice by placing orders through the web UI. There is also a REST interface, which gives other microservices or external clients use of the user functionality. The web UI, the REST interface, and the test adapter are three adapters for the user functionality of the microservice. The implementation with three adapters emphasizes that REST and web UI are just two ways to use the same functionality. It also leads to microservices that are implemented to integrate UI and REST. Technically the adapters can still be implemented in separate microservices.

Another interface is the order events. They announce to the Delivery microservice whenever new orders arrive so that the orders can be delivered. Through this interface the Delivery microservice also communicates when an order has been delivered or when delays have occurred. In addition, this interface can be served by an adapter for tests. This means that the interface to the delivery microservice does not just write data but can also introduce changes to the orders. This means the interface works in both directions: It calls other microservices but can also be used by other microservices to change data.

The hexagonal architecture has a domain-based distribution into an interface for user functionality and an interface for order events. That way, the architecture underlines the domain-based design.

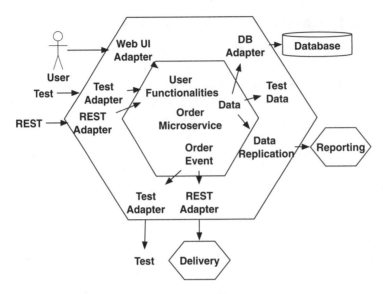

Figure 9.4 *The Order Microservice as an Example for Hexagonal Architecture*

The state of the orders is saved in a database. There is also an interface where test data can be used for tests instead of the database. This interface corresponds to the persistence layer of a traditional architecture.

Finally, there is an interface that uses data replication to transmit order information to reporting. There statistics can be generated from the orders. Reporting appears to be a persistence interface but is really more: The data is not just stored, but changed to enable quick generation of statistics.

As the example shows, a hexagonal architecture creates a good domain-based distribution into different domain-based interfaces. Each domain-based interface and each adapter can be implemented as a separate microservice. This makes possible the division of the application into numerous microservices, if necessary.

Try and Experiment

Choose a project you know.

- Which individual hexagons would there be?

- Which ports and adapters would the hexagons have?

- Which advantages would a hexagonal architecture offer?

- What would the implementation look like?

9.5 Resilience and Stability

In a well-designed microservices-based system, the failure of a single microservice should have a minimal impact on the availability of other microservices in the system. As microservice-based systems are, by their very nature, distributed, the danger of a failure is fundamentally higher than with other architectural styles: Networks and servers are unreliable. As microservices are distributed onto multiple servers, the number of servers is higher per system, and this also increases the chances of a failure. When the failure of one microservice results in the failure of additional microservices, a cascade effect can result in the entire system breaking down. This should be avoided.

For this reason, microservices have to be shielded from the failure of other microservices. This property is called resilience. The necessary measures to achieve resilience have to be part of the microservice. Stability is a broader term that denotes high software availability. *Release It!*[4] lists several patterns on this topic.

Timeout

Timeouts help to detect when a target system is unavailable during a communication with that system. If no response has been returned after the timeout period, the system being called is considered to be unavailable. Unfortunately, many APIs do not have methods to define timeouts, and some default timeouts are very high. For example, at the operating system level, default TCP timeouts can be as high as five minutes. During this time the microservice cannot respond to callers since the service is waiting for the other microservice. This may lead to requests to the calling microservice appearing to have failed. It is also possible that the request can block a thread during this time. At some point all threads are blocked, and the microservice can no longer receive any further requests. This type of cascade effect needs to be avoided. When the API intends a timeout to be used for accessing another system or a database, this timeout should be set. An alternative option is to let all requests to external systems or databases take place in an extra thread and to terminate this thread after a timeout.

Circuit Breaker

A circuit breaker is a safety device used in electrical circuits. In the event of a short circuit the circuit breaker interrupts the flow of electricity to avoid a dangerous situation occurring, such as overheating or fire. This idea can be applied to software as well: When another system is no longer available or returns errors, a *Circuit Breaker*

---

4. Michael T. Nygard. 2007. *Release It!: Design and Deploy Production-Ready Software*. Raleigh, NC: Pragmatic Programmers.

design feature prevents calls going to that system. After all, there is no point in making calls to a broken system.

Normally the *Circuit Breaker* is closed and calls are forwarded to the target system. When an error occurs, depending on the error frequency, the *Circuit Breaker* will be opened. Calls will no longer be sent on to the target system but will instead return an error. The *Circuit Breaker* can also be combined with a timeout. When the timeout parameters are exceeded, the *Circuit Breaker* is opened.

This takes load off the target system and means that the calling system does not need to wait for a timeout to occur, as the error is returned immediately. After some set period, the *Circuit Breaker* will close again. Incoming calls will once again be forwarded to the target system. If the error persists, the *Circuit Breaker* will open again.

The state of the *Circuit Breakers* in a system can highlight where problems are currently occurring to operations staff. An open *Circuit Breaker* indicates that a microservice is no longer able to communicate with another microservice. Therefore, the state of the *Circuit Breaker* should be part of the monitoring done by operations.

When the *Circuit Breaker* is open, an error does not necessarily have to be generated. It is also possible to simply degrade the functionality. Let us assume that an automated teller machine (ATM) cannot verify whether an account contains enough money for the desired withdrawal because the system that is responsible is not reachable. Nevertheless, cash withdrawals can be permitted up to a certain limit so that customers do not get annoyed by the failure, and the bank can continue to make the associated withdrawal fees. Whether a cash withdrawal is allowed and up to what limit is a business decision. The possible damage has to be balanced against the potential for profit. There can also be other rules applied in case of the failure of a system. Calls can be answered from a cache, for instance. More important than the technical options is the domain-based requirement for deciding on the appropriate handling of a system failure.

Bulkhead

A bulkhead is a special door on a ship which can be closed in a watertight manner. It divides the ship into several areas. When water gets in, only a part of the ship should be affected, and therefore the ship stays afloat.

Similar approaches are applicable to software: the entire system can be divided into individual areas. A breakdown or a problem in one area should not affect the other areas. For example, there can be several different instances of a microservice for different clients. If a client overloads the microservices, the other clients will not be negatively affected. The same is true for resources like database connections or threads. When different parts of a microservice use different pools for these resources, one part cannot block the other parts, even if it uses up all its resources.

In microservices-based architectures the microservices themselves form separate areas. This is particularly true when each microservice brings its own virtual machine along. Even if the microservice causes the entire virtual machine to crash or overloads it, the other microservices will not be affected. They run on different virtual machines and are therefore separate.

Steady State

The term steady state is used to describe systems that are built in a way that makes possible their continuous operation. For instance, this would mean that a system should not store increasing amounts of data. Otherwise the system will have used up its entire capacity at some point and break down. Log files, for example, have to be deleted at some point. Usually they are only interesting during a certain time interval anyway. Another example is caching: when a cache keeps growing, it will at some point fill all available storage space. Therefore, values in the cache have to be flushed at some point to keep the cache size from continuously increasing.

Fail Fast

Timeouts are necessary only because another system may need a long time to respond. The idea behind *Fail Fast* is to address the problem from the other side: Each system should recognize errors as quickly as possible and indicate them immediately. When a call requires a certain service and that service is unavailable at the moment, the call can be directly answered with an error message. The same is true when other resources are not available at the time. Also, a call should be validated right at the start. When it contains errors, there is nothing to be gained by processing it and an error message can be returned immediately. The benefits of *Fail Fast* are identical to those offered by timeouts: A rapid failure uses up less resources and therefore results in a more stable system.

Handshaking

Handshaking in a protocol serves to initiate communication. This feature of protocols gives servers the opportunity to reject additional calls when the server is overloaded. This can help to avoid additional overload, a breakdown, or responses that are too slow. Unfortunately, protocols like HTTP do not support this. Therefore, the application has to mimic the functionality with, for instance, health checks. An application can signal that it is, in principle, reachable but has so much load at the moment that it is unable to handle further calls. Protocols that build on socket connections can implement these type of approaches by themselves.

Test Harness

A *Test Harness* can be used to find out how an application behaves in certain error situations. Those problems might be at the level of TCP/IP or, say, responses of other systems that contain an HTTP header but no HTTP body. Theoretically, something like that should never occur since the operating system or network stack should deal with it. Nevertheless, such errors can occur in practice and have dramatic consequences if applications are not prepared to handle them. A *Test Harness* can be an extension of the tests that are discussed in section 10.8.

Uncoupling via Middleware

Calls in a single program only ever function on the same host at the same time in the same process. Synchronous distributed communication (REST) enables communication between different hosts and different processes at the same time. Asynchronous communication via messaging systems (section 8.4) also enables an uncoupling over time. A system should not wait for the response of an asynchronous process. The system should continue working on other tasks instead of just waiting for a response. Errors that cause one system after another to break down like dominoes are much less likely when using asynchronous communication. The systems are forced to deal with long response times since asynchronous communication often means long response times.

Stability and Microservices

Stability patterns like *Bulkheads* restrict failures to a unit. Microservices are the obvious choice for a unit. They run on separate virtual machines and are therefore already isolated with regard to most issues. This means that the bulkhead pattern arises very naturally in a microservices-based architecture. Figure 9.5 shows an overview: A microservice using *Bulkheads*, *Circuit Breakers*, and *Timeouts* can safeguard the use of other microservices. The used microservice can additionally implement fail fast. The safeguarding can be implemented via patterns in those parts of a microservice that are responsible for communicating with other microservices. This enables this aspect to be implemented in one area of the code and not distributed across the entire code.

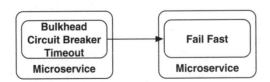

Figure 9.5 *Stability in the Case of Microservices*

On a technical level the patterns can be implemented in different ways. For micro-services there are the following options:

- *Timeouts* are easy to implement. When another system is accessed, an individual thread is started that is terminated after a timeout.

- At first glance *Circuit Breakers* are not very complex and can be developed in your own code. However, any implementation must work under high load and has to offer an interface for operations to enable monitoring. This is not trivial. Therefore, a home-grown implementation is often not sensible.

- *Bulkheads* are an inherent feature of microservices since a problem is, in many cases, already limited to just one microservice. For instance, a memory leak will only cause one microservice to fail.

- *Steady State*, *Fail Fast*, *Handshaking* and *Test Harness* have to be implemented by each microservice.

- Uncoupling via middleware is an option for shared communication of microservices.

Resilience and Reactive

The Reactive Manifesto[5] lists resilience as an essential property of a Reactive application. Resilience can be implemented in an application by processing calls asynchronously. Each part of an application which processes messages (actor) has to be monitored. When an actor does not react anymore, it can be restarted. This enables errors to be handled and makes applications more resilient.

Hystrix

Hystrix[6] implements *Timeout* and *Circuit Breaker*. To achieve this, developers have to encapsulate calls in commands. Alternatively, Java annotations can be used. The calls take place in individual thread pools, and several thread pools can be created. If there is one thread pool per called microservice, the calls to the microservices can be separated from each other in such a manner that a problem with one microservice does not affect the use of the other microservices. This is in line with the Bulkhead concept. Hystrix is a Java library that is made available under the Apache license and originates from the Netflix stack. The example application uses Hystrix together with Spring Cloud (see section 13.10). In combination with a sidecar, Hystrix can also be used for applications that are not written in Java (see section 7.9). Hystrix

---

5. http://www.reactivemanifesto.org/
6. https://github.com/Netflix/Hystrix/

supplies information about the state of the thread pools and the Circuit Breaker for monitoring and operational purposes. This information can be displayed in a special monitoring tool—the Hystrix dashboard. Internally, Hystrix uses the Reactive Extensions for Java (RxJava). Hystrix is the most widely used library in the area of resilience.

Try and Experiment

- This chapter introduced eight patterns for stability. Prioritize these patterns. Which properties are indispensable? Which are important? Which are unimportant?

- How can it be verified that the microservices actually implement the patterns?

9.6 Technical Architecture

The technical architecture of each microservice can be individually designed. Frameworks or programming languages do not have to be uniform for all microservices. Therefore, each microservice may well use different platforms. However, certain technical infrastructures fit microservices better than others.

Process Engines

Process engines, which typically serve to orchestrate services in an SOA (section 6.1), can be used within a microservice to model a business process. The important point is that one microservice should implement only one domain—that is, one *Bounded Context*. A microservice should not end working purely to integrate or orchestrate other microservices without its own logic. When this happens, changes will affect not just the responsible microservice but also the microservice responsible for integration/orchestration. However, it is a central objective of microservice-based architectures that changes should be limited to one microservice whenever possible. If multiple business processes have to be implemented, different microservices should be used for these. Each of these microservices should implement one business process together with the dependent services. Of course, it will not always be possible to avoid other microservices having to be integrated to implement a business process. However, a microservice that just represents an integration is not sensible.

Statelessness

Stateless microservices are very beneficial. To put it more clearly, microservices should not save any state in their logic layer. States held in a database or on the client side are acceptable. When using a stateless approach, the failure of an individual instance does not have a big impact. The instance can just be replaced by a new instance. In addition, the load can be distributed between multiple instances without having to take into consideration which instance processed the previous calls of the user. Finally, the deployment of a new version is easier since the old version can just be stopped and replaced without having to migrate its state.

Reactive

Implementing microservices with Reactive[7] technologies can be particularly useful. These approaches are comparable to Erlang (see section 14.7): Applications consist of actors. In Erlang they are called processes. Work in each actor is sequential; however, different actors can work in parallel on different messages. This enables the parallel processing of tasks. Actors can send messages to other actors that end up in the mailboxes of these actors. I/O operations are not blocking in Reactive applications: A request for data is sent out. When the data is there, the actor is called and can process the data. In the meantime, the actors can work on other requests.

Essential properties according to the Reactive Manifesto:

- Responsive: The system should react to requests as fast as possible. This has among others advantages for fail fast and therefore for stability (see section 9.5). Once the mailbox is filled to a certain predetermined degree, the actor can, for instance, reject or accept additional messages. This results in the sender being slowed down and the system does not get overloaded. Other requests can still be processed. The aim of being responsive is also helped if blocking I/O operations are not used.

- Resilience and its relationship with Reactive applications has already been discussed in section 9.5.

---

7. http://www.reactivemanifesto.org/

- Elastic means that new systems can be started at run times that share the load. To achieve this, the system has to be scalable, and it has to be possible to change the system at run time in such a way that the load can be distributed to the different nodes.

- Message Driven means that the individual components communicate with each other via messages. As described in section 8.4, this communication fits well with microservices. Reactive applications also use very similar approaches within the application itself.

Reactive systems are particularly easy to implement using microservices and the concepts from Reactive fit neatly with microservices' concepts. However, similarly good results can also be achieved by the use of more traditional technologies.

Some examples of technologies from the Reactive arena are:

- The programming language Scala[8] with the Reactive framework Akka[9] and the web framework Play[10] is based on it. These frameworks can also be used with Java.

- There are Reactive extensions[11] for practically all popular programming languages. Among them are RxJava[12] for Java or RxJS[13] for JavaScript.

- Similar approaches are also supported by Vert.x[14] (see also section 14.6). Even though this framework is based on the JVM, it supports many different programming languages like Java, Groovy, Scala, JavaScript, Clojure, Ruby, and Python.

Microservices without Reactive?

Reactive is only one way to implement a system with microservices. The traditional programming model with blocking I/O, without actors, and with synchronous calls is also suitable for this type of system. As previously discussed, resilience can be implemented via libraries. Elasticity can be achieved by starting new instances of the microservices, for instance, as virtual machines or Docker containers. Additionally,

---

8. http://www.scala-lang.org/

9. http://akka.io/

10. https://www.playframework.com/

11. http://reactivex.io/

12. https://github.com/ReactiveX/RxJava

13. https://github.com/Reactive-Extensions/RxJS

14. http://vertx.io/

traditional applications can also communicate with each other via messages. Reactive applications have benefits for responsiveness. However, in that case it has to be guaranteed that operations really do not block. For I/O operations Reactive solutions can usually ensure that. However, a complex calculation can block the system. This may mean that no messages can be processed anymore, and the entire system is blocked. A microservice does not have to be implemented with Reactive technologies, but they are certainly an interesting alternative.

Try and Experiment

Get more information about Reactive and microservices.

• How exactly are the benefits achieved and implemented?

• Is there a Reactive extension for your preferred programming language? Which features does it offer? How does this help with implementing microservices?

9.7 Conclusion

The team implementing a particular microservice is also responsible for its domain-based architecture. There should be only a small number of guidelines restricting team decisions so that the independence of the teams is maintained.

Low cohesion can be an indication of a problem with the domain-based design of a microservice. Domain-driven design (DDD) is an interesting way to structure a microservice. Transactions can also provide clues for an optimized domain-based division: An operation of a microservice should be a transaction (section 9.1).

CQS (command–query separation) divides operations of a microservice or a class into read operations (queries) and write operations (commands). CQRS (command–query responsibility segregation) (section 9.2) separates data changes via commands from query handlers, which process requests. This means that microservices or classes are created that can only implement reading or writing services. Event Sourcing (section 9.3) stores events and does not focus on the current state but on the history of all events. These approaches are useful for building up microservices because they enable the creation of smaller microservices that implement only read or write operations. This enables independent scaling and optimizations for both types of operations.

Hexagonal architecture (section 9.4) focuses on a kernel that can be called via adapters, for instance, by a UI or an API, as the center point of each microservice. Likewise, adapters can enable the use of other microservices or of databases. For microservices this results in an architecture that supports a UI and a REST interface in a microservice.

Section 9.5 presented patterns for Resilience and Stability. The most important of those are Circuit Breaker, Timeout and Bulkhead. A popular implementation is Hystrix.

Section 9.6 introduced certain technical choices for microservices: For instance, the use of process engines is a possibility for a microservice. Statelessness is beneficial. And finally, reactive approaches are a good basis for the implementation of microservices.

In summary, this chapter explained some essential considerations for the implementation of individual microservices.

Essential Points

- Microservices within a microservice-based system can have different domain-based architectures.

- Microservices can be implemented internally with Event Sourcing, CQRS, or hexagonal architectures.

- Technical properties like stability can only be implemented individually by each microservice.

Chapter 10

Testing Microservices and Microservice-Based Systems

The division of a system into microservices has an impact on testing. Section 10.1 explains the motivation behind software tests. Section 10.2 discusses fundamental approaches to testing broadly, not just with regard to microservices. Section 10.3 explains why there are particular challenges when testing microservices that are not present in other architectural patterns. For example, in a microservice-based system the entire system consisting of all microservices has to be tested (section 10.4). This can be difficult when there are a large number of microservices. Section 10.5 describes the special case of a legacy application that is being replaced by microservices. In that situation the integration of microservices and the legacy application has to be tested—testing just the microservices is not sufficient. Another way to safeguard the interfaces between microservices are consumer-driven contract tests (section 10.7). They reduce the effort required to test the system as a whole—although, of course, the individual microservices still have to be tested as well. In this context the question arises of how individual microservices can be run in isolation without other microservices (section 10.6). Microservices provide technology freedom; nevertheless, there have to be certain standards, and tests can help to enforce the technical standards (section 10.8) that have been defined in the architecture.

10.1 Why Tests?

Even though testing is an essential part of every software development project, questions about the goals of testing are rarely asked. Ultimately, tests are about risk management. They are supposed to minimize the risk that errors will appear in production systems and be noticed by users or do other damage.

With this in mind, there are a number of things to consider:

- Each test has to be evaluated based on the risk it minimizes. In the end, a test is only meaningful when it helps to avoid concrete error scenarios that could otherwise occur in production.

- Tests are not the only way to deal with risk. The impact of errors that occur in production can also be minimized in other ways. An important consideration is how long it takes for a certain error to be corrected in production. Usually, the longer an error persists, the more severe the consequences. How long it takes to put a corrected version of the services into production depends on the Deployment approach. This is one place where testing and Deployment strategies impact on each other.

- Another important consideration is the time taken before an error in production is noticed. This depends on the quality of monitoring and logging.

There are many measures that can address errors in production. Just focusing on tests is not enough to ensure that high-quality software is delivered to customers.

Tests Minimize Expenditure

Tests can do more than just minimize risk. They can also help to minimize or avoid expenditure. An error in production can incur significant expense. The error may also affect customer service, something that can result in extra costs. Identifying and correcting errors in production is almost always more difficult and time-consuming than during tests. Access to the production systems is normally restricted, and developers will have moved on to work on other features and will have to reacquaint themselves with the code that is causing errors.

In addition, using the correct approach for tests can help to avoid or reduce expenditures. Automating tests may appear time-consuming at first glance. However, when tests are so well defined that results are reproducible, the steps needed to achieve complete formalization, and automation are small. When the costs for the execution of the tests are negligible it becomes possible to test more frequently, which leads to improved quality.

Tests = Documentation

A test defines what a section of code is supposed to do and therefore represents a form of documentation. Unit tests define how the production code is supposed to be used and also how it is intended to behave in exceptional and borderline cases.

Acceptance tests reflect the requirements of the customers. The advantage of tests over documentation is that they are executed. This ensures that the tests actually reflect the current behavior of the system and not an outdated state or a state that will only be reached in the future.

Test-Driven Development

Test-driven development is an approach to development that makes use of the fact that tests represent requirements: In this approach developers initially write tests and then write the implementation. This ensures that the entire codebase is safeguarded by tests. It also means that tests are not influenced by knowledge of the code because the code does not exist when the test is written. When tests are implemented after code has been written, developers might not test for certain potential problems because of their knowledge about the implementation. This is unlikely when using test-driven development. Tests turn into a very important base for the development process. They push the development: before each change there has to be a test that does not work. Code can only be adjusted when the test was successful. This is true not only at the level of individual classes, which are safeguarded by previously written unit tests, but also at the level of requirements that are ensured by previously written acceptance tests.

10.2 How to Test?

There are different types of tests that handle different types of risks. The next sections will look into each type of test and which risk it addresses.

Unit Tests

Unit tests examine the individual units that compose a system—just as their name suggests. They minimize the risk that an individual unit contain errors. Unit tests are intended to check small units, such as individual methods or functions. In order to achieve this, any dependencies that exist in the unit have to replaced so that only the unit under test is being exercised and not all its dependencies. There are two ways to replace the dependencies:

- **Mocks** simulate a certain call with a certain result. After the call the test can verify whether the expected calls have actually taken place. A test can, for instance, define a mock that will return a defined customer for a certain customer number. After the test it can evaluate whether the correct customer has actually been fetched by the code. In another test scenario the mock can simulate an error if asked for a customer. This enables unit tests to simulate error situations that might otherwise be hard to reproduce.

- **Stubs**, on the other hand, simulate an entire microservice, but with limited functionality. For example, the stub may return a constant value. This means that a test can be performed without the actual dependent microservice. For example, a stub can be implemented that returns test customers for certain customer numbers—each with certain properties.

The responsibility for creating unit tests lies with developers. To support them there are unit testing frameworks that exist for all popular programming languages. The tests use knowledge about the internal structure of the units. For example, they replace dependencies by mocks or stubs. Also, this knowledge can be employed to run through all code paths for code branches within the tests. The tests are white box tests because they exploit knowledge about the structure of the units. Logically, one should really call it a transparent box; however, white box is the commonly used term.

One advantage of unit tests is their speed: even for a complex project the unit tests can be completed within a few minutes. This enables, literally, each code change to be safeguarded by unit tests.

Integration Tests

Integration tests check the interplay of the components. This is to minimize the risk that the integration of the components contains errors. They do not use stubs or mocks. The components can be tested as applications via the UI or via special test frameworks. At a minimum, integration tests should evaluate whether the individual parts are able to communicate with each other. They should go further, however, and, for example, test the logic based on business processes.

In situations where they test business processes the integration tests are similar to acceptance tests that check the requirements of the customers. This area is covered by tools for BDD (behavior-driven design) and ATDD (acceptance test-driven design). These tools make possible a test-driven approach where tests are written first and then the implementation—even for integration and acceptance tests.

Integration tests do not use information about the system under test. They are called black box tests, for they do not exploit knowledge about the internal structure of the system.

UI Tests

UI tests check the application via the user interface. In principle, they only have to test whether the user interface works correctly. There are numerous frameworks and tools for testing the user interface. Among those are tools for web UIs and also for desktop and mobile applications. The tests are black box tests. Since they test the user interface, the tests tend to be fragile: changes to the user interface can cause problems even if the logic remains unchanged. Also this type of testing often requires a complete system setup and can be slow to run.

Manual Tests

Finally, there are manual tests. They can either minimize the risk of errors in new features or check certain aspects like security, performance, or features that have previously caused quality problems. They should be explorative: They look at problems in certain areas of the applications. Tests that are aimed at detecting whether a certain error shows up again (regression tests) should never be done manually since automated tests find such errors more easily and in a more cost-efficient and reproducible manner. Manual testing should be limited to explorative tests.

Load Tests

Load tests analyze the behavior of the application under load. Performance tests check the speed of a system, and capacity tests examine how many users or requests the system is able to handle. All of these tests evaluate the efficiency of the application. For this purpose, they use similar tools that measure response times and generate load. Such tests can also monitor the use of resources or check whether errors occur under a certain load. Tests that investigate whether a system is able to cope with high load over an extended period of time are called endurance tests.

Test Pyramid

The distribution of tests is illustrated by the test pyramid (Figure 10.1): The broad base of the pyramid represents the large number of unit tests. They can be rapidly performed, and most errors can be detected at this level. There are fewer integration tests since they are more difficult to create and take longer to run. There are also fewer potential problems related to the integration of the different parts of the system. The logic itself is also safeguarded by the unit tests. UI tests only have to verify the correctness of the graphical user interface. They are even more difficult to create since automating UI is complicated, and a complete environment is necessary. Manual tests are only required now and then.

Test-driven development usually results in a test pyramid: For each requirement there is an integration test written, and for each change to a class a unit test is written. This leads to many integration tests and even more unit tests being created as part of the process.

The test pyramid achieves high quality with low expenditure. The tests are automated as much as possible. Each risk is addressed with a test that is as simple as

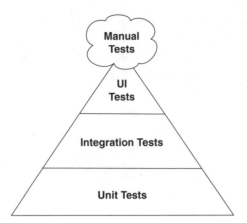

Figure 10.1 *Test Pyramid: The Ideal*

possible: is tested by simple and rapid unit tests. More difficult tests are restricted to areas that cannot be tested with less effort.

Many projects are far from the ideal of the test pyramid. Unfortunately, in reality tests are often better represented by the ice-cream cone shown in Figure 10.2. This leads to the following challenges:

- There are comprehensive manual tests since such tests are very easy to implement, and many testers do not have sufficient experience with test automation. If the testers are not able to write maintainable test code, it is very difficult to automate tests.

- Tests via the user interface are the easiest type of automation because they are very similar to the manual tests. When there are automated tests, it is normally largely UI tests. Unfortunately, automated UI tests are fragile: Changes to the graphical user interface often lead to problems. Since the tests are testing the entire system, they are slow. If the tests are parallelized, there are often failures resulting from excessive load on the system rather than actual failures of the test.

- There are few integration tests. Such tests require a comprehensive knowledge about the system and about automation techniques, which testers often lack.

- There can actually be more unit tests than presented in the diagram. However, their quality is often poor since developers often lack experience in writing unit tests.

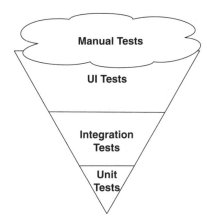

Figure 10.2 *Test Ice-Cream Cone: Far Too Common*

Other common problems include unnecessarily complex tests that are often used for certain error sources and UI tests or manual tests being used to test logic. For this purpose, however, unit tests would normally be sufficient and much faster. When testing, developers should try to avoid these problems and the ice-cream cone. Instead the goal should be to implement a test pyramid.

The test approach should be adjusted according to the risks of the respective software and should provide tests for the right properties. For example, a project where performance is key should have automated load or capacity tests. Functional tests might not be so important in this scenario.

Try and Experiment

- In which places does the approach in your current project correspond to the ice-cream cone rather than the test pyramid?

- Where are manual tests used? Are the most important tests automated?

- What is the relationship of UI to integration and unit tests?

- How is the quality of the different tests?

- Is test-driven development used? For individual classes or also for requirements?

Continuous Delivery Pipeline

The continuous delivery pipeline (Figure 4.2, section 4.1) illustrates the different test phases. The unit tests from the test pyramid are executed in the commit phase. UI tests can be part of the acceptance tests or could also be run in the commit phase. The capacity tests use the complete system and can therefore be regarded as integration tests from the test pyramid. The explorative tests are the manual tests from the test pyramid.

Automating tests is even more important for microservices than in other software architectures. The main objective of microservice-based architectures is independent and frequent software Deployment. This can only be achieved when the quality of microservices is safeguarded by tests. Without these, Deployment into production will be too risky.

10.3 Mitigate Risks at Deployment

An important benefit of microservices is that they can be deployed quickly because of the small size of the deployable units. Resilience helps to ensure that the failure of an individual microservice doesn't result in other microservices or the entire system failing. This results in lower risks should an error occur in production despite the microservice passing the tests.

However, there are additional reasons why microservices minimize the risk of a Deployment:

- It is much faster to correct an error, for only one microservice has to be redeployed. This is far faster and easier than the Deployment of a Deployment monolith.

- Approaches like Blue/Green Deployment or Canary Releasing (section 11.4) further reduce the risk associated with Deployments. Using these techniques, a microservice that contains a bug can be removed from production with little cost or time lost. These approaches are easier to implement with microservices since it requires less effort to provide the required environments for a microservice than for an entire Deployment monolith.

- A service can participate in production without doing actual work. Although it will get the same requests as the version in production, changes to data that the new service would trigger are not actually performed but are compared to the changes made by the service in production. This can, for example, be achieved by modifications to the database driver or the database itself. The service could also use a copy of the database. The main point is that in this phase the microservice will not change the data in production. In addition, messages that the microservice sends to the outside can be compared with the messages of the microservices in production instead of sending them on to the recipients. With this approach the microservice runs in production against all the special cases of the real life data—something that even the best test cannot cover completely. Such a procedure can also provide more reliable information regarding performance, although data is not actually written, so performance is not entirely comparable. These approaches are very difficult to implement with a Deployment monolith because of the difficulty of running the entire Deployment monolith in another instance in production. This would require a lot of resources and a very complex configuration because the Deployment monolith could introduce changes to data in numerous locations. Even with microservices this approach is still complex, and comprehensive support is necessary in software and Deployment. Extra code has to be written for calling the old and the new version and to compare the changes and outgoing messages of both versions. However, this approach is at least feasible.

- Finally, the service can be closely examined via monitoring in order to rapidly recognize and solve problems. This shortens the time before a problem is noticed and addressed. This monitoring can act as a form of acceptance criteria of load tests. Code that fails in a load test should also create an alarm during monitoring in production. Therefore, close coordination between monitoring and tests is sensible.

In the end the idea behind these approaches is to reduce the risk associated with bringing a microservice into production instead of addressing the risk with tests. When the new version of a microservice cannot change any data, its Deployment is practically free of risk. This is difficult to achieve with Deployment monoliths since the Deployment process is much more laborious and time consuming and requires more resources. This means that the Deployment cannot be performed quickly and therefore cannot be easily rolled back when errors occur.

The approach is also interesting because some risks are difficult to eliminate with tests. For example, load and performance tests can be an indicator of the behavior of the application in production. However, these tests cannot be completely reliable since the volume of data will be different in production, user behavior is different, and hardware is often differently sized. It is not feasible to cover all these aspects in one test environment. In addition, there can be errors that only occur with data sets from production—these are hard to simulate with tests. Monitoring and rapid Deployment can be a realistic alternative to tests in a microservices environment. It is important to think about which risk can be reduced with which type of measure—tests or optimizations of the Deployment pipeline.

10.4 Testing the Overall System

In addition to the tests for each of the individual microservices, the system as a whole also has to be tested. This means that there are multiple test pyramids: one for each individual microservice and one for the system in its entirety (see Figure 10.3). For the complete system there will also be integration tests of the microservices, UI tests of the entire application and manual tests. Unit tests at this level are the tests of the microservices since they are the units of the overall system. These tests consist of a complete test pyramid of the individual microservices.

The tests for the overall system are responsible for identifying problems that occur in the interplay of the different microservices. Microservices are distributed systems. Calls can require the interplay of multiple microservices to return a result to the user. This is a challenge for testing: distributed systems have many more sources of errors, and tests of the overall system have to address these risks. However, when testing microservices another approach is chosen: with resilience the individual microservices should still work even if there are problems with other microservices. So a

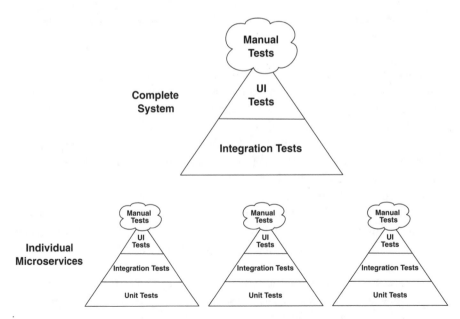

Figure 10.3 *Test Pyramid for Microservices*

failure of parts of the system is expected and should not have severe consequences. Functional tests can be performed with stubs or mocks of the other microservices. In this way microservices can be tested without the need to build up a complex distributed system and examine it for all possible error scenarios.

Shared Integration Tests

Before being deployed into production, each microservice should have its integration with other microservices tested. This requires changes to the continuous delivery pipeline as it was described in section 5.1: At the end of the Deployment pipeline each microservice should be tested together with the other microservices. Each microservice should run through this step on its own. When new versions of multiple microservices are tested together at this step and a failure occurs it will not be clear which microservice has caused the failure. There may be situations where new versions of multiple microservices can be tested together and the source of failures will always be clear. However, in practice such optimizations are rarely worth the effort.

This reasoning leads to the process illustrated in Figure 10.4: The continuous delivery pipelines of the microservices end in a common integration test into which each microservice has to enter separately. When a microservice is in the integration test phase, the other microservices have to wait until the integration test is completed. To ensure that only one microservice at a time runs through the integration tests the tests can be performed in a separate environment. Only one new version of a microservice may be delivered into this environment at a given point in time, and the environment enforces the serialized processing of the integration tests of the microservices.

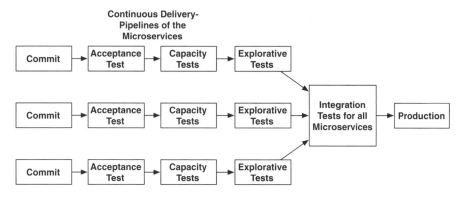

Figure 10.4 *Integration Tests at the End of the Continuous Delivery Pipelines*

Such a synchronization point slows down the Deployment and therefore the entire process. If the integration test lasts for an hour, for example, it will only be possible to put eight microservices through the integration test and into production per eight-hour work day. If there are eight teams in the project, each team will only be able to deploy a microservice once a day. This is not sufficient to achieve rapid error correction in production. Besides, this weakens an essential advantage of microservices: It should be possible to deploy each microservice independently. Even though this is in principle still possible, the Deployment takes too long. Also, the microservices now have dependencies to each other because of the integration tests—not at the code level but in the Deployment pipelines. In addition, things are not balanced when the continuous delivery without the last integration test requires, for example, only one hour, but it is still not possible to get more than one release into production per day.

Avoiding Integration Tests of the Overall System

This problem can be solved with the test pyramid. It moves the focus from integration tests of the overall system to integration tests of the individual microservices and unit tests. When there are fewer integration tests of the overall system, they will not take as much time to run. In addition, less synchronization is necessary, and the Deployment into production is faster. The integration tests are only meant to test the interplay between microservices. It is sufficient when each microservice can reach all dependent microservices. All other risks can then be taken care of before this last test. With consumer-driven contract tests (section 10.7) it is even possible to exclude errors in the communication between the microservices without having to test the microservices together. All these measures help to reduce the number of integration tests and therefore their total duration. In the end there is no reduction in overall testing—the testing is just moved to other phases: to the tests of the individual microservices and to the unit tests.

The tests for the overall system should be developed by all teams working together. They form part of the macro architecture because they concern the system as a whole and cannot therefore be the responsibility of an individual team (see section 12.3).

The complete system can also be tested manually. However, it is not feasible for each new version of a microservice to only go into production after a manual test with the other microservices. The delays will just be too long. Manual tests of the system can, for example, address features that are not yet activated in production. Alternatively, certain aspects like security can be tested in this manner if problems have occurred in these areas previously.

10.5 Testing Legacy Applications and Microservices

Microservices are often used to replace legacy applications. The legacy applications are usually Deployment monoliths. Therefore, the continuous delivery pipeline of the legacy application tests many functionalities that have to be split into microservices. Because of the many functionalities the test steps of the continuous delivery pipeline for Deployment monoliths take a very long time. Accordingly, the Deployment in production is very complex and takes a long time. Under such conditions it is unrealistic that each small code change to the legacy application goes into production. Often there are Deployments at the end of a sprint of 14 days or even only one release per quarter. Nightly tests inspect the current state of the system. Tests can be transferred from the continuous delivery pipeline into the nightly tests. In that case the continuous delivery pipeline will be faster, but certain errors are only recognized during the nighttime testing. Then the question arises of which of the changes of the past day is responsible for the error.

Relocating Tests of the Legacy Application

When migrating from a legacy application to microservices, tests are especially important. If just the tests of the legacy application are used, they will test a number of functionalities that meanwhile have been moved to microservices. In that case these tests have to be run at each release of a microservice—which takes much too long. The tests have to be relocated. They can turn into integration tests for the microservices (see Figure 10.5). However, the integration tests of the microservices should run rapidly. In this phase it is not necessary to use tests for functionalities, which reside in a single microservice. Then the tests of the legacy application have to turn into integration tests of the individual microservices or even into unit tests. In that case they are much faster. Additionally, they run as tests for a single microservice so that they do not slow down the shared tests of the microservices.

Not only the legacy application has to be migrated, but also the tests. Otherwise fast Deployments will not be possible in spite of the migration of the legacy application.

The tests for the functionalities that have been transferred to microservices can be removed from the tests of the legacy application. Step by step this will speed up the Deployment of the legacy application. Consequently, changes to the legacy application will also get increasingly easier.

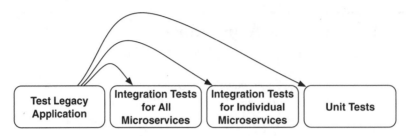

Figure 10.5 *Relocating Tests of Legacy Applications*

Integration Test: Legacy Application and Microservices

The legacy application also has to be tested together with the microservices. The microservices have to be tested together with the version of the legacy production that is in production. This ensures that the microservices will also work in production together with the legacy application. For this purpose, the version of the legacy application running in production can be integrated into the integration tests of the microservices. It is the responsibility of each microservice to pass the tests without any errors with this version (see Figure 10.6).

When the Deployment cycles of the legacy application last days or weeks, a new version of the legacy application will be in development in parallel. The microservices also have to be tested with this version. This ensures that there will not suddenly be errors occurring upon the release of the new legacy application. The version of the legacy application that is currently in development runs an integration test with the current microservices as part of its own Deployment pipeline (Figure 10.7). For this the versions of the microservices that are in production have to be used.

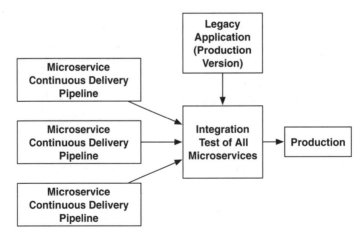

Figure 10.6 *Legacy Application in the Continuous Delivery Pipelines*

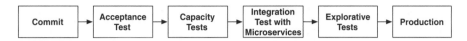

Figure 10.7 *Microservices in the Continuous Delivery Pipeline of the Legacy Application*

The versions of the microservices change much more frequently than the version of the legacy application. A new version of a microservice can break the continuous delivery pipeline of the legacy application. The team of the legacy application cannot solve these problems since it does not know the code of the microservices. This version of the microservice is possibly already in production though. In that case a new version of the microservice has to be delivered to eliminate the error—although the continuous delivery pipeline of the microservice ran through successfully.

An alternative would be to also send the microservices through an integration test with the version of the legacy application that is currently in development. However, this prolongs the overarching integration test of the microservices and therefore renders the development of the microservices more complex.

The problem can be addressed by consumer-driven contract tests (section 10.7). The expectations of the legacy application to the microservices and of the microservices to the legacy application can be defined by consumer-driven contract tests so that the integration tests can be reduced to a minimum.

In addition, the legacy application can be tested together with a stub of the microservices. These tests are not integration tests since they only test the legacy application. This enables reduction of the number of overarching integration tests. This concept is illustrated in section 10.6 using tests of microservices as example. However, this means that the tests of the legacy application have to be adjusted.

10.6 Testing Individual Microservices

Tests of the individual microservices are the duty of the team that is responsible for the respective microservice. The team has to implement the different tests such as unit tests, load tests, and acceptance tests as part of their own continuous delivery pipeline—as would also be the case for systems that are not microservices.

However, for some functionalities microservices require access to other microservices. This poses a challenge for the tests: It is not sensible to provide a complete environment with all microservices for each test of each microservice. On the one hand, this would use up too many resources. On the other hand, it is difficult to supply all these environments with the up-to-date software. Technically, lightweight virtualization approaches like Docker can at least reduce the expenditure in terms of resources. However, for 50 or 100 microservices this approach will not be sufficient anymore.

Reference Environment

A reference environment in which the microservices are available in their current version is one possible solution. The tests of the different microservices can use the microservices from this environment. However, errors can occur when multiple teams test different microservices in parallel with the microservices from the reference environment. The tests can influence each other and thereby create errors. Besides the reference environment has to be available. When a part of the reference environment breaks down due to a test, in extreme cases tests might be impossible for all teams. The microservices have to be hold available in the reference environment in their current version. This generates additional expenditure. Therefore, a reference environment is not a good solution for the isolated testing of microservices.

Stubs

Another possibility is the simulation of the used microservice. For the simulation of parts of a system for testing there are two different options as section 10.2 presented, namely stubs and mocks. Stubs are the better choice for the replacement of microservices. They can support different test scenarios. The implementation of a single stub can support the development of all dependent microservices.

If stubs are used, the teams have to deliver stubs for their microservices. This ensures that the microservices and the stubs really behave largely identically. When consumer-driven contract tests also validate the stubs (see section 10.7), the correct simulation of the microservices by the stubs is ensured.

The stubs should be implemented with a uniform technology. All teams that use a microservice also have to use stubs for testing. Handling the stubs is facilitated by a uniform technology. Otherwise a team that employs several microservices has to master a plethora of technologies for the tests.

Stubs could be implemented with the same technology as the associated microservices. However, the stubs should use fewer resources than the microservices. Therefore, it is better when the stubs utilize a simpler technology stack. The example in section 13.13 uses for the stubs the same technology as the associated microservices. However, the stubs deliver only constant values and run in the same process as the microservices that employ the stub. Thereby the stubs use up less resources.

There are technologies that specialize on implementing stubs. Tools for client-driven contract tests can often also generate stubs (see section 10.7).

- mountebank[1] is written in JavaScript with Node.js. It can provide stubs for TCP, HTTP, HTTPS, and SMTP. New stubs can be generated at run time. The definition of the stubs is stored in a JSON file. It defines under which conditions which responses are supposed to be returned by the stub. An extension with JavaScript is likewise possible. mountebank can also serve as proxy. In that case it forwards requests to a service—alternatively, only the first request is forwarded and the response is recorded. All subsequent requests will be answered by mountebank with the recorded response. In addition to stubs, mountebank also supports mocks.

- WireMock[2] is written in Java and is available under the Apache 2 license. This framework makes it very easy to return certain data for certain requests. The behavior is determined by Java code. WireMock supports HTTP and HTTPS. The stub can run in a separate process, in a servlet container or directly in a JUnit test.

- Moco[3] is likewise written in Java and is available under the MIT license. The behavior of the stubs can be expressed with Java code or with a JSON file. It supports HTTP, HTTPS, and simple socket protocols. The stubs can be started in a Java program or in an independent server.

- stubby4j[4] is written in Java and is available under the MIT license. It utilizes a YAML file for defining the behavior of the stub. HTTPS is supported as protocol in addition to HTTP. The definition of the data takes place in YAML or JSON. It is also possible to start an interaction with a server or to program the behavior of stubs with Java. Parts of the data in the request can be copied into the response.

Try and Experiment

Use the example presented in Chapter 13, "Example of a Microservice-Based Architecture," and supplement stubs with a stub framework of your choice. The example application uses the configuration file application-test.properties. In this configuration it is defined which stub is used for the tests.

---

1. http://www.mbtest.org/
2. http://wiremock.org/
3. https://github.com/dreamhead/moco
4. https://github.com/azagniotov/stubby4j

10.7 Consumer-Driven Contract Tests

Each interface of a component is ultimately a contract: the caller expects that certain side effects are triggered or that values are returned when it uses the interface. The contract is usually not formally defined. When a microservice violates the expectations, this manifests itself as error that is either noticed in production or in integration tests. When the contract can be made explicit and tested independently, the integration tests can be freed from the obligation to test the contract without incurring a larger risk for errors during production. Besides, then it would get easier to modify the microservices because it would be easier to anticipate which changes cause problems with using other microservices.

Often changes to system components are not performed because it is unclear which other components use that specific component and how they us it. There is a risk of errors during the interplay with other microservices, and there are fears that the error will be noticed too late. When it is clear how a microservice is used, changes are much easier to perform and to safeguard.

Components of the Contract

These aspects belong to the contract[5] of a microservice:

- The data formats define in which format information is expected by the other microservices and how they are passed over to a microservice.

- The interface determines which operations are available.

- Procedures or protocols define which operations can be performed in which sequence with which results.

- Finally, there is meta information associated with the calls that can comprise for example a user authentication.

- In addition, there can be certain nonfunctional aspects like the latency time or a certain throughput.

Contracts

There are different contracts between the consumers and the provider of a service:

- The **Provider Contract** comprises everything the service provider provides. There is one such contract per service provider. It completely defines the entire service. It can, for instance, change with the version of the service (see section 8.6).

---

5. http://martinfowler.com/articles/consumerDrivenContracts.html

- The **Consumer Contract** comprises all functionalities that a service user really utilizes. There are several such contracts per service—at least one with each user. The contract comprises only the parts of the service that the user really employs. It can change through modifications to the service consumer.

- The **Consumer-Driven Contract** (CDC) comprises all user contracts. Therefore, it contains all functionalities that any service consumer utilizes. There is only one such contract per service. Since it depends on the user contracts, it can change when the service consumers add new calls to the service provider or when there are new requirements for the calls.

Figure 10.8 summarizes the differences.

The Consumer-Driven Contract makes clear which components of the provider contracts are really used. This also clarifies where the microservice can still change its interface and which components of the microservice are not used.

Implementation

Ideally, a Consumer-Driven Contract turns into a consumer-driven contract test that the service provider can perform. It has to be possible for the service consumer to change these tests. They can be stored together in the version control with the microservice of the service provider. In that case the service consumers have to get access to the version control of the service provider. Otherwise the tests can also be stored in the version control of the service consumers. In that case the service provider has to fetch the tests out of the version control and execute them with each version of the software. However, in that case it is not possible to perform version control on the tests together with the tested software since tests and tested software are in two separate projects within the version control system.

The entirety of all tests represents the Consumer-Driven Contract. The tests of each team correspond to the Consumer Contract of each team. The consumer-driven

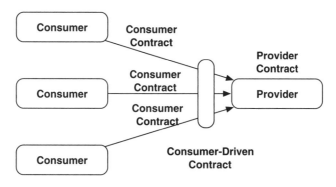

Figure 10.8 *Differences between Consumer and Provider Contracts*

contract tests can be performed as part of the tests of the microservice. If they are successful, all service consumers should be able to successfully work together with the microservice. The test precludes that errors will only be noticed during the integration test. Besides, modifications to the microservices get easier because requirements for the interfaces are known and can be tested without special expenditure. Therefore, the risk associated with changes that affect the interface is much smaller since problems will be noticed prior to integration tests and production.

Tools

To write consumer-driven contract tests a technology has to be defined. The technology should be uniform for all projects because a microservice can use several other microservices. In that case a team has to write tests for different other microservices. This is easier when there is a uniform technology. Otherwise the teams have to know numerous different technologies. The technology for the tests can differ from the technology used for implementation.

- An **arbitrary test framework** is an option for implementing the consumer-driven contract tests. For load tests additional tools can be defined. In addition to the functional requirements there can also be requirements with regard to the load behavior. However, it has to be clearly defined how the microservice is provided for the test. For example, it can be available at a certain port on the test machine. In this way the test can take place via the interface that is also used for access by other microservices.

- In the example application (section 13.13), simple **JUnit** tests are used for testing the microservice and for verifying whether the required functionalities are supported. When incompatible changes to data formats are performed or the interface is modified in an incompatible manner, the tests fail.

- There are tools especially designed for the implementation of consumer-driven contract tests. An example is **Pacto**.[6] It is written in Ruby and is available under the MIT license. Pacto supports REST/HTTP and supplements such interfaces with a contract. Pacto can be integrated into a test structure. In that case Pacto compares the header with expected values and the JSON data structures in the body with JSON schemas. This information represents the contract. The contract can also be generated out of a recorded interaction between a client and a server. Based on the contract Pacto can validate the calls and responses of a system. In addition, Pacto can create with this information simple stubs.

---

6. http://thoughtworks.github.io/pacto/

Moreover, Pacto can be used in conjunction with RSpec to write tests in Ruby. Also test systems that are written in other languages than Ruby can be tested in this way. Without RSpec, Pacto offers the possibility to run a server. Therefore it is possible to use Pacto outside of a Ruby system also.

- **Pact**[7] is likewise written in Ruby and under MIT license. The service consumer can employ Pact to write a stub for the service and to record the interaction with the stub. This results in a Pact file that represents the contract. It can also be used for testing whether the actual service correctly implements the contract. Pact is especially useful for Ruby, however **pact-jvm**[8] supports a similar approach for different JVM languages like Scala, Java, Groovy or Clojure.

Try and Experiment

- Use the example presented in Chapter 13 and supplement consumer-driven contracts with a framework of your choice. The example application has the configuration application-test.properties. In this configuration which stub is used for the tests is defined. Verify also the contracts in the production environment.

10.8 Testing Technical Standards

Microservices have to fulfill certain technical requirements. For example, microservices should register themselves in Service Discovery and keep functioning even if other microservices break down. Tests can verify these properties. This entails a number of advantages:

- The guidelines are unambiguously defined by the test. Therefore, there is no discussion how precisely the guidelines are meant.

- They can be tested in an automated fashion. Therefore it is clear at any time whether a microservice fulfills the rules or not.

---

7. https://github.com/realestate-com-au/pact
8. https://github.com/DiUS/pact-jvm

- New teams can test new components concerning whether they comply with the rules or not.

- When microservices do not employ the usual technology stack, it can still be ensured that they behave correctly from a technical point of view.

Among the possible tests are:

- The microservices have to register in the Service Discovery (section 7.11). The test can verify whether the component registers at service registry upon starting.

- Besides, the shared mechanisms for configuration and coordination have to be used (section 7.10). The test can control whether certain values from the central configuration are read out. For this purpose, an individual test interface can be implemented.

- A shared security infrastructure can be checked by testing the use of the microservice via a certain token (section 7.14).

- With regard to documentation and metadata (section 7.15) whether a test can access the documentation via the defined path can be tested.

- With regard to monitoring (section 11.3) and logging (section 11.2) whether the microservice provides data to the monitoring interfaces upon starting and delivers values resp. log entries can be examined.

- With regard to Deployment (section 11.4) it is sufficient to deploy and start the microservice on a server. When the defined standard is used for this, this aspect is likewise correctly implemented.

- As test for control (section 11.6) the microservice can simply be restarted.

- To test for resilience (section 9.5) in the simplest scenario whether the microservice at least boots also in absence of the dependent microservices and displays errors in monitoring can be checked. The correct functioning of the microservice upon availability of the other microservices is ensured by the functional tests. However, a scenario where the microservice cannot reach any other service is not addressed in normal tests.

In the easiest case the technical test can just start and deploy the microservice. Therefore Deployment and control are already tested. Dependent microservices do not have to be present for that. Starting the microservice should also be possible without dependent microservices due to resilience. Subsequently, logging and monitoring can be examined that should also work and contain errors in this situation.

Finally, the integration in the shared technical services like Service Discovery, configuration and coordination, or security can be checked.

Such a test is not hard to write and can render many discussions about the precise interpretation of the guidelines superfluous. Therefore, this test is very useful. Besides, it tests scenarios that are usually not covered by automated tests—for instance, the breakdown of dependent systems.

This test does not necessarily provide complete security that the microservice complies with all rules. However, it can at least examine whether the fundamental mechanisms function.

Technical standards can easily be tested with scripts. The scripts should install the microservice in the defined manner on a virtual machine and start it. Afterwards the behavior, for instance with regard to logging and monitoring, can be tested. Since technical standards are specific for each project, a uniform approach is hardly possible. Under certain conditions a tool like Serverspec[9] can be useful. It serves to examine the state of a server. Therefore, it can easily determine whether a certain port is used or whether a certain service is active.

10.9 Conclusion

Reasons for testing include, on the one hand, the risk that problems are only noticed in production and, on the other hand, that tests serve as an exact specification of the system (section 10.1).

Section 10.2 illustrated how using the concept of the test pyramid tests should be structured: The focus should be on fast, easily automatable unit tests. They address the risk that there are errors in the logic. Integration tests and UI tests then only ensure the integration of the microservices with each other and the correct integration of the microservices into the UI.

As section 10.3 showed, microservices can additionally deal with the risk of errors in production in a different manner: microservice Deployments are faster, they influence only a small part of the system, and microservices can even run blindly in production. Therefore the risk of Deployment decreases. Thus it can be sensible instead of comprehensive tests to rather optimize the Deployment in production to such an extent that it is, for all practical purposes, free of risk. In addition, the section discussed that there are two types of test pyramids for microservice-based systems: one per microservice and one for the overall system.

Testing the overall system entails the problem that each change to a microservice necessitates a run through this test. Therefore, this test can turn into a bottleneck

---

9. http://serverspec.org/

and should be very fast. Thus, when testing microservices, one objective is to reduce the number of integration tests across all microservices (section 10.4).

When replacing legacy applications not only their functionality has to be transferred into microservices, but also the tests for the functionalities have to be moved into the tests of the microservices (section 10.5). Besides, each modification to a microservice has to be tested in the integration with the version of the legacy application used in production. The legacy application normally has a much slower release cycle than the microservices. Therefore, the version of the legacy application that is at the time in development has to be tested together with the microservices.

For testing individual microservices the other microservices have to be replaced by stubs. This enables you to uncouple the tests of the individual microservices from each other. Section 10.6 introduced a number of concrete technologies for creating stubs.

In section 10.7 client-driven contract tests were presented. With this approach the contracts between the microservices get explicit. This enables a microservice to check whether it fulfills the requirements of the other microservices—without the need for an integration test. Also for this area a number of tool are available.

Finally, section 10.8 demonstrated that technical requirements to the microservices can likewise be tested in an automated manner. This enables unambiguous establishment of whether a microservice fulfills all technical standards.

Essential Points

- Established best practices like the test pyramid are also sensible for microservices.

- Common tests across all microservices can turn into a bottleneck and therefore should be reduced, for example, by performing more consumer-driven contract tests.

- With suitable tools stubs can be created from microservices.

Chapter 11

Operations and Continuous Delivery of Microservices

Deployment and operation are additional components of the continuous delivery pipeline (see section 10.1). When the software has been tested in the context of the pipeline, the microservices go into production. There, monitoring and logging collect information that can be used for the further development of the microservices.

The operation of a microservice-based system is more laborious than the operation of a deployment monolith. There are many more deployable artifacts that all have to be surveilled. Section 11.1 discusses the typical challenges associated with the operation of microservice-based systems in detail. Logging is the topic of section 11.2. Section 11.3 focuses on the monitoring of the microservices. Deployment is treated in section 11.4. Section 11.6 shows necessary measures for directing a microservice from the outside, and finally, section 11.7 describes suitable infrastructures for the operation of microservices.

The challenges associated with operation should not be underestimated. It is in this area where the most complex problems associated with the use of microservices frequently arise.

11.1 Challenges Associated with the Operation of Microservices

There are a number of challenges associated with the operation of microservices. The main challenges are covered in this section.

Numerous Artifacts

Teams that have so far only run deployment monoliths are confronted with the problem that there are many additional deployable artifacts in microservices-based systems. Each microservice is independently brought into production and therefore a separate deployable artifact. Fifty, one hundred, or more microservices are definitely possible. The concrete number depends on the size of the project and the size of the microservices. Such a number of deployable artifacts is hardly met with outside of microservices-based architectures. All these artifacts have to be versioned independently because only then can which code runs currently in production be tracked. Besides, this enables bringing a new version of each microservice independently into production.

When there are so many artifacts, there has to be a correspondingly high number of continuous delivery pipelines. They comprise not only the deployment in production but also the different testing phases. In addition, many more artifacts have to be surveilled in production by logging and monitoring. This is only possible when all these processes are mostly automated. For a small number of artifacts, manual interventions might still be acceptable. Such an approach is simply not possible any more for the large number of artifacts contained in a microservice-based architecture.

The challenges in the areas of deployment and infrastructure are the most difficult ones encountered when introducing microservices. Many organizations are not sufficiently proficient in automation although automation is also very advantageous in other architectural approaches and should already be routine.

There are different approaches for achieving the necessary automation.

Delegate into Teams

The easiest option is to delegate this challenge to the teams that are responsible for the development of the microservices. In that case each team has not only to develop its microservice but also to take care of its operation. They have the choice to either use appropriate automation for it or to adopt automation approaches from other teams.

The team does not even have to cover all areas. When there is no need to evaluate log data to achieve reliable operation, the team can decide not to implement a system for evaluating log data. A reliable operation without surveilling the log output is hardly possible, though. However, this risk is then within the responsibility of the respective team.

This approach only works when the teams have a lot of knowledge regarding operation. Another problem is that the wheel is invented over and over again by the different teams: each team implements automation independently and might use different tools for it. This approach entails the danger that the laborious operation of the microservices gets even more laborious due to the heterogeneous approaches taken by the teams. The teams have to do this work. This interferes with the rapid implementation of new features. However, the decentralized decision about which technologies to use increases the independence of the teams.

Unify Tools

Because of the higher efficiency, unification can be a sensible approach for deployment. The easiest way to obtain uniform tools is to prescribe one tool for each area—deployment, test, monitoring, logging, and deployment pipeline. In addition, there will be guidelines and best practices such as immutable server or the separation of build environment and deployment environment. This enables the identical implementation of all microservices and will facilitate operation since the teams only need to be familiar with one tool for each area.

Specify Behavior

Another option is to specify the behavior of the system. For example, when log output is supposed to be evaluated in a uniform manner across services, it is sufficient to define a uniform log format. The log framework does not necessarily have to be prescribed. Of course, it is sensible to offer a configuration that generates this output format for at least one log framework. This increases the motivation of the teams to use this log framework. In this way uniformity is not forced but emerges on its own since the teams will minimize their own effort. When a team regards the use of another log framework or programming language that necessitates another log framework as more advantageous, it can still use these technologies.

Defining uniform formats for log output has an additional advantage: the information can be delivered to different tools that process log files differently. This enables operations to screen log files for errors while the business stakeholders create statistics. Operation and business stakeholders can use different tools that use the uniform format as shared basis.

Similarly, behavior can be defined for the other areas of operation such as deployment, monitoring, or the deployment pipeline.

Micro and Macro Architecture

Which decisions can be made by the team and which have to be made for the overall project correspond to the separation of the architecture into micro and macro architecture (see section 12.3). Decisions the team can make belong to micro architecture while decisions that are made across all teams for the overall project are part of the macro architecture. Technologies or the desired behavior for logging can be either part of the macro or the micro architecture.

Templates

Templates offer the option to unify microservices in these areas and to increase the productivity of the teams. Based on a very simple microservice, a template demonstrates how the technologies can be used and how microservices are integrated into the operation infrastructure. The example can simply respond to a request with a constant value since the domain logic is not the point here.

The template will make it easy and fast for a team to implement a new microservice. At the same time, each team can easily make use of the standard technology stack. So the uniform technical solution is at the same time the most attractive for the teams. Templates achieve a large degree of technical uniformity between microservices without prescribing the technology used. In addition, a faulty use of the technology stack is avoided when the template demonstrates the correct use.

A template should contain the complete infrastructure in addition to the code for an exemplary microservice. This refers to the continuous delivery pipeline, the build, the continuous integration platform, the deployment in production, and the necessary resources for running the microservice. Especially build and continuous delivery pipeline are important since the deployment of a large number of microservices is only possible when these are automated.

The template can be very complex when it really contains the complete infrastructure—even if the respective microservice is very simple. It is not necessarily required to provide a complete and perfect solution at once. The template can also be built up in a stepwise manner.

The template can be copied into each project. This entails the problem that changes to the template are not propagated into the existing microservices. On the other hand, this approach is much easier to implement than an approach that enables the automated adoption of changes. Besides, such an approach would create dependencies between the template and practically all microservices. Such dependencies should be avoided for microservices.

The templates fundamentally facilitate the generation of new microservices. Accordingly, teams are more likely to create new microservices. Therefore, they can more easily distribute microservices in multiple smaller microservices. Thus templates help to keep microservices small. When the microservices are rather small, the advantages of a microservice-based architecture can be exploited even better.

11.2 Logging

By logging, an application can easily provide information about which events occurred. These can be errors, but they can also be events like the registration of a new user that are mostly interesting for statistics. Finally, log data can help developers to locate errors by providing detailed information.

In normal systems logs have the advantage that they can be written very easily and that the data can be persisted without huge effort. Besides, log files are human-readable and can be easily searched.

Logging for Microservices

For microservices writing and analyzing log files is hardly sufficient:

- Many requests can only be handled by the interplay of multiple microservices. In that case the log file of a single microservice is not sufficient to understand the complete sequence of events.

- The load is often distributed across multiple instances of one microservice. Therefore, the information contained in the log file of an individual instance is not very useful.

- Finally, due to increased load, new releases, or crashes, new instances of a microservice start constantly. The data from a log file can get lost when a virtual machine is shut down and its hard disk is subsequently deleted.

It is not necessary for microservices to write logs into their file system because the information cannot be analyzed there anyhow. Only writing to the central log server is definitely necessary. This has also the advantage that the microservices utilize less local storage.

Usually, applications just log text strings. The centralized logging parses the strings. During parsing relevant pieces of information like time stamps or server names are extracted. Often parsing goes even beyond that and scrutinizes the texts more closely. If it is possible, for instance, to determine the identity of the current user from the logs, all information about a user can be selected from the log data of the microservices. In a way the microservice hides the relevant information in a string that the log system subsequently takes apart again. To facilitate the parsing log data can be transferred into a data format like JSON. In that case the data can already be structured during logging. They are not first packaged into a string that then has to be laboriously parsed. Likewise, it is sensible to have uniform standards: When a microservice logs something as an error, then an error should really have occurred. In addition, the semantics of the other log levels should be uniform across all microservices.

Technologies for Logging via the Network

Microservices can support central logging by sending log data directly via the network. Most log libraries support such an approach. Special protocols like GELF (Graylog Extended Log Format)[1] can be used for this or long-established protocols like syslog, which is the basis for logging in UNIX systems. Tools like the logstash-forwarder,[2] Beaver,[3] or Woodchuck[4] are meant to send local files via the network to a central log server. They are sensible in cases where the log data is supposed to be also locally stored in files.

ELK for Centralized Logging

Logstash, Elasticsearch, and Kibana can serve as tools for the collection and processing of logs on a central server (see Figure 11.1). These tools form the ELK stack (Elasticsearch, Logstash, Kibana).

- With the aid of Logstash[5] log files can be parsed and collected by servers in the network. Logstash is a very powerful tool. It can read data from a source, modify or filter data, and finally write it into a sink. Apart from importing logs from the network and storage in Elasticsearch, Logstash supports many other data sources and data sinks. For example, data can be read from message queues or databases or written into them. Finally, Logstash can also parse data and supplement it—for example, time stamps can be added to each log entry, or individual fields can be cut out and further processed.

- Elasticsearch[6] stores log data and makes it available for analyses. Elasticsearch cannot only search the data with full text search, but it can also search in individual fields of structured data and permanently store the data like a database. Finally, Elasticsearch offers statistical functions and can use those to analyze

---

1. https://www.graylog.org/
2. https://github.com/elastic/logstash-forwarder
3. https://github.com/python-beaver/python-beaver
4. https://github.com/danryan/woodchuck
5. https://www.elastic.co/products/logstash
6. https://www.elastic.co/products/elasticsearch

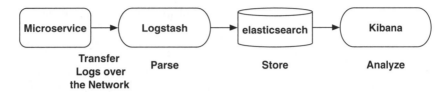

Figure 11.1 *ELK Infrastructure for Log Analysis*

data. As a search engine Elasticsearch is optimized for fast response times so that the data can be analyzed quasi-interactively.

- Kibana[7] is a web user interface that enables analysis of data from Elasticsearch. In addition to simple queries, statistical evaluations, visualizations and diagrams can be created.

All three tools are open source projects and are available under the Apache 2.0 license.

Scaling ELK

Especially in case of microservices, log data often accumulates in large amounts. Therefore, in microservice-based architectures the system for the central processing of logs should be highly scalable. Good scalability is one of the advantages of the ELK stack:

- **Elasticsearch** can distribute the indices into shards. Each data set is stored in a single shard. As the shards can be located on different servers, this makes possible load balancing. In addition, shards can be replicated across several servers to improve fail-safe qualities of the system. Besides, a read access can be directed to an arbitrary replica of the data. Therefore, replicas can serve to scale read access.

- **Logstash** can write logs into different indices. Without an additional configuration Logstash would write the data for each day into a different index. Since the current data usually is read more frequently, this enables reduction of the amount of data that has to be searched for a typical request and therefore improves performance. Besides, there are still other possibilities to distribute the data to indices—for instance, according to the geographic origin of the

---

7. https://www.elastic.co/products/kibana

user. This also promotes the optimization of the data amounts that has to be searched.

- Log data can be buffered in a **broker** prior to processing by Logstash. The broker serves as buffer. It stores the messages when there are so many log messages that they cannot be immediately processed. Redis[8] is often used as broker. It is a fast in memory database.

Graylog

The ELK stack is not the only solution for the analysis of log files. Graylog[9] is also an open source solution and likewise utilizes Elasticsearch for storing log data. Besides it uses MongoDB for metadata. Graylog defines its own format for the log messages: The already mentioned GELF (Graylog Extended Log Format) standardizes the data that is transmitted via the network. For many log libraries and programming languages there are extensions for GELF. Likewise, the respective information can be extracted from the log data or surveyed with the UNIX tool syslog. Also Logstash supports GELF as in- and output format so that Logstash can be combined with Graylog. Graylog has a web interface that makes it possible to analyze the information from the logs.

Splunk

Splunk[10] is a commercial solution that has already been on the market for a long time. Splunk presents itself as a solution that not only analyzes log files but can generally analyze machine data and big data. For processing logs Splunk gathers the data via a forwarder, prepares it via an indexer for searching, and search heads take over the processing of search requests. Its intention to serve as an enterprise solution is underlined by the security concept. Customized analysis, but also alerts in case of certain problems, are possible. Splunk can be extended by numerous plugins. Besides there are apps that provide ready-made solutions for certain infrastructures, such as Microsoft Windows Server. The software does not necessarily have to be installed in your own computing center, but is also available as a cloud solution.

---

8. http://redis.io/
9. https://www.graylog.org/
10. http://www.splunk.com/

Stakeholders for Logs

There are different stakeholders for logging. However, the analysis options of the log servers are so flexible and the analyses so similar that one tool is normally sufficient. The stakeholders can create their own dashboards with the information that is relevant to them. For specific requirements the log data can be passed on to other systems for evaluation.

Correlation IDs

Often multiple microservices work together on a request. The path the request takes through the microservices has to be traceable for analysis. For filtering all log entries to a certain customer or to a certain request, a correlation ID can be used. This ID unambiguously identifies a request to the overall system and is passed along during all communication between microservices. In this manner log entries for all systems to a single request are easy to find in the central log system, and the processing of the requests can be tracked across all microservices.

Such an approach can, for instance, be implemented by transferring a request ID for each message within the headers or within the payloads. Many projects implement the transfer in their own code without using a framework. For Java there is the library tracee,[11] which implements the transfer of the IDs. Some log frameworks support a context that is logged together with each log message. In that case it is only necessary to put the correlation ID into the context when receiving a message. This obliterates the need to pass the correlation ID on from method to method. When the correlation ID is bound to the thread, problems can arise when the processing of a request involves several threads. Setting the correlation ID in the context ensures that all log messages contain the correlation ID. How the correlation ID is logged has to be uniform across all microservices so that the search for a request in the logs works for all microservices.

Zipkin: Distributed Tracing

Also in regard to performance, evaluations have to be made across microservices. When the complete path of the requests is traceable, which microservice represents a bottleneck and requires an especially long time for processing requests can be identified. With the aid of distributed tracing which microservice needs how much time for answering a request and where optimization should start can be determined.

---

11. https://github.com/tracee/tracee

Zipkin[12] enables exactly this type of investigations.[13] It comprises support for different network protocols so that a request ID is automatically passed on via these protocols. In contrast to the correlation IDs, the objective is not to correlate log entries, but to analyze the time behavior of the microservices. For this purpose, Zipkin offers suitable analysis tools.

Try and Experiment

- Define a technology stack that enables a microservice-based architecture to implement logging:

  - How should the log messages be formatted?

  - Define a logging framework if necessary.

  - Determine a technology for collecting and evaluating logs.

  This section listed a number of tools for the different areas. Which properties are especially important? The objective is not a complete product evaluation, but a general weighing of advantages and disadvantages.

- Chapter 13, "Example of a Microservice-Based Architecture," shows an example for a microservice-based architecture, and in section 13.15 there are suggestions about how the architecture can be supplemented with a log analysis.

- How does your current project handle logging? Is it possible to implement parts of these approaches and technologies in your project also?

11.3 Monitoring

Monitoring surveils the metrics of a microservice and uses information sources other than logging. Monitoring uses mostly numerical values that provide information about the current state of the application and indicate how this state changes over time. Such values can represent the number of processed calls over a certain time, the time needed for processing the calls, or also system values like the CPU or memory

---

12. https://github.com/openzipkin/zipkin
13. https://blog.twitter.com/2012/distributed-systems-tracing-with-zipkin

utilization. If certain thresholds are surpassed or not reached, this indicates a problem and can trigger an alarm so that somebody can solve the problem. Or even better: The problem is solved automatically. For example, an overload can be addressed by starting additional instances.

Monitoring offers feedback from production that is not only relevant for operation but also for developers or the users of the system. Based on the information from monitoring they can better understand the system and therefore make informed decisions about how the system should be developed further.

Basic Information

Basic monitoring information should be mandatory for all microservices. This makes it easier to get an overview of the state of the system. All microservices should deliver the required information in the same format. Besides, components of the microservice system can likewise use the values. Load balancing, for instance, can use a health check to avoid accessing microservices that cannot process calls.

The basic values all microservices should provide can comprise the following:

- There should be a value that indicates the availability of the microservice. In this manner the microservice signals whether it is capable of processing calls at all ("alive").

- Detailed information regarding the availability of the microservice is another important metric. One relevant piece of information is whether all microservices used by the microservice are accessible and whether all other resources are available ("health"). This information does not only indicate whether the microservice functions but also provide hints about which part of a microservice is currently unavailable and why it failed. Importantly, it becomes apparent whether the microservice is unavailable because of the failure of another microservice or because the respective microservice itself is having a problem.

- Information about the version of a microservice and additional meta information like the contact partner or libraries used and their versions as well as other artifacts can also be provided as metrics. This can cover part of the documentation (see section 7.15). Alternatively, which version of the microservice is actually currently in production can be checked. This facilitates the search for errors. Besides, an automated continuous inventory of the microservices and other software used is possible, which simply inquires after these values.

Additional Metrics

Additional metrics can likewise be recorded by monitoring. Among the possible values are, for instance, response times, the frequency of certain errors, or the number of calls. These values are usually specific for a microservice so that they do not necessarily have to be offered by all microservices. An alarm can be triggered when certain thresholds are reached. Such thresholds are different for each microservice.

Nevertheless, a uniform interface for accessing the values is sensible when all microservices are supposed to use the same monitoring tool. Uniformity can reduce expenditure tremendously in this area.

Stakeholders

There are different stakeholders for the information from monitoring:

- **Operations** wants to be informed about problems in a timely manner to enable a smooth operation of the microservice. In case of acute problems or failures it wants to get an alarm—at any time of day or night—via different means like a pager or SMS. Detailed information is only necessary when the error has to be analyzed more closely—often together with the developers. Operations is interested not only in observing the values from the microservice itself, but also in monitoring values of the operating system, the hardware, or the network.

- **Developers** mostly focus on information from the application. They want to understand how the application functions in production and how it is utilized by the users. From this information they deduce optimizations, especially at the technical level. Therefore, they need very specific information. If the application is, for instance, too slow in responding to a certain type of call, the system has to be optimized for this type of call. To do so it is necessary to obtain as much information as possible about exactly this type of call. Other calls are not as interesting. Developers evaluate this information in detail. They might even be interested in analyzing calls of just one specific user or a circle of users.

- The **business stakeholders** are interested in the business success and the resulting business numbers. Such information can be provided by the application specifically for the business stakeholders. The business stakeholders then generate statistics based on this information and therefore prepare business decisions. On the other hand, they are usually not interested in technical details.

The different stakeholders are not only interested in different values but also analyze them differently. Standardizing the data format is sensible to support different tools and enables all stakeholders to access all data.

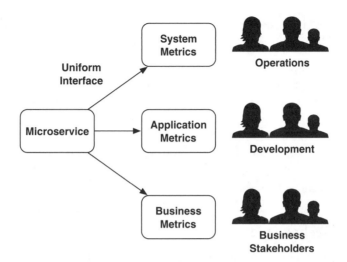

Figure 11.2 *Stakeholders and Their Monitoring Data*

Figure 11.2 shows an overview of a possible monitoring of a microservice-based system. The microservice offers the data via a uniform interface. Operations uses monitoring to surveil for instance threshold values. Development utilizes a detailed monitoring to understand processes within the application. Finally, the business stakeholders look at the business data. The individual stakeholders might use more or less similar approaches: The stakeholders can, for instance, use the same monitoring software with different dashboards or entirely different software.

Correlate with Events

In addition, it can be sensible to correlate data with an event, such as a new release. This requires that information about the event has to be handed over to monitoring. When a new release creates markedly more revenue or causes decisively longer response times, this is an interesting realization.

Monitoring = Tests?

In a certain way monitoring is another version of testing (see section 10.4). While tests look at the correct functioning of a new release in a test environment, monitoring examines the behavior of the application in a production environment. The integration tests should also be reflected in monitoring. When a problem causes an integration test to fail, there can be an associated alarm in monitoring. Besides, monitoring should also be activated for test environments to pinpoint problems already in the tests. When the risk associated with deployments is reduced by suitable measures (see section 11.4), the monitoring can even take over part of the tests.

Dynamic Environment

Another challenge when working with microservice-based architectures is that microservices come and go. During the deployment of a new release, an instance can be stopped and started anew with a new software version. When servers fail, instances shut down, and new ones are started. For this reason, monitoring has to occur separately from the microservices. Otherwise the stopping of a microservice would influence the monitoring infrastructure or may even cause it to fail. Besides, microservices are a distributed system. The values of a single instance are not telling in themselves. Only by collecting values of multiple instances does the monitoring information become relevant.

Concrete Technologies

Different technologies can be used for monitoring microservices:

- Graphite[14] can store numerical data and is optimized for processing time-series data. Such data occurs frequently during monitoring. The data can be analyzed in a web application. Graphite stores the data in its own database. After some time, the data is automatically deleted. Monitoring values are accepted by Graphite in a very simple format via a socket interface.
- Grafana[15] extends Graphite by alternative dashboards and other graphical elements.
- Seyren[16] extends Graphite by a functionality for triggering alarms.
- Nagios[17] is a comprehensive solution for monitoring and can be an alternative to Graphite.
- Icinga[18] has originally been a fork of Nagios and therefore covers a very similar use case.
- Riemann[19] focuses on the processing of event streams. It uses a functional programming language to define logic for the reaction to certain events. For this purpose, a fitting dashboard can be configured. Messages can be sent by SMS or email.

---

14. http://graphite.wikidot.com/
15. http://grafana.org/
16. https://github.com/scobal/seyren
17. http://www.nagios.org/
18. https://www.icinga.org/
19. http://riemann.io/

- Packetbeat[20] uses an agent that records the network traffic on the computer to be monitored. This enables Packetbeat to determine with minimal effort which requests take how long and which nodes communicate with each other. It is especially interesting that Packetbeat uses Elasticsearch for data storage and Kibana for analysis. These tools are also widely used for analyzing log data (see section 11.2). Having only one stack for the storage and analysis of logs and monitoring reduces the complexity of the environment.

- In addition, there are different commercial tools. Among those are HP's Operations Manager,[21] IBM Tivoli,[22] CA Opscenter[23] and BMC Remedy.[24] These tools are very comprehensive, have been on the market for a long time, and offer support for many different software and hardware products. Such platforms are often used enterprise-wide, and introducing them into an organization is usually a very complex project. Some of these solutions can also analyze and monitor log files. Due to their large number and the high dynamics of the environment, it can be sensible for microservices to establish their own monitoring tools, even if an enterprise-wide standard exists already. When the established processes and tools require a high manual expenditure for administration, this expenditure might not be feasible any more in the face of the large number of microservices and the dynamics of the microservice environment.

- Monitoring can be moved to the Cloud. In this manner no extra infrastructure has to be installed. This facilitates the introduction of tools and monitoring the applications. An example is NewRelic.[25]

These tools are, first of all, useful for operations and for developers. Business monitoring can be performed with different tools. Such monitoring is not only based on current trends and data, but also on historical values. Therefore, the amount of data is markedly larger than for operations and development. The data can be exported into a separate database or investigated with big data solutions. In fact, the analysis of data from web servers is one of the areas where big data solutions have first been used.

---

20. https://www.elastic.co/products/beats

21. http://www8.hp.com/us/en/software-solutions/operations-manager-infrastructure-monitoring/

22. http://www-01.ibm.com/software/tivoli/

23. http://www3.ca.com/us/opscenter.aspx

24. http://www.bmc.com/it-solutions/remedy-itsm.html

25. http://newrelic.com/

Enabling Monitoring in Microservices

Microservices have to deliver data that is displayed in the monitoring solutions. It is possible to provide the data via a simple interface like HTTP with a data format such as JSON. Then the monitoring tools can read the data out and import it. For this purpose, adaptors can be written as scripts by the developers. This makes it possible to provide different tools via the same interface with data.

Metrics

In the Java world, the Metrics[26] framework can be used. It offers functionalities for recording custom values and sending them to a monitoring tool. This makes it possible to record metrics in the application and to hand them over to a monitoring tool.

StatsD

StatsD[27] can collect values from different sources, perform calculations, and hand over the results to monitoring tools. This enables condensing of data before it is passed on to the monitoring tool in order to reduce the load on the monitoring tool. There are also many client libraries for StatsD that facilitate the sending of data to StatsD.

collectd

collectd[28] collects statistics about a system—for instance, the CPU utilization. The data can be analyzed with the front end or it can be stored in monitoring tools. collectd can collect data from a HTTP JSON data source and send it on to the monitoring tool. Via different plugins, collectd can collect data from the operating system and the basic processes.

Technology Stack for Monitoring

A technology stack for monitoring comprises different components (see Figure 11.3):

- Within the microservice itself data has to be recorded and provided to monitoring. For this purpose, a library can be used that directly contacts the monitoring tool. Alternatively, the data can be offered via a uniform interface—for

---

26. https://github.com/dropwizard/metrics
27. https://github.com/etsy/statsd
28. https://collectd.org/

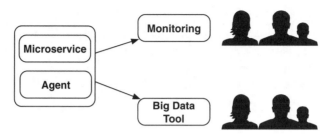

Figure 11.3 *Parts of a Monitoring System*

example JSON via HTTP– and another tool collects the data and sends it on to the monitoring tool.

- In addition, if necessary, there should be an agent to record the data from the operating system and the hardware and pass it on to monitoring.

- The monitoring tool stores and visualizes the data and can, if needed, trigger an alarm. Different aspects can be covered by different monitoring applications.

- For analyses of historical data or by complex algorithms a solution based on big data tools can be created in parallel.

Effects on the Individual Microservice

A microservice also has to be integrated into the infrastructure. It has to hand over monitoring data to the monitoring infrastructure and provide some mandatory data. This can be ensured by a suitable template for the microservice and by tests.

Try and Experiment

- Define a technology stack that enables implementation of monitoring in a microservice-based architecture. To do so define the stakeholders and the data that is relevant for them. Each of the stakeholders needs to have a tool for analyzing the data that is relevant for him/her. Finally, with which tools the data can be recorded and how it is stored has to be defined. This section listed a number of tools for the different areas. In conjunction with further research it is possible to assemble a technology stack that is well suited for individual projects.

(continued)

> - Chapter 13 shows an example for a microservice-based architecture, and in section 13.15 there is also a suggestion about how the architecture can be extended by monitoring. How does your current project handle monitoring? Can some of the technologies presented in this section also be advantageous for your project? Which? Why?

11.4 Deployment

Independent deployment is a central aim of microservices. Besides, the deployment has to be automated because manual deployment or even just manual corrections are not feasible due to the large number of microservices.

Deployment Automation

There are different possibilities for automating deployment:

- **Installation scripts** can be used that only install the software on the computer. Such scripts can, for instance, be implemented as shell scripts. They can install necessary software packages, generate configuration files, and create user accounts. Such scripts can be problematic when they are called repeatedly. In that case the installation finds a computer on which the software is already installed. However, an update is different from a fresh installation. In such a situation a script can fail, for example, because user accounts or configuration files might already be present and cannot easily be overwritten. When the scripts are supposed to handle updates, development and testing the scripts get more laborious.

- **Immutable servers** are an option to handle these problems. Instead of updating the software on the servers, the server is completely deployed anew. This facilitates not only the automation of deployment but also the exact reproduction of the software installed on a server. It is sufficient to consider fresh installations. A fresh installation is easier to reproduce than an update, which can be started from many different configuration states and should lead to the same state from any of those. Approaches like Docker[29] make it possible to tremendously reduce the expenditure for installing software. Docker is a kind

---

29. https://www.docker.com/

of lightweight virtualization. It also optimizes the handling of virtual hard drives. If there is already a virtual hard drive with the correct data, it is recycled instead of installing the software anew. When installing a package like Java, first a virtual hard drive is looked for that already has this installation. Only when one does not exist is the installation really performed. Should there only be a change in a configuration file when going from an old to a new version of an immutable server, Docker will recycle the old virtual hard drives behind the scenes and only supplement the new configuration file. This does not only reduce the consumption of hard drive space, but also profoundly speeds up the installation of the servers. Docker also decreases the time a virtual team needs for booting. These optimizations turn immutable server in conjunction with Docker into an interesting option. The new deployment of the servers is very fast with Docker, and the new server can also rapidly be booted.

- Other possibilities are tools like **Puppet**,[30] **Chef**,[31] **Ansible**,[32] or **Salt**.[33] They are specialized for installing software. Scripts for these tools describe what the system is supposed to look like after the installation. During an installation run the tool will take the necessary steps to transfer the system into the desired state. During the first run on a fresh system the tool completely installs the software. If the installation is run a second time immediately afterwards, it will not change the system any further since the system is already in the desired state. Besides, these tools can uniformly install a large number of servers in an automated manner and are also able to roll out changes to a large number of servers.

- Operating systems from the Linux area possess package managers like **rpm** (RedHat), **dpkg** (Debian/Ubuntu), or **zypper** (SuSE). They make it possible to centrally roll out software onto a large number of servers. The file formats used are very simple, so that it is very easy to generate a package in a fitting format. The configuration of the software poses a problem, though. Package managers usually support scripts that are executed during installation. Such scripts can generate the necessary configuration files. However, there can also be an extra package with the individual configurations for each host. The installation tools mentioned under the last bullet point can also use package manager for installing the actual software so that they themselves only generate the configuration files.

---

30. http://puppetlabs.com/
31. https://www.chef.io/
32. http://www.ansible.com/
33. http://www.saltstack.com/

Installation and Configuration

Section 7.10 already described tools that can be used for configuring microservices. In general, it is hard to separate the installation from the software configuration. The installation has to generate a configuration. Therefore, many of the tools such as Puppet, Chef, Ansible, or Salt can also create configurations and roll them out onto servers. Thus, these solutions are an alternative to the configuration solutions that are specialized for microservices.

Risks Associated with Microservice Deployments

Microservices are supposed to make possible an easy and independent deployment. Nevertheless, it can never be excluded that problems arise in production. The microservice-based architecture by itself will already help to reduce the risk. When a microservice fails as a result of a problem with a new version, this failure should be limited to the functionality of this microservice. Apart from that, the system should keep working. This is made possible by stability patterns and resilience described in section 9.5. Already for this reason the deployment of a microservice is much less risky than the deployment of a monolith. In cases of a monolith it is much harder to limit a failure to a certain functionality. If a new version of the deployment monolith has a memory leak, this will cause the entire process to break down so that the entire monolith will not be available any more. A memory leak in a microservice only influences this microservice. There are different challenges for which microservices are not helpful per se: schema changes in relational databases are, for instance, problematic because they often take very long and might fail—especially when the database already contains a lot of data. As microservices have their own data storage, a schema migration is always limited to just one microservice.

Deployment Strategies

To further reduce the risk associated with a microservice deployment there are different strategies:

- A **rollback** brings the old version of a microservice back into production. Handling the database can be problematic: Often the old version of the microservice does not work anymore with the database schema created by the newer version. When there are already data in the database that use the new schema, it can get very difficult to recreate the old state without losing the new data. Besides, the rollback is hard to test.

- A **roll forward** brings a new version of a microservice in production that does not contain the error any more. The procedure is identical to the procedure for the deployment of any other new version of the microservice so that no special measures are necessary. The change is rather small so that deployment and the passage through the continuous delivery pipeline should rapidly take place.

- **Continuous deployment** is even more radical: Each change to a microservice is brought into production when the continuous delivery pipeline was passed successfully. This further reduces the time necessary for the correction of errors. Besides, this entails that there are fewer changes per release, which further decreases the risk and makes it easier to track that changes to the code caused a problem. Continuous deployment is the logical consequence when the deployment process works so well that going into production is just a formality. Moreover, the team will pay more attention to the quality of their code when each change really goes into production.

- A **blue/green deployment** builds up a completely new environment with the new version of a microservice. The team can completely test the new version and then bring it into production. Should problems occur, the old version can be used again, which is kept for this purpose. Also in this scenario there are challenges in case of changes to the database schema. When switching from the one version to the other version of the microservice, the database has to be switched also. Data that has been written into the old database between the built-up of the new environment and the switch has to be transferred into the new database.

- **Canary releasing** is based on the idea to deploy the new version initially just on one server in a cluster. When the new version runs without trouble on one server, it can also be deployed on the other servers. The database has to support the old and the new version of the microservice in parallel.

- **Microservices** can also run blindly in production. In that case they get all requests, but they may not change data, and calls that they send out are not passed on. By monitoring, log analyses, and comparison with the old version, it is possible to determine whether the new service has been correctly implemented.

Theoretically, such procedures can also be implemented with deployment monoliths. However, in practice this is very difficult. With microservices it is easier since they are much smaller deployment units. Microservices require less comprehensive tests. Installing and starting microservices is much faster. Therefore, microservices can more rapidly pass through the continuous delivery pipeline into production.

This will have positive effects for roll forward or rollback because problems require less time to fix. A microservice needs fewer resources in operation. This is helpful for canary releasing or blue/green deployment since new environments have to be built up. If this is possible with fewer resources, these approaches are easier to implement. For a deployment monolith it is often very difficult to build up an environment at all.

11.5 Combined or Separate Deployment? (Jörg Müller)

by Jörg Müller, Hypoport AG

The question whether different services are rolled out together or independently from each other is of greater relevance than sometimes suspected. This is an experience we had to make in the context of a project that started approximately five years ago.

The term "microservices" was not yet important in our industry. However, achieving a good modularization was our goal right from the start. The entire application consisted initially of a number of web modules coming in the shape of typical Java web application archives (WAR). These comprised in turn multiple modules that had been split based on domain as well as technical criteria. In addition to modularization we relied from the start on continuous deployment as a method for rolling out the application. Each commit goes straight into production.

Initially, it seemed an obvious choice to build an integrated deployment pipeline for the entire application. This enabled integration tests across all components. A single version for the entire application enabled controlled behavior, even if multiple components of the applications were changed simultaneously. Finally, the pipeline itself was easier to implement. The latter was an important reason: Since there were relatively few tools for continuous deployment at the time, we had to build most ourselves.

However, after some time the disadvantages of our approach became obvious. The first consequence was a longer and longer run time of our deployment pipeline. The larger the number of components that were built, tested, and rolled out, the longer the process took. The advantages of continuous deployments rapidly diminished when the run time of the pipeline became longer. The first countermeasure was the optimization that only changed components were built and tested. However, this increased the complexity of the deployment pipeline tremendously. At the same time other problems like the runtime for changes to central components or the size of the artifacts could not be improved this way.

But there was also a subtler problem. A combined rollout with integrative tests offered a strong security net. It was easy to perform refactorings across multiple modules. However, this often changed interfaces between modules just because it was so easy to do. This is, in principle, a good thing. However, it had the consequence that it became very frequently necessary to start the entire system. Especially when working on the developer machine, this turned into a burden. The requirements for the hardware got very high, and the turnaround times lengthened considerably.

The approach got even more complicated when more than one team worked with this integrated pipeline. The more components were tested in one pipeline, the more frequently errors were uncovered. This blocked the pipeline since the errors had to be fixed first. At the time when only one team was dependent on the pipeline, it was easy to find somebody who took over responsibility and fixed the problem. When there were several teams, this responsibility was not so clear any more. This meant that errors in the pipeline persisted for a longer time. Simultaneously, the variety of technologies increased. Again, the complexity rose. This pipeline now needed very specialized solutions. Therefore, the expenditure for maintenance increased, and the stability decreased. The value of continuous deployment got hard to put into effect.

At this time it became obvious that the combined deployment in one pipeline could not be continued any more. All new services, regardless of whether they were microservices or larger modules, now had their own pipeline. However, it caused a lot of expenditure to separate the previous pipeline that was based on shared deployment into multiple pipelines.

In a new project it can be the right decision to start with a combined deployment. This especially holds true when the borders between the individual services and their interfaces are not yet well known. In such a case good integrative tests and simple refactoring can be very useful. However, starting at a certain size an independent deployment is obligatory. Indications for this are the number of modules or services, the run time and stability of the deployment pipeline, and last, but not least, the how many teams work on the overall system. If these indications are overlooked and the right point in time to separate the deployment is missed, it can easily happen that one builds a monolith that consists of many small microservices.

11.6 Control

Interventions in a microservice might be necessary at run time. For instance, a problem with a microservice might require restarting the respective microservice. Likewise, a start or a stop of a microservice might be necessary. These are ways for operation to intervene in case of a problem or for a load balancer to terminate instances that cannot process requests any more.

Different measures can be used for control:

- When a microservice runs in a **virtual machine**, the virtual machine can be shut down or restarted. In that case the microservice itself does not have to make special arrangements.

- The operating system supports **services** that are started together with the operating system. Usually, services can also be stopped, started, or restarted by means of the operating system. In that case the installation only has to register the microservice as service. Working with services is nothing unusual for operation, which is sufficient for this approach.

- Finally, an **interface** can be used that enables restarting or shutting down, for instance via REST. Such an interface has to be implemented by the microservice itself. This is supported by several libraries in the microservices area—for instance by Spring Boot, which is used to implement the example in Chapter 13. Such an interface can be called with simple HTTP tools like curl.

Technically, the implementation of control mechanisms is not a big problem, but they have to be present for operating the microservices. When they are identically implemented for all microservices, this can reduce the expenditure for operating the system.

11.7 Infrastructure

Microservices have to run on a suitable platform. It is best to run each microservice in a separate virtual machine (VM). Otherwise it is difficult to assure an independent deployment of the individual microservices.

When multiple microservices run on a virtual machine, the deployment of one microservice can influence another microservice. The deployment can generate a high load or introduce changes to the virtual machine that also concern other microservices running on the virtual machine.

Besides, microservices should be isolated from each other to achieve a better stability and resilience. When multiple microservices are running on one virtual machine, one microservice can generate so much load that the other microservices fail. However, precisely that should be prevented: When one microservice fails, this failure should be limited to this one microservice and not affect additional microservices. The isolation of virtual machines is helpful for limiting the failure or the load to one microservice.

Scaling microservices is likewise easier when each microservice runs in an individual virtual machine. When the load is too high, it is sufficient to start a new virtual machine and register it with the load balancer.

In case of problems it is also easier to analyze the error when all processes on a virtual machine belong to one microservice. Each metric on the system then unambiguously belongs to this microservice.

Finally, the microservice can be delivered as hard drive image when each microservice runs on its own virtual machine. Such a deployment has the advantage that the entire environment of the virtual machine is exactly in line with the requirements of the microservice and that the microservice can bring along its own technology stack up to its own operating system.

Virtualization or Cloud

It is hardly possible to install new physical hardware upon the deployment of a new microservice. Besides, microservices profit from virtualization or a Cloud, since this renders the infrastructures much more flexible. New virtual machines for scaling or testing environments can easily be provided. In the continuous delivery pipeline microservices are constantly started to perform different tests. Moreover, in production new instances have to be started depending on the load.

Therefore, it should be possible to start a new virtual machine in a completely automated manner. Starting new instances with simple API calls is exactly what a Cloud offers. A cloud infrastructure should be available in order to really be able to implement a microservice-based architecture. Virtual machines that are provided by operation via manual processes are not sufficient. This also demonstrates that microservices can hardly be run without modern infrastructures.

Docker

When there is an individual virtual machine for each microservice, it is laborious to generate a test environment containing all microservices. Even creating an environment with relatively few microservices can be a challenge for a developer machine. The usage of RAM and CPU is very high for such an environment. In fact, it is hardly sensible to use an entire virtual machine for one microservice. In the end, the microservice should just run and integrate in logging and monitoring. Therefore, solutions like Docker are convenient: Docker does not comprise many of the normally common operating system features.

Instead Docker[34] offers a very lightweight virtualization. To this purpose Docker uses different technologies:

- In place of a complete virtualization Docker employs Linux Containers.[35] Support for similar mechanisms in Microsoft Windows has been announced. This enables implementation of a lightweight alternative to virtual machines: All containers use the same kernel. There is only one instance of the kernel in memory. Processes, networks, data systems, and users are separate from each other. In comparison to a virtual machine with its own kernel and often also many operating system services, a container has a profoundly lower overhead. It is easily possible to run hundreds of Linux containers on a simple laptop. Besides, a container starts much more rapidly than a virtual machine with its own kernel and complete operating system. The container does not have to boot an entire operating system; it just starts a new process. The container itself does not add a lot of overhead since it only requires a custom configuration of the operating system resources.

- In addition, the file system is optimized: basic read-only file systems can be used. At the same time additional file systems can be added to the container, which also enables writing. One file system can be put on top of another file system. For instance, a basic file system can be generated that contains an operating system. If software is installed in the running container or if files are modified, the container only has to store these additional files in a small container-specific file system. In this way the memory requirement for the containers on the hard drive is significantly reduced.

Besides, additional interesting possibilities arise: For example, a basic file system can be started with an operating system, and subsequently software can be installed. As mentioned, only changes to the file system are saved that are introduced upon the installation of the software. Based on this delta a file system can be generated. Then a container can be started that puts a file system with this delta on top of the basic file system containing the operating system—and afterwards additional software can be installed in yet another layer. In this manner each "layer" in the file system can contain specific changes. The real file system at run time can be composed from numerous such layers. This enables recycling software installations very efficiently.

---

34. https://www.docker.com/
35. https://linuxcontainers.org/

Figure 11.4 *Filesystems in Docker*

Figure 11.4 shows an example for the file system of a running container: The lowest level is an Ubuntu Linux installation. On top there are changes that have been introduced by installing Java. Then there is the application. For the running container to be able to write changes into the file system, there is a file system on top into which the container writes files. When the container wants to read a file, it will move through the layers from top to bottom until it finds the respective data.

Docker Container versus Virtualization

Docker containers offer a very efficient alternative to virtualization. However, they are not "real" virtualization since each container has separate resources, its own memory, and its own file systems, but all share, for instance, one kernel. Therefore, this approach has some disadvantages. A Docker container can only use Linux and only the same kernel as the host operating system—consequently Windows applications, for instance, cannot be run on a Linux machine this way. The separation of the containers is not as strict as in the case of real virtual machines. An error in the kernel would, for example, affect all containers. Moreover, Docker also does not run on Mac OS X or Windows. Nevertheless, Docker can directly be installed on these platforms. Behind the scenes a virtual machine with Linux is being used. Microsoft has announced a version for Windows that can run the Windows container.

Communication between Docker Containers

Docker containers have to communicate with each other. For example, a web application communicates with its database. For this purpose, containers export network ports that other containers use. Besides, file systems can be used together. There containers write data that can be read by other containers.

Docker Registry

Docker images comprise the data of a virtual hard drive. Docker registries enable saving and downloading Docker images. This makes it possible to save Docker images as result of a build process and subsequently to roll them out on servers. Because of the efficient storage of images, it is easily possible to distribute even complex installations in a performant manner. Besides, many cloud solutions can directly run Docker containers.

Docker and Microservices

Docker constitutes an ideal running environment for microservices. It hardly limits the technology used, as every type of Linux software can run in a Docker container. Docker registries make it possible to easily distribute Docker containers. At the same time the overhead of a Docker container is negligible in comparison to a normal process. Since microservices require a multitude of virtual machines, these optimizations are very valuable. On the one hand, Docker is very efficient, and on the other hand, it does not limit the technology freedom.

Try and Experiment

- At https://docs.docker.com/engine/getstarted/ the Docker online tutorial can be found. Complete the tutorial—it demonstrates the basics of working with Docker. The tutorial can be completed quickly.

Docker and Servers

There are different possibilities to use Docker for servers:

- On a **Linux server** Docker can be installed, and afterwards one or multiple Docker containers can be run. Docker then serves as solution for the provisioning of the software. For a cluster new servers are started on which, again, the Docker containers are installed. Docker only serves for the installation of the software on the servers.

- Docker containers are run directly on a **cluster**. Which physical computer a certain Docker is located on is decided by the software for cluster administration. Such an approach is supported by the scheduler Apache Mesos.[36] It administrates a cluster of servers and directs jobs to the respective servers.

---

36. http://mesos.apache.org/

Mesosphere[37] enables running of Docker containers with the aid of the Mesos scheduler. Besides Mesos supports many additional kinds of jobs.

- Kubernetes[38] likewise supports the execution of Docker containers in a cluster. However, the approach taken is different from Mesos. Kubernetes offers a service that distributes pods in the cluster. Pods are interconnected Docker containers, which are supposed to run on a physical server. As basis Kubernetes requires only a simple operating system installation—Kubernetes implements the cluster management.

  - CoreOS[39] is a very lightweight server operating system. With etcd it supports the cluster-wide distribution of configurations. fleetd enables the deployment of services in a cluster—up to redundant installation, failure security, dependencies, and shared deployment on a node. All services have to be deployed as Docker containers while the operating system itself remains essentially unchanged.

  - Docker Machine[40] enables the installation of Docker on different virtualization and cloud systems. Besides, Docker machine can configure the Docker command line tool in such a manner that it communicates with such a system. Together with Docker Compose[41] multiple Docker containers can be combined to an overall system. The example application employs this approach—compare section 13.6 and section 13.7. Docker Swarm[42] adds a way to configure and run clusters with this tool stack: Individual servers can be installed with Docker Machine and combined to a cluster with Docker Swarm. Docker Compose can run each Docker container on a specific machine in the cluster.

Kubernetes, CoreOS, Docker Compose, Docker Machine, Docker Swarm, and Mesos, of course, influence the running of the software so that the solutions require changes in the operation procedures in contrast to virtualization. These technologies solve challenges that were previously addressed by virtualization solutions. Modern virtualization technology run virtual machines on a node in a cluster and do the cluster management. The container technologies mentioned above distribute containers in the cluster. So the cluster handling is done by different software which requires a fundamental change in the operations procedures.

---

37. http://mesosphere.com/
38. http://kubernetes.io/
39. http://coreos.com/
40. https://docs.docker.com/machine/
41. http://docs.docker.com/compose/
42. http://docs.docker.com/swarm/

PaaS

PaaS (platform as a service) is based on a fundamentally different approach. The deployment of an application can be done simply by updating the application in version control. The PaaS fetches the changes, builds the application, and rolls it out on the servers. These servers are installed by PaaS and represent a standardized environment. The actual infrastructure—that is, the virtual machines—are hidden from the application. PaaS offers a standardized environment for the application. The environment also takes care, for instance, of the scaling and can offer services like databases and messaging systems. Because of the uniform platform PaaS systems limit the technology freedom that is normally an advantage of microservices. Only technologies that are supported by PaaS can be used. On the other hand, deployment and scaling are further facilitated.

Microservices impose high demands on infrastructure. Automation is an essential prerequisite for operating the numerous microservices. A PaaS offers a good basis for this since it profoundly facilitates automation. To use a PaaS can be especially sensible when the development of a home-grown automation is too laborious and there is not enough knowledge about how to build the necessary infrastructure. However, the microservices have to restrict themselves to the features that are offered by the PaaS. When the microservices have been developed for the PaaS from the start, this is not very laborious. However, if they have to be ported, considerable expenditure can ensue.

Nanoservices (Chapter 14, "Technologies for Nanoservices") have different operating environments, which, for example, even further restrict the technology choice. On the other hand, they are often even easier to operate and even more efficient in regards to resource usage.

11.8 Conclusion

Operating a microservice-based system is one of the central challenges when working with microservices (section 11.1). A microservice-based system contains a tremendous number of microservices and therefore operating system processes. Fifty or one hundred virtual machines are no rarity. The responsibility for operation can be delegated to the teams. However, this approach creates a higher overall expenditure. Standardizing operations is a more sensible strategy. Templates are a possibility to achieve uniformity without exerting pressure. Templates turn the uniform approach into the easiest one.

For logging (section 11.2) a central infrastructure has to be provided that collects logs from all microservices. There are different technologies available for this. To trace a call across the different microservices a correlation ID can be used that unambiguously identifies a call.

Monitoring (section 11.3) has to offer at least basic information such as the availability of the microservice. Additional metrics can, for instance, provide an overview of the overall system or can be useful for load balancing. Metrics can be individually defined for each microservice. There are different stakeholders for the monitoring: operations, developers, and business stakeholders. They are interested in different values and use, where necessary, their own tools for evaluating the microservices data. Each microservice has to offer an interface with which the different tools can fetch values from the application. The interface should be identical for all microservices.

The deployment of microservices (section 11.4) has to be automated. Simple scripts, especially in conjunction with immutable server, special deployment tools, and package manager can be used for this purpose.

Microservices are small deployment units. They are safeguarded by stability and resilience against the failure of other microservices. Therefore, the risk associated with deployments is already reduced by the microservice-based architecture itself. Strategies like rollback, roll forward, continuous deployment, blue/green-deployment, or a blind moving along in production can further reduce the risk. Such strategies are easy to implement with microservices since the deployment units are small and the consumption of resources by microservices is low. Therefore, deployments are faster, and environments for blue/green-deployment or canary releasing are much easier to provide.

Control (section 11.6) comprises simple intervention options like starting, stopping, and restarting of microservices.

Virtualization or Cloud are good options for infrastructures for microservices (section 11.7). On each VM only a single microservice should run to achieve a better isolation, stability, and scaling. Especially interesting is Docker because the consumption of resources by a Docker container is much lower than that of a VM. This makes it possible to provide each microservice with its own Docker container even if the number of microservices is large. PaaS are likewise interesting. They enable a very simple automation. However, they also restrict the choice of technologies.

This section only focuses on the specifics of continuous delivery and operation in a microservices environment. Continuous delivery is one of the most important reasons for the introduction of microservices. At the same time operation poses the biggest challenges.

Essential Points

- Operation and continuous delivery are central challenges for microservices.

- The microservices should handle monitoring, logging, and deployment in a uniform manner. This is the only way to keep the effort reasonable.

- Virtualization, Cloud, PaaS, and Docker are interesting infrastructure alternatives for microservices.

Chapter 12

Organizational Effects
of a Microservices-Based
Architecture

It is an essential feature of the microservice-based approach that one team is responsible for each microservice. Therefore, when working with microservices, it is necessary to look not only at the architecture but also at the organization of teams and the responsibilities for the individual microservices. This chapter discusses the organizational effects of microservices.

In section 12.1 organizational advantages of microservices are described. Section 12.2 shows that collective code ownership presents an alternative to devising teams according to Conway's Law, which states that an organization can only generate architectures that mirror its communication structures. The independence of the teams is an important consequence of microservices. Section 12.3 defines micro and macro architecture and shows how these approaches offer a high degree of autonomy to the teams and let them make independent decisions. Closely connected is the question about the role of the technical leadership (section 12.4). DevOps is an organizational approach that combines development (Dev) and operations (Ops) (section 12.5). DevOps has synergies with microservices. Since microservices focus on independent development from a domain perspective, they also influence product owners and business stakeholders—for example, the departments of the business that uses the software. Section 12.7 discusses how these groups can handle microservices. Reusable code can only be achieved in microservice systems via organizational measures as illustrated in section 12.8. Finally, section 12.9 follows up on the question whether an introduction of microservices is possible without changing the organization.

12.1 Organizational Benefits of Microservices

Microservices are an approach for tackling large projects with small teams. As the teams are independent of each other, less coordination is necessary between them. In particular the communication overhead renders the work of large teams inefficient. Microservices are an approach on the architectural level for solving this problem. The architecture helps to reduce the need for communication and to let many small teams work in the project instead of one large one. Each domain-based team can have the ideal size: the Scrum guide[1] recommends three to nine members.

Besides, modern enterprises stress self-organization and teams that are themselves active directly at the market. Microservices support this approach because each service is in the responsibility of an individual team consistent with Conway's Law (Section 3.2). Therefore, microservices fit well to self-organization. Each team can implement new features independently of other teams and can evaluate the success on the market by themselves.

On the other hand, there is a conflict between independence and standardization: when the teams are supposed to work on their own, they have to be independent. Standardization restricts independence. This concerns, for instance, the decision about which technologies should be used. If the project is standardized in regard to a certain technology stack, the teams cannot decide independently anymore which technology they want to use. In addition, independence conflicts with the wish to avoid redundancy: if the system is supposed to be free of redundancy, there has to be coordination between the teams in order to identify the redundancies and to eliminate them. This, in turn, limits the independence of the teams.

Technical Independence

An important aspect is the technological decoupling. Microservices can use different technologies and can have entirely different structures internally. This means that developers have less need to coordinate. Only fundamental decisions have to be made together. All other technical decisions can be made by the teams.

Separate Deployment

Each microservice can be brought into production independently of the other microservices. There is also no need to coordinate release dates or test phases across

---

1. http://www.scrumguides.org/scrum-guide.html#team

teams. Each team can choose its own speed and its own dates. A delayed release date of one team does not influence the other teams.

Separate Requirement Streams

The teams should each implement independent stories and requirements. This enables each team to pursue its own business objectives.

Three Levels of Independence

Microservices enable independence on three levels:

- Decoupling via independent releases: each team takes care of one or multiple microservices. The team can bring them into production independently of the other teams and the other microservices.

- Technological decoupling: the technical decisions made by a certain team concern, first of all, their microservices and none of the other microservices.

- Domain-based decoupling: the distribution of the domain in separate components enables each team to implement their own requirements.

For deployment monoliths, in contrast, the technical coordination and deployment concerns the entire monolith (see Figure 12.1). This necessitates such a close coordination between the developers that in the end all developers working on the monolith have to act like one team.

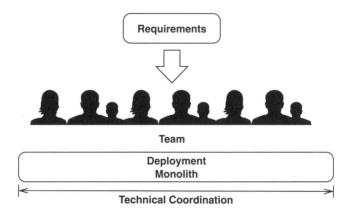

Figure 12.1 *Deployment Monolith*

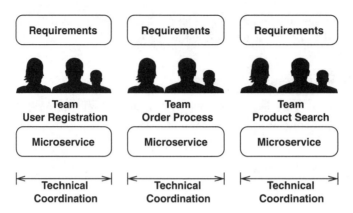

Figure 12.2 *Separation into Microservices*

A prerequisite for the independence of the microservice teams is that the architecture really offers the necessary independence of the microservices. This requires, first of all, good domain architecture. This architecture also enables independent requirement streams for each team.

There are the following teams in the example from Figure 12.2:

- The team "user registration" takes care of how users can register in the e-commerce shop. A possible business objective is to achieve a high number of registrations. New features aim at optimizing this number. The components of the team are the processes that are necessary for the registration and the UI elements. The team can change and optimize them at will.

- The team "order process" addresses how the shopping cart turns into an order. Here, a possible objective is that as many shopping carts as possible turn into orders. The entire process is implemented by this team.

- The team "product search" improves the search for products. The success of this team depends on how many search processes lead to items being put into a shopping cart.

Of course, there can be additional teams with other goals. Overall this approach distributes the task of developing an e-commerce shop onto multiple teams, which all have their own objectives. The teams can largely independently pursue their objectives because the architecture of the system is distributed into microservices that each team can develop independently—without much need for coordination.

In addition, small projects have many more advantages:

- Estimations are more accurate since estimates concerning smaller efforts are easier to make.
- Small projects are easier to plan.
- The risk decreases because of the more accurate estimates and because of the better forecast reliability.
- If there still is a problem, its effects are smaller because the project is smaller.

In addition, microservices offer much more flexibility. This makes decisions faster and easier because the risk is smaller, and changes can be implemented more rapidly. This ideally supports agile software development that relies on such flexibility.

12.2 An Alternative Approach to Conway's Law

Section 3.2 introduced Conway's Law. According to this law, an organization can only generate architectures that mirror its communication structures. In microservice-based architectures the teams are built according to the microservices. Each team develops one or multiple microservices. Thus each microservice is only developed by exactly one team. This ensures that the domain architecture is not only implemented by the distribution into microservices but also supported by the organizational distribution. This renders violations of the architecture practically impossible. Moreover, the teams can independently develop features when the features are limited to one microservice. For this to work the distribution of domains between the microservices has to be of very high quality.

The Challenges Associated with Conway's Law

However, this approach also has disadvantages:

- The teams have to remain stable in the long run. Especially when the microservices use different technologies, the ramp-up time for an individual microservice is very long. Developers cannot easily switch between teams. Especially in teams containing external consultants, long-term stability is often hard to ensure. Already the usual fluctuation of personnel can turn into a challenge when working with microservices. In the worst case, if there is nobody left to maintain a specific microservice, it is still possible to rewrite the respective microservice. Microservices are easy to replace due to their limited size. Of course, this still entails some expenditure.

- Only the team understands the component. When team members quit, knowledge about one or multiple microservices can get lost. In that case the microservice cannot be modified anymore. Such islands of knowledge need to be avoided. In such a case it will not be an option to replace the microservice since an exact knowledge of the domain is necessary for this.

- Changes are difficult whenever they require the coordinated work of multiple teams. When a team can implement all changes for a feature in its own microservices, architecture and scaling of development will work very well. However, when the feature concerns another microservice also and therefore another team, the other team needs to implement the changes to the respective microservice. This requires not only communication, but the necessary changes also have to be prioritized versus the other requirements of the team. If the teams work in sprints, a team can deliver the required changes without prematurely terminating the current sprint earliest in the following sprint—this causes a marked delay. In case of a sprint length of two weeks the delay can amount to two weeks—if the team prioritizes the change high enough so that it is taken care of in the next sprint. Otherwise the ensuing delay can be even longer.

Collective Code Ownership

When it is always only the responsible team that can introduce changes to a microservice, a number of challenges result as described. Therefore, it is worthwhile to consider alternatives. Agile processes have led to the concept of "collective code ownership." Here, each developer has not only the right, but even the duty to alter any code—for example when he/she considers the code quality as insufficient in a certain place. Therefore, all developers take care of code quality. Besides, technical decisions are better communicated because more developers understand them due to their reading and changing code. This leads to the critical questioning of decisions so that the overall quality of the system increases.

Collective code ownership can relate to a team and its microservices. Since the teams are relatively free in their organization, such an approach is possible without much coordination.

Advantages of Collective Code Ownership

However, in principle teams can also modify microservices that belong to other teams. This approach is used by some microservice projects to deal with the discussed challenges because it entails a number of advantages:

- Changes to a microservice of another team can be faster and more easily implemented. When a modification is necessary, the change does not to be introduced by another team. Instead the team requiring the change can implement it by itself. It is not necessary anymore to prioritize the change in regard to other changes to the component.

- Teams can be put together more flexibly. The developers are familiar with a larger part of the code—at least superficially due to changes that they have introduced in the code. This makes it easier to replace team members or even an entire team— or to enlarge a team. The developers do not have to ramp up from the very basics. A stable team is still the best option—however, often this cannot be achieved.

- The distribution in microservices is easy to change. Because of the broader knowledge of the developers it is easier to move responsibility for a microservice to a different team. This can be sensible when microservices have a lot of dependencies on each other but are in the responsibility of different teams that then have to closely and laboriously coordinate. If the responsibility for the microservices is changed so that the same team is responsible for both of the closely coupled microservices, coordination is easier than in the case where two teams were working on these microservices. Within one team the team members often sit in the same office. Therefore, they can easily and directly communicate with each other.

Disadvantages of Collective Code Ownership

However, there also disadvantages associated with this approach:

- Collective code ownerships are in contrast to technology freedom: when each team uses other technologies, it is difficult for developers outside of a team to change the respective microservices. They might not even know the technology used in the microservice.

- The teams can lose their focus. The developers acquire a larger overview of the full system. However, it might be better when the developers concentrate on their own microservices instead.

- The architecture is not as solid anymore. By knowing the code of other components developers can exploit the internals and, therefore, rapidly create dependencies that had not been intended in the architecture. Finally, the distribution of the teams according to Conway's Law is supposed to support the architecture by turning interfaces between domain components into interfaces between teams. However, the interfaces between the teams lose importance when everybody can change the code of every other team.

Pull Requests for Coordination

Communication between teams is still necessary; in the end, the team responsible for the respective microservice has the most knowledge about the microservice. So changes should be coordinated with the respective team. This can be safeguarded technically: the changes of the external teams can initially be introduced separately from other changes and subsequently be sent to the responsible team via a pull request. Pull requests bundle changes to the source code. In the open source community they are an especially popular approach to enable external contributions without giving up control of the project. The responsible team can accept the pull request or demand fixes. This means that there is a review for each change by the responsible team. This enables the responsible team to ensure that the architecture and design of the microservice remain sound.

Since there is still the need for communication between teams, Conway's Law is not violated by this approach. It is just a different way of playing the game. In case of a bad split among teams in a microservice-based architecture all options are associated with tremendous disadvantages. To correct the distribution is difficult as larger changes across microservices are laborious, as discussed in section 7.4. Due to the unsuitable distribution, the teams are forced to communicate a lot with each other. Therefore, productivity is lost. Also, there is no option to leave the distribution as it is. Collective code ownership can be used to limit the need for communication. The teams directly implement requirements in the code of other teams. This causes less need for communication and better productivity. To do so the technology freedom should be restricted. The changes to the microservices still have to be coordinated—at least reviews are definitely necessary. However, if the architecture had been set up appropriately from the start, this measure would not be necessary as a workaround at all.

Try and Experiment

- Did you already encounter collective code ownership? Which experiences did you have with it?

- Which restrictions are there in your current project when a developer wants to change some code that has been written by another developer in the same team or by a developer from another team? Are changes to the code of other teams not meant to occur? In that case, how is it still possible to implement the necessary changes? Which problems are associated with this course of action?

12.3 Micro and Macro Architecture

Microservices enable you to largely avoid overarching architecture decisions. Each team can choose the optimal type of architecture for its microservices.

The basis for this is the microservices architecture. It provides a large degree of technical freedom. While normally due to technical reasons, uniform technologies are mandatory, microservices do not have these restrictions. However, there can be other reasons for uniformity. The question is which decision is made by whom. There are two layers of decision making:

- Macro architecture comprises the decisions that concern the overall system. These are at least the decisions presented in Chapter 7, "Architecture of Microservice-Based Systems," regarding the domain architecture and basic technologies, which have to be used by all microservices, as well as communication protocols (Chapter 8, "Integration and Communication"). The properties and technologies of individual microservices can also be preset (Chapter 9, "Architecture of Individual Microservices"). However, this does not have to be the case. Decisions about the internals of the individual microservices do not have to be made in the macro architecture.

- The micro architecture deals with decisions each team can make by itself. These should address topics that concern only the microservices developed by the respective team. Among these topics can be all aspects presented in Chapter 9 as long as they have not already been defined as part of the macro architecture.

The macro architecture cannot be defined once and for all but has to undergo continuous development. New features can require a different domain architecture or new technologies. Optimizing the macro architecture is a permanent process.

Decision = Responsibility

The question is, who defines macro and micro architecture and takes care of their optimization? It is important to keep in mind that each decision is linked to responsibility. Whoever makes a decision is responsible for its consequences—good or bad. In turn the responsibility for a microservice entails the necessity to make the required decisions for its architecture. When the macro architecture defines a certain technology stack, the responsibility for this stack rests with the persons responsible for the macro architecture—not with the teams that use them in the microservices and might later have problems with this technology stack. Therefore, a strong restriction of the technology freedom of the individual microservices by the macro architecture is often not helpful. It only shifts decisions and responsibility to a level that does not have much to do with the individual microservices. This can lead to an ivory-tower architecture that is not based on the real requirements. In the best case it is ignored. In the worst case it causes serious problems in the application. Microservices enable you to largely do without macro architecture decisions in order to avoid such an ivory-tower architecture.

Who Creates the Macro Architecture?

For defining the macro architecture, decisions have to be made that affect all microservices. Such decisions cannot be made by a single team since the teams only carry responsibility for their respective microservices. Macro architecture decisions go beyond individual microservices.

The macro architecture can be defined by a team that is composed from members of each individual team. This approach seems to be obvious at first glance: It enables all teams to voice their perspectives. Nobody dictates certain approaches. The teams are not left out of the decision process. There are many microservice projects that very successfully employ this approach.

However, this approach has also disadvantages:

- For decisions at the macro architecture level, an overview of the overall system and an interest to develop the system in its entirety are necessary. Members of the individual teams often have a strong focus on their own microservices. That is, of course, very sensible since the development of these microservices is their primary task. However, this can make it hard for them to make overarching decisions since those require a different perspective.

- The group can be too large. Effective teams normally have five to ten members at maximum. If there are many teams and each is supposed to participate with at least one member, the macro architecture team will get too large and thus cannot work effectively anymore. Large teams are hardly able to define and maintain the macro architecture.

The alternative is to have a single architect or an architecture team that is exclusively responsible for shaping the macro architecture. For larger projects this task is so demanding that an entire architecture team certainly is needed to work on it. This architecture team takes the perspective of the overall project. However, there is a danger that the architecture team distances itself too much from the real work of the other teams and consequently makes ivory-tower decisions or solves problems the teams do not actually have. Therefore, the architecture team should mainly moderate the process of decision making and make sure that the viewpoints of the different teams are all considered. It should not set a certain direction all by itself. In the end the different microservices teams will have to live with the consequences of the architecture team's decisions.

Extent of the Macro Architecture

There is no one and only way to divide the architecture into micro and macro architecture. The company culture, the degree of self-organization, and other organizational criteria play a prominent role. A highly hierarchical organization will give the teams less freedom. When as many decisions as possible are made on the level of the micro architecture, the teams will gain more responsibility. This often has positive effects because the teams really feel responsible and will act accordingly.

The NUMMI car factory[2] in the United States, for instance, was a very unproductive factory that was known for drug abuse and sabotage. By the company focusing more on teamwork and trust, the same workers could be turned into a very productive workforce. When teams are able to make more decisions on their own and have more freedom of choice, the work climate as well as productivity will profoundly benefit.

Besides, by delegating decisions to teams, less time is spent on coordination so that the teams can work more productively. To avoid the need for communication by delegating more decisions to the teams and therefore to micro architecture is an essential point for architecture scaling.

However, when the teams are very restricted in their choices, one of the main advantages of microservices is not realized. Microservices increase the technical complexity of the system. This only makes sense if the advantages of microservices are really exploited. Consequently, when the decision for microservices has been made, there should also be a decision for having as much micro architecture and as little macro architecture as possible.

The decision for more or less macro architecture can be made for each area differently.

---

2. http://en.wikipedia.org/wiki/NUMMI#Background

Technology: Macro/Micro Architecture

For the technologies the following decisions can be made concerning macro versus micro architecture:

- Uniform security (section 7.14), service discovery (section 7.11), and communication protocols (Chapter 8) are necessary to enable microservices to communicate with each other. Therefore, decisions in these areas clearly belong to macro architecture. Among these are also the decisions for the use and details of downwards compatible interfaces that are required for the independent deployment of microservices.

- Configuration and coordination (Section 7.10) do not necessarily have to be determined globally for the complete project. When each microservice is operated by its respective team, the team can also handle the configuration and use its own tool of choice for it. However, a uniform tool for all microservices has clear advantages. Besides, there is hardly any sensible reason why each team should use a different mechanism.

- The use of resilience (section 9.5) or load balancing (section 7.12) can be defined in the macro architecture. The macro architecture can either define a certain standard technology or just enforce that these points have to be addressed during the implementation of the microservices. This can, for instance, be ensured by tests (section 10.8). The tests can check whether a microservice is still available after a dependent microservice failed. In addition, they can check whether the load is distributed to multiple microservices. The decision for the use of resilience or load balancing can theoretically be left to the teams. When they are responsible for the availability and the performance of their service, they have to have the freedom to use their choice of technologies for it. When their microservices are sufficiently available without resilience and load balancing, their strategy is acceptable. However, in the real world such scenarios are hard to imagine.

- In regard to platform and programming language the decision can be made at the level of macro or micro architecture. The decision might not only influence the teams but also operations, since operations needs to understand the technologies and to be able to deal with failures. It is not necessarily required to prescribe a programming language. Alternatively, the technology can be restricted, for example, to the JVM (Java Virtual Machine) that supports a number of programming languages. In regard to the platform a potential compromise is that a certain database is provided by operations, but the teams can also use and operate different ones. Whether the macro architecture defines platform and programming language depends also on whether developers need to be able to change between teams. A shared platform facilitates transferring the responsibility for a microservice from one team to another team.

Figure 12.3 shows which decisions are part of the macro architecture—they are on the right side. The micro architecture parts are on the left side. The areas in the middle can be either part of the macro or micro architecture. Each project can handle them differently.

Operations

In the area of operations (see Figure 12.4) there is control (section 11.6), monitoring (section 11.3), logging (section 11.2), and deployment (section 11.4). To reduce the complexity of the environment and to enable a uniform operations solution, these areas have to be defined by macro architecture. The same holds true for platform and programming language. However, standardizing is not obligatory; when the entire operations of the microservices rests with the teams, theoretically each team can use a different technology for each of the mentioned areas. But while this scenario does

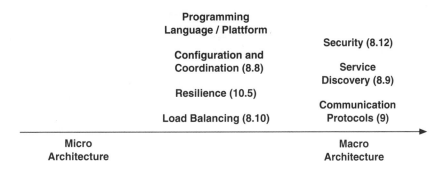

Figure 12.3 *Technology: Macro and Micro Architecture*

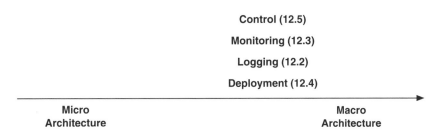

Figure 12.4 *Operations: Macro and Micro Architecture*

not generate many advantages, it creates a huge technological complexity. However, it is, for example, possible that the teams use their own special solution for certain tasks. When, for instance, the revenue is supposed to be transferred in a different way into the monitoring for the business stakeholders, this is certainly doable.

Domain Architecture

In the context of domain architecture (see Figure 12.5) the distribution of domains to teams is part of the macro architecture (section 7.1). It not only influences the architecture but also decides which teams are responsible for which domains. Therefore, this task cannot be moved into the micro architecture. However, the domain architecture of the individual microservices has to be left to the teams (sections 9.1–9.4). To dictate the domain architecture of the individual microservices to the teams would be equivalent to treating microservices at the organizational level like monoliths because the entire architecture is centrally coordinated. In that case one could as well develop a deployment monolith, which is technically easier. Such a decision would not make sense.

Tests

In the area of testing (see Figure 12.6) integration tests (section 10.4) belong to the macro architecture. In practice whether there should be an integration test for a

Figure 12.5 *Architecture: Macro and Micro Architecture*

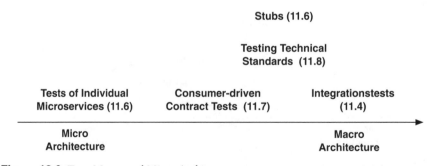

Figure 12.6 *Test: Macro and Micro Architecture*

certain domain and who should implement it has to be decided. Integration tests only make sense when they concern functionalities across teams. The respective teams can test all other functionalities on their own. Therefore, integration tests have to be globally coordinated across teams. Technical tests (section 10.8) can be dictated to the teams by the macro architecture. They are a good option to enforce and control global standards and technical areas of macro architecture. Consumer-driven contract tests (CDC) (section 10.7) and stubs (section 10.6) can be coordinated between the teams themselves. A shared technological foundation as part of macro architecture can profoundly facilitate development. Uniform technologies are especially sensible in this area since teams have to use the CDCs and stubs of other teams. When only one technology is used, work is markedly easier. However, it is not obligatory that technologies are rigidly prescribed by the macro architecture.

How to test the respective microservices should be up to the individual teams as they have the responsibility for the quality of the microservices.

In many areas decisions can be made either at the level of macro or at the level of micro architecture. It is a central objective of microservice-based architectures to give the individual teams as much independence as possible. Therefore, as many decisions as possible should be made on the level of micro architecture and therefore by the individual teams. However, in regard to operations the question arises whether the teams really profit from the freedom to use their own distinct tools. It seems more likely that the technology zoo just gets bigger without real advantages. In this area there is a connection to DevOps (section 12.5). Depending on the degree of cooperation between developers and operations there can be different degrees of freedom. In case of a clear division between development and operations, operations will define many standards in macro architecture. In the end operations will have to take care of the microservices in production. When all microservices employ a uniform technology, this task is easier.

When defining programming language and platform, one should likewise weigh the advantages of specialized technology stacks versus the disadvantages of having heterogeneous technologies in the overall system. Depending on the circumstances the decision to prescribe a technology stack might be as sensible as the decision to leave the technology choice to the individual teams. A uniform technology stack can facilitate operations and make it easier for developers to change between microservices and teams. Specialized technology stacks make it easier to handle special challenges and motivate employees who thus have the possibility to use cutting-edge technologies.

Whether a microservice really conforms to the macro architecture can be evaluated by a test (see section 10.8). This test can be an artifact that is likewise part of the macro architecture. The group responsible for the macro architecture can use this artifact to unambiguously define the macro architecture. This enables you to check whether all microservices are in line with macro architecture.

12.4 Technical Leadership

The division in micro and macro architecture completely changes the technical leadership teams and is an essential advantage of microservices. The macro architecture defines technical duties and freedom. The freedom of choice entails also the responsibility for the respective decisions.

For example, a database can be prescribed. In that case the team can delegate the responsibility for the database to the technical leadership team. If the database decision were part of the micro architecture, the database would be run by the team since it made the decision for the technology. No other team would need to deal with potential consequences of this decision (see section 7.9). Whoever makes the decision also has the responsibility. The technical leadership team certainly can make such decisions, but by doing so it takes away responsibility from the microservices teams and therefore independence.

A larger degree of freedom entails more responsibility. The teams have to be able to deal with this and also have to want this freedom. Unfortunately, this is not always the case. This can either argue for more macro architecture or for organizational improvements that in the end lead to more self-organization and thus less macro architecture. It is one of the objectives of the technical leadership team to enable less macro architecture and to lead the way to more self-organization.

Developer Anarchy

The approach Developer[3] Anarchy[4] is even more radical in regards to the freedom of the teams. It confers the entire responsibility to the developers. They cannot only freely choose technologies but even rewrite code if they deem it necessary. Besides, they communicate directly with the stakeholders. This approach is employed in very fast growing enterprises and works very well there. Behind this idea is Fred George, who has collected more than 40 years of experience while working in many different companies. In a model like this, macro architecture and deployment monoliths are abolished so that the developers can do what they think is best. This approach is very radical and shows how far the idea can be extended.

---

3. http://www.infoq.com/news/2012/02/programmer-anarchy
4. https://www.youtube.com/watch?v=uk-CF7klLdA

> **Try and Experiment**
>
> - In Figures 12.3–12.5 areas are marked that can belong to either micro or macro architecture. These are the elements that are depicted in the center of the respective figures. Look through these elements and decide whether you would place them in micro or macro architecture. Most important is your reasoning for the one or the other alternative. Take into consideration that making decisions at the level of the micro architecture rather than the level of the macro architecture corresponds to the microservice idea of independent teams.

12.5 DevOps

DevOps denotes the concept that development (Dev) and operations (Ops) merge into one team (DevOps). This is an organizational change: each team has developers and operations experts. They work together in order to develop and operate a microservice. This requires a different mindset, since operations-associated topics are often unfamiliar to developers while people working in operations often do not work in projects but usually run systems independently of projects. Ultimately, the technical skills become very similar: operations works more on automation and associated suitable tests—and this is, in the end, software development. At the same time monitoring, log analysis, or deployment also turn more and more into topics for developers.

DevOps and Microservices

DevOps and microservices ideally complement each other:

- The teams cannot only take care of the development but also of the operations of the microservices. This requires that the teams have knowledge in the areas of operations and development.

- Orienting the teams in line with features and microservices represents a sensible organizational alternative to the division into operations and development.

- Communication between operations and development gets easier when members of both areas work together in one team. Communication within a team is easier than between teams. This is in line with the aim of microservices to reduce the need for coordination and communication.

DevOps and microservices fit very well together. In fact, the aim that teams deploy microservices up to production and keep taking care of them in production can only be achieved with DevOps teams. This is the only way to ensure that teams have the necessary knowledge about both areas.

Do Microservices Necessitate DevOps?

DevOps is such a profound change in organization that many enterprises are still reluctant to take this step. Therefore the question arises whether microservices can also be implemented without introducing DevOps. In fact, this is possible:

- Via the macro versus micro architecture division, operations can define standards. Then technical elements like logging, monitoring, or deployment belong to the macro architecture. When these standards are conformed to, operations can take over the software and make it part of the standard operations processes.

- In addition, platform and programming language can be defined as much as needed for operations. When staff from operations only feels comfortable running Java applications on a Tomcat, this can be prescribed as the platform in the macro architecture. The same holds true for infrastructure elements like databases or messaging systems.

- Moreover, there can be organizational requirements. For example, operations can ask that members of the microservices teams are available at certain times so that problems arising in production can be referred to the teams. To put it concretely, whoever wants to deploy on his/her own has to provide a phone number and will be called at night in case of problems. If the call is not answered, the manager for that developer can be called next. This increases the likelihood that developers actually answer such calls.

In such a context the teams cannot be responsible anymore for bringing all microservices up to production. Access and responsibility rest with operations. There has to be a point in the continuous delivery pipeline where the microservices are passed on to operations and then are rolled out in production. At this point the microservice passes into the responsibility of operations that has to coordinate with the respective team about their microservices. A typical point for the transfer to operations is immediately after the test phases, prior to possible explorative tests. Operations is at least responsible for the last phase, that is, the rollout in production. Operations can turn into a bottleneck if a high number of modified microservices have to be brought into production.

Overall, DevOps and microservices have synergies; however, it is not necessarily required to also introduce DevOps when deciding for microservices.

12.6 When Microservices Meet Classical IT Organizations (Alexander Heusingfeld)

by Alexander Heusingfeld, innoQ

The "microservices" topic has meanwhile reached numerous IT departments and is discussed there. Interestingly, initiatives for introducing microservices are often started by middle management. However, frequently too little thought is spent on the effect a microservice architecture has on the (IT) organization of enterprises. Because of this I would like to tell of a number of "surprises" that I experienced during the introduction of such an architecture approach.

Pets versus Cattle

"Pets vs. cattle"[5] is a slogan that reached a certain fame at the outset of the DevOps movement. Its basic message is that in times of Cloud and virtualization, servers should not be treated like pets but rather like a herd of cattle. If a pet gets sick, the owner will likely nurse it back to health. Sick cattle, on the other hand, are killed immediately in order not to endanger the health of the entire herd.

Thus the point is to avoid the personification of servers—for example, by giving them names (like Leviathan, Pollux, Berlin, or Lorsch). If you assign such "pet" names to servers, there will be a tendency to care for them like pets and thus provide individual updates, scripts, adjustments, or other specific modifications. However, it is well known that this has negative consequences for the reproducibility of installations and server state. Especially considering auto-scaling and failover features as they are required for microservice-based architectures, this is a deal breaker.

One of my projects addressed this problem in a very interesting manner. The server and virtual machines still had names. However, the administration of these systems was completely automated via Puppet. Puppet downloaded the respective scripts from an SVN repository. In this repository individual scripts for each server were stored. This scenario could be called "Puppets for automated pet care." The advantage is that crashed servers can quickly be replaced by exact copies.

However, requirements for scalability are not taken into consideration at all, since there can always only be one instance of a "pet server" named Leviathan.

---

5. http://www.slideshare.net/randybias/architectures-for-open-and-scalable-clouds

An alternative is to switch to parameterized scripts and to use templates like "production VM for app XYZ." At the same time this also enables more flexible deployment scenarios like Blue/Deployments. In that case it is not relevant anymore whether the VM app-xyz-prod08.zone1.company.com or app-xyz-prod045.zone1.company.com gets the job done. The only relevant point is that eight instances of this service are constantly available, and at times of high load additional instances can be started. How these instances are named does not matter.

Us versus Them

"Monitoring is our concern!"

"You shouldn't care about that!"

"That is none of your business; it's our area!"

Unfortunately, I frequently hear sentences like these in so-called cross-functional teams. These are teams composed of architects, developers, testers, and administrators. Especially if the members previously worked in other, purely functional teams within the same company, old trench wars and prejudices are carried along into the new team—often subconsciously. Therefore, it is important to be aware of the social aspects right from the start and to counter these proactively. For example, in my experience letting newly set-up teams work in the same office for the first two to four weeks has very positive effects. This enables the new teammates to get to know each other's human side and to directly experience the colleague's body language, character, and humor. This will markedly facilitate communication during the later course of the project, and misunderstandings can be avoided.

In addition, team-building measures during the first weeks that require that the team members rely on each other can help to break the ice, to get an idea of the strengths and weaknesses of the individual members, and to build up and strengthen trust within the team. If these points are neglected, there will be noticeable adverse consequences throughout the run time of the project. People who do not like each other or do not trust each other will not rely on each other, even if only subconsciously. And this means that they will not be able to work 100 percent as a team.

Development versus Test versus Operations: Change of Perspective

In many companies there are initiatives for a change of perspective. For example, employees from sales may work in the purchasing department for a day to get to know the people and the processes there. The expectation is that the employees will develop a better understanding for their colleagues and to let that become part of their daily work so that cross-department processes harmonize better. The motto is: "On 'the other side' you get to know a new perspective!"

Such a change of perspective can also be advantageous in IT. A developer could, for instance, get a new perspective with regard to the use cases or test cases. This might motivate them to enforce a modularization in the development, which is easier to test. Or they might consider early in development which criteria will be needed later on to better monitor the software in production or to more easily find errors. A deeper insight into the internal processes of the application can help an administrator to develop a better understanding for implementing a more specific and more efficient monitoring. Each perspective that deviates from one's own perspective can raise questions that previously were not considered in this section of the application life cycle. These questions will help the team to evolve as a whole and deliver better software.

For Operations There Is Never an "Entirely Green Field"

Certainly, microservices are a topical subject and bring along new technologies, concepts, and organizational changes. However, one should always consider that enterprises introducing microservices hardly ever start from scratch! There are always some kinds of legacy systems or entire IT environments that already exist and might better not be replaced in a Big Bang approach. Usually these legacy systems have to be integrated into the brave new world of microservices; at least they will have to coexist.

For this reason, it is important to take these systems into consideration when planning a microservices-based architecture, especially in regards to IT costs. Can the existing hardware infrastructure really be restructured for the microservices or is there a legacy system that relies exactly on this infrastructure? These are often questions that get caught on the infrastructure or operations team—if there is such an organizational unit in the company. Otherwise it might happen that these questions first arise when a deployment to the system test or production environment is supposed to be done. To recognize these questions early on, I recommend dealing with the deployment pipeline as early as possible in the reorganization project. The deployment pipeline should already be in place before the first business functionality is implemented by the teams. A simple "Hello World" program will often be sufficient, which then is brought towards production by the combined forces of the entire team. While doing so, the team will almost always encounter open questions, which in the worst case will have effects on the design of the systems. However, as not much is implemented at this stage early on during the project, such changes are still comparably cost-efficient to implement.

Conclusion

Up to now the organizational changes with regard to Conway's Law that accompany the introduction of microservices are often underestimated. Old habits, prejudices, and maybe even trench wars are often deep-rooted, especially if the new teammates were previously assigned to different departments. However, "one team" has to be more than just a buzzword. If the team manages to bury their prejudices and put their different experiences to good use, it can advance together. Everyone has to understand that all of them now share the task and responsibility to bring a stable software into production for the customer. Everybody can profit from the experiences of the others when everybody acts on the premise: "Everybody voices their concerns, and we will solve it jointly."

12.7 Interface to the Customer

To ensure that the development can really be scaled to multiple teams and microservices, each team needs to have its own product owner. In line with Scrum approaches, he/she is responsible for the further development of the microservice. For this purpose, he/she defines stories that are implemented in the microservice. The product owner is the source of all requirements and prioritizes them. This is especially easy when a microservice only comprises features that are within the responsibility of a single department at the business level (see Figure 12.7). Usually this objective is achieved by adjusting microservices and teams to the organization of departments. Each department gets its product owner and therefore its team and its microservices.

When the microservices have a good domain architecture, they can be independently developed. Ultimately, each domain should be implemented in one or many microservices, and the domain should only be of interest to one department. The architecture has to take the organization of the departments into consideration when distributing the domains into microservices. This ensures that each department has its own microservices that are not shared with other domains or departments.

Unfortunately, the architecture often is not perfect. Besides, microservices have interfaces—an indication that functionalities might span multiple microservices. When multiple functionalities concern one microservice and therefore multiple departments want to influence the development of a microservice, the product owner has to ensure a prioritization that is coordinated with the different departments. This can be a challenge because departments can have different priorities. In that case the product owner has to coordinate between the concerned departments.

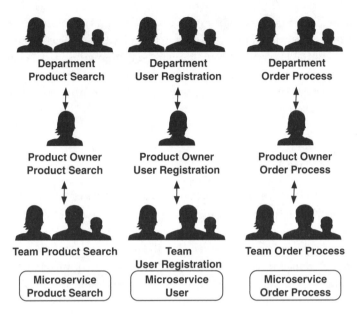

Figure 12.7 *Department, Product Owner, and Microservices*

Let us assume that there is a department that takes care of sales campaigns in an e-commerce shop. It starts a campaign where orders containing a certain item get a rebate on the delivery cost. The required modification concerns the order team: tt has to find out whether an order contains such an item. This information has to be transmitted to the delivery microservice, which has to calculate the costs for the delivery. Accordingly, the product owners of these two teams have to prioritize these changes in regards to the changes desired by the departments in charge of delivery and orders. Unfortunately, many of these sales campaigns combine different functionalities so that such a prioritization is often required. The departments for orders and deliveries have their own microservices, while the department in charge of sales campaigns does not have its own microservices. Instead it has to introduce its features into the other microservices.

Architecture Leads to Departments

The microservice architecture can thus be a direct result of the departmental organization of the company. However, there are also cases where a new department is created around an IT system, which then takes care of this system from the business side. In such a case one can argue that the microservices architecture directly influences the organization. For instance, there might be a new Internet market place that is implemented by an IT system. If it is successful, a department can be created that takes over the further development of this marketplace. This department will continue to develop the IT system from a domain and from a business perspective. In this case the marketplace was developed first, and subsequently the department has been created. Therefore, the system architecture has defined the departmental structure of the organization.

12.8 Reusable Code

At first sight the reuse of code is a technical problem. Section 7.3 already described the challenges that arise when two microservices use the same library. When the microservices use the library in such a way that a new release of the library necessitates a new deployment of the microservices, the result is a deployment dependency. This has to be avoided to enable an independent deployment of the microservices. There is additional expenditure because the teams responsible for the microservices have to coordinate their changes to the library. New features for the different microservices have to be prioritized and developed. These also represent dependencies between the teams, which should be avoided.

Client Libraries

Client libraries that encapsulate calls from a microservice can be acceptable. When the interfaces of the microservices are downwards compatible, the client library does not have to be replaced in case of a new version of the microservice. In such a scenario client libraries do not cause problems because a new deployment of the called microservices does not lead to an update of the client library or a new deployment of the calling microservice.

However, when the client library also contains domain objects, problems can occur. When a microservice wants to change the domain model, the team has to coordinate this change with the other users of the client library and therefore cannot develop independently anymore. The boundaries between a simplified use of the interface, which can be sensible, and a shared implementation of logic or other deployment dependencies, which can be problematic, is not clear cut. One option is to entirely forbid shared code.

Reuse Anyhow?

However, obviously, projects can reuse code. Hardly any project nowadays manages without some open source library. Using this code is obviously easy and thus facilitates work. Problems like the ones arising upon reusing code between microservices are unlikely for a number of reasons:

- Open source projects in general are of high quality. Developers working in different companies use the code and therefore spot errors. Often they even remove the errors so that the quality permanently increases. To publish source code and therefore provide insight into internals is often already motivation enough to increase the quality.

- The documentation enables you to immediately start to use the code without a need to directly communicate with the developers. Without good documentation open source projects hardly find enough users or additional developers since getting started would be too hard.

- There is a coordinated development with a bug tracker and a process for accepting code changes introduced by external developers. Therefore, errors and their fixes can be tracked. In addition, it is clear how changes from the outside can be incorporated into the code basis.

- Moreover, in case of a new version of the open source library it is not necessary for all users to use the new version. The dependencies in regard to the library are not so pronounced that a deployment dependency ensues.

- Finally, there are clear rules how one's own supplements can be incorporated into the open source library.

In the end the difference between a shared library and an open source project is mainly a higher quality in regard to different aspects. Besides, there is also an organizational aspect: there is a team that takes care of the open source project. It directs the project and keeps developing it. This team does not necessarily make all changes, but it coordinates them. Ideally, the team has members from different organizations and projects so that the open source project is developed under different viewpoints and in the context of different use cases.

Reuse as Open Source

With open source projects as role models in mind there are different options for reusable code in a microservices project:

- The organization around reusable libraries is structured like in an open source project. There are employees responsible for the continued code development, the consolidation of requirements and for incorporating the changes of other employees. The team members ideally come from different microservice teams.

- The reusable code turns into a real open source project. Developers outside of the organization can use and extend the project.

Both decisions can result into a significant investment since markedly more effort has to go into quality and documentation, etc. Besides, the employees working on the project have to get enough freedom to do so in their teams. The teams can control the prioritization in the open source project by only making their members available for certain tasks. Due to the large investment and potential problems with prioritization the decision to establish an open source project should be well considered. The idea itself is not new—experiences[6] in this area have already been collected for quite some time.

If the investment is very high, it means that the code is hardly reusable for the moment, and using the code in its current state causes quite some effort. Probably the code is not only hard to reuse, but hard to use at all. The question is why team members would accept such a bad code quality. Investing into code quality in order to make the code reusable can pay off already by reusing it just once.

At first glance it does not appear very sensible to make code available to external developers. This requires that code quality and documentation are of high enough quality for external developers to be able to use the code without direct contact to the developers of the open source project. Only the external developers seem to profit from this approach as they get good code for free.

However, a real open source project has a number of advantages:

- External developers find weak spots by using the code. Besides, they will use the code in different projects so that it gets more generalized. This will improve quality as well as documentation.

- Maybe external developers contribute to the further development of the code. However, this is the exception rather than the norm. But having external feedback via bug reports and requests for new features can already represent a significant advantage.

- Running open source projects is great marketing for technical competence. This can be useful for attracting employees as well as customers. Important is the extent of the project. If it is only a simple supplement of an existing open source project, the investment can be manageable. An entirely new open source framework is a very different topic.

---

6. http://dirkriehle.com/2015/05/20/inner-source-in-platform-based-product-engineering/

Blueprints such as documentation for certain approaches, represent elements that are fairly easy to reuse. This can be elements of macro architecture, like a document detailing the correct approach for logging. Likewise, there can be templates that contain all necessary components of a microservice including a code skeleton, a build script and a continuous delivery pipeline. Such artifacts can rapidly be written and are immediately useful.

Try and Experiment

- Maybe you have already previously used your own technical libraries in projects or even developed some yourself. Try to estimate how large the expenditure would be to turn these libraries into real open source libraries. Apart from a good code quality this also necessitates documentation about the use and the extension of the code. Besides, there has to be a bug tracker and forums. How easy would it be to reuse it in the project itself? How high would be the quality of the library?

12.9 Microservices without Changing the Organization?

Microservices are more than just an approach for software architecture. They have pronounced effects on organization. Changes to the organization are often very difficult. Therefore, the question arises whether microservices can be implemented without changing the organization.

Microservices without Changing the Organization

Microservices make independent teams possible. The domain-focused teams are responsible for one or multiple microservices—this ideally includes their development as well as operations. Theoretically it is possible to implement microservices without dividing developers into domain-focused teams. In that case the developers could modify each microservice—an extension of the ideas presented in section 12.2. It would even be possible that technically focused teams work on microservices that are split according to domain-based criteria. In this scenario there would be a UI, a middle tier, and a database team that work on domain microservices such as order process or registration. However, a number of advantages usually associated with microservices cannot be exploited anymore in that case. First, it is not possible anymore to scale the agile processes via microservices. Second, it will be necessary to restrict the technology freedom since the teams will not be able to handle the different microservices if they all employ different technologies. Besides, each team can modify each microservice. This entails the danger that though a distributed system is created, there are dependencies that prevent the independent development of individual microservices. The necessity for independent microservices is obliterated because a team can change multiple microservices together and therefore also can handle microservices having numerous dependencies. However, even under these conditions sustainable development, an easier start with continuous delivery, independent scaling of individual microservices, or a simple handling of legacy systems can still be implemented because the deployment units are smaller.

Evaluation

To put it clearly, introducing microservices without creating domain-focused teams does not lead to the main benefits meant to be derived from microservices. It is always problematic to implement only some parts of a certain approach as only the synergies between the different parts will generate the overall value. Although implementing microservices without domain-focused teams is a possible option—it is certainly not recommended.

Departments

As already discussed in section 12.7, the microservice structure should ideally extend to the departments. However, in reality this is sometimes hard to achieve since the microservice architecture often deviates too much from the organizational structure of the departments. It is unlikely that the organization of the departments will adapt to the distribution into microservices. When the distribution of the microservice cannot be adjusted, the respective product owners have to take care of prioritization and coordinate the wishes of the departments that concern multiple microservices in such a way that all requirements are unambiguously prioritized for the teams. If this is not possible, a collective code ownership approach (section 12.2) can limit the problem. In this case the product owner and his/her team can also modify microservices that do not really belong to their sphere of influence. This can be the better alternative in contrast to a coordination across teams—however, both solutions are not optimal.

Operations

In many organizations there is a separate team for operations. The teams responsible for the microservices should also take care of the operations of their microservices following the principle of DevOps. However, as discussed in section 12.5, it is not a strict requirement for microservices to introduce DevOps. If the separation between operations and development is supposed to be maintained, operations has to define the necessary standards for the microservices in the macro architecture to ensure a smooth operations of the system.

Architecture

Often architecture and development are likewise kept separated. In a microservices environment there is the area of macro architecture where architects make global decisions for all teams. Alternatively, the architects can be distributed to the different teams and work together with the teams. In addition, they can found an overarching committee that defines topics for macro architecture. In that case it has to be ensured that the architects really have time for this task and are not completely busy with work in their team.

Try and Experiment

- What does the organization of a project you know look like?

  - Is there a special organizational unit that takes care of architecture? How would they fit into a microservices-based architecture?

  - How is operations organized? How can the organization of operations best support microservices?

  - How well does the domain-based division fit to the departments? How could it be optimized?

  - Can a product owner with fitting task area be assigned to each team?

12.10 Conclusion

Microservices enable the independence of teams in regard to technical decisions and deployments (section 12.1). This enables the teams to independently implement requirements. In the end this makes it possible for numerous small teams to work together on a large project. This reduces the communication overhead between the teams. Since the teams can deploy independently, the overall risk of the project is reduced.

Ideally the teams should be put together in a way that enables them to work separately on different domain aspects. If this is not possible or requires too much coordination between the teams, collective code ownership can be an alternative (section 12.2). In that case each developer can change all of the code. Still, one team has the responsibility for each microservice. Changes to this microservice have to be coordinated with the responsible team.

Section 12.3 described that microservices have a macro architecture that comprises decisions that concern all microservices. In addition, there is the micro architecture, which can be different for each microservice. In the areas of technology, operations, domain architecture, and testing there are decisions that can either be attributed to micro or macro architecture. Each project has the choice to delegate them to teams (micro architecture) or to centrally define them (macro architecture). Delegating into teams is in line with the objective to achieve a large degree of independence and is therefore often the better option. A separate architecture team can define the macro architecture; alternatively, the responsible team is assembled from members of the different microservice teams.

Responsibility for the macro architecture is closely linked to a concept for technical leadership (section 12.4). Less macro architecture means more responsibility for the microservice teams and less responsibility for the central architecture team.

Though microservices profit from merging operations and development to DevOps (section 12.5), it is not strictly required to introduce DevOps to do microservices. If DevOps is not possible or desired, operations can define guidelines in the context of macro architecture to unify certain aspects in order to ensure a smooth operation of the microservice-based system.

Microservices should always implement their own separate requirements. Therefore, it is best when each microservice can be assigned to a certain department on the business side (section 12.7). If this is not possible, the product owners have to coordinate the requirements coming from different departments in such a way that each microservice has clearly prioritized requirements. When collective code ownership is used, a product owner and his/her team can also change microservices of other teams, which can limit the communication overhead. Instead of coordinating priorities, a team will introduce the changes that are necessary for a new feature by itself—even if they concern different microservices. The team responsible for the modified microservice can review the introduced changes and adjust them if necessary.

Code can be reused in a microservices project if the code is treated like an open source project (section 12.8). An internal project can be handled like an internal open source project—or can in fact be turned into a public open source project. The effort for a real open source project is high, which has to be considered. Therefore, it can be more efficient not to reuse code. Besides, the developers of the open source project have to prioritize domain requirements versus changes to the open source project, which can be a difficult decision at times.

Section 12.9 discussed that an introduction of microservices without changes to the organizational structure at the development level does not work in real life. When there are no domain-focused teams that can develop certain domain aspects independently of other teams, it is practically impossible to develop multiple features in parallel and thus to bring more features to the market within the same time. However, this is just what microservices were meant to achieve. Sustainable development, an easy introduction of continuous delivery, independent scaling of individual microservices, or a simple handling of legacy systems are still possible. Operations and an architecture team can define the macro architecture so that changes to the organizational structure in this area are not strictly required. Ideally, the requirements of the departments are always reflected by one microservice. If that is not possible, the product owners have to coordinate and prioritize the required changes.

Essential Points

- Microservices have significant effects on the organization. Independent small teams that work together on a large project are an important advantage of microservices.

- Viewing the organization as part of the architecture is an essential innovation of microservices.

- A combination of DevOps and microservices is advantageous but not obligatory.

PART IV

Technologies

Part IV moves away from the theoretical to show the technologies involved in actual implementations of microservices.

Chapter 13, "Example of a Microservices-Based Architecture," contains a complete example of a microservices architecture based on Java, Spring, Spring Boot, Spring Cloud, the Netflix stack, and Docker. The example is a good starting point for your own implementation or experiments. Many of the technological challenges discussed in Part III are solved in this part with the aid of concrete technologies—for instance, build, deployment, service discovery, communication, load balancing, and tests.

Even smaller than microservices are the nanoservices discussed in **Chapter 14, "Technologies for Nanoservices."** They require special technologies and a number of compromises. The chapter introduces technologies that can implement very small services—Amazon Lambda for JavaScript, Python and Java; OSGi for Java; Java EE; and Vert.x on the JVM (Java Virtual Machine) with support for languages like Java, Scala, Clojure, Groovy, Ceylon, JavaScript, Ruby, and Python. The programming language Erlang can also be used for very small services, and it is able to integrate with other systems. Seneca is a specialized JavaScript framework for the implementation of nanoservices.

At the close of the book **Chapter 15, "Getting Started with Microservices,"** concludes by reiterating the benefits of using microservices and discusses how you might go about starting to use them.

Chapter 13

Example of a Microservices-Based Architecture

This chapter provides an example of an implementation of a microservices-based architecture. It aims at demonstrating concrete technologies in order to lay the foundation for experiments. The example application has a very simple domain architecture containing a few compromises. Section 13.1 deals with this topic in detail.

For a real system with a comparable low complexity as in the presented example application, an approach without microservices would be better suited. However, the low complexity makes the example application easy to understand and simple to extend. Some aspects of a microservice environment, such as security, documentation, monitoring, or logging are not illustrated in the example application—but these aspects can be relatively easily addressed with some experiments.

Section 13.2 explains the technology stack of the example application. The build tools are described in section 13.3. Section 13.4 deals with Docker as a technology for the deployment. Docker needs to run in a Linux environment. Section 13.5 describes Vagrant as a tool for generating such environments. Section 13.6 introduces Docker Machine as alternative tool for the generation of a Docker environment, which can be combined with Docker Compose for the coordination of several Docker containers (section 13.7). The implementation of Service Discovery is discussed in section 13.8. The communication between the microservices and the user interface is the main topic of section 13.9. Thanks to resilience other microservices are not affected if a single microservice fails. In the example application resilience is implemented with Hystrix (section 13.10). Load Balancing (section 13.11), which can distribute the load onto several instances of a microservice, is closely related to that. Possibilities for the integration of non-Java-technologies are detailed in section 13.12, and testing is discussed in section 13.13.

The code of the example application can be found at https://github.com/ewolff/microservice. It is Apache-licensed, and can, accordingly, be used and extended freely for any purpose.

13.1 Domain Architecture

The example application has a simple web interface, with which users can submit orders. There are three microservices (see Figure 13.1):

- **"Catalog"** keeps track of products. Items can be added or deleted.
- **"Customer"** performs the same task in regards to customers: It can register new customers or delete existing ones.
- **"Order"** can not only show orders but also create new orders.

For the orders the microservice "Order" needs access to the two other microservices, "Customer" and "Catalog." The communication is achieved via REST. However, this interface is only meant for the internal communication between the microservices. The user can interact with all three microservices via the HTML-/HTTP-interface.

Separate Data Storages

The data storages of the three microservices are completely separate. Only the respective microservice knows the information about the business objects. The microservice "Order" saves only the primary keys of the items and customers, which are necessary for the access via the REST interface. A real system should use

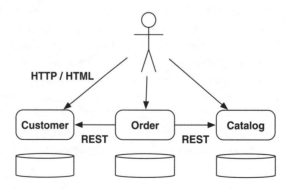

Figure 13.1 *Architecture of the Example Application*

artificial keys as the internal primary keys so that they do not become visible to the outside. These are internal details of the data storage that should be hidden. To expose the primary keys, the class `SpringRestDataConfig` within the microservices configures Spring Data REST accordingly.

Lots of Communication

Whenever an order needs to be shown, the microservice "Customer is called for the customer data and the microservice "Catalog" for each line of the order in order to determine the price of the item. This can have a negative influence on the response times of the application as the display of the order cannot take place before all requests have been answered by the other microservices. As the requests to the other services take place synchronously and sequentially, latencies will add up. This problem can be solved by using asynchronous parallel requests.

In addition, a lot of computing power is needed to marshal the data for sending and receiving. This is acceptable in case of such a small example application. When such an application is supposed to run in production, alternatives have to be considered.

This problem can, for instance, be solved by caching. This is relatively easy as customer data will not change frequently. Items can change more often—still, not so fast that caching would pose a problem. Only the amount of data can interfere with this approach. The use of microservices has the advantage that such a cache can be implemented relatively simply at the interface of the microservices, or even at the level of HTTP, if this protocol is used. An HTTP cache, like the one used for websites, can be added to REST services in a transparent manner and without much programming effort.

Bounded Context

Caching will solve the problem of too long response times technically. However, very long response times can also be a sign of a fundamental problem. Section 3.3 argued that a microservice should contain a *Bounded Context*. A specific domain model is only valid in a *Bounded Context*. The modularization into microservices in this example contradicts this idea: The domain model is used to modularize the system into the microservices "Order" for orders, "Catalog" for items, and "Customer" for customers. In principle the data of these entities should be modularized in different *Bounded Context*s.

The described modularization implements, in spite of low domain complexity, a system consisting of three microservices. In this manner the example application is easy to understand while still having several microservices and demonstrating the communication between microservices. In a real system the microservice "Order" can also handle information about the items that is relevant for the order process such as the price. If necessary, the service can replicate the data from another microservice into its own database in order to access it efficiently. This is an alternative to the aforementioned caching. There are different possibilities how the domain models can be modularized into the different *Bounded Context*s "Order," "Customer," and "Catalog."

This design can cause errors: when an order has been put into the system and the price of the item is changed afterwards, the price of the order changes as well, which should not happen. In case the item is deleted, there is even an error when displaying the order. In principle the information concerning the item and the customer should become part of the order. In that case the historical data of the orders including customer and item data would be transferred into the service "Order."

Don't Modularize Microservices by Data!

It is important to understand the problem inherent in architecting a microservices system by domain model. Often the task of a global architecture is misunderstood: The team designs a domain model, which comprises, for instance, objects such as customers, orders, and items. Based on this model microservices are defined. That is how the modularization into microservices could have come about in the example application, resulting in a huge amount of communication. A modularization based on processes such as ordering, customer registration, and product search might be more advantageous. Each process could be a *Bounded Context* that has its own domain model for the most important domain objects. For product search the categories of items might be the most relevant, while for the ordering process, data like weight and size might matter more.

The modularization by data can also be advantageous in a real system. When the microservice "Order" gets too big in combination with the handling of customer and product data, it is sensible to modularize data handling. In addition, the data can be used by other microservices. When devising the architecture for a system, there is rarely a single right way of doing things. The best approach depends on the system and the properties the system should have.

13.2 Basic Technologies

Microservices in the example application are implemented with Java. Basic functionalities for the example application are provided by the Spring Framework.[1] This

---

1. http://projects.spring.io/spring-framework/

framework offers not only dependency injection, but also a web framework, which enables the implementation of REST-based services.

HSQL Database

The database HSQLDB handles and stores data. It is an in-memory database, which is written in Java. The database stores the data only in RAM so that all data is lost upon restarting the application. In line with this, this database is not really suited for production use, even if it can write data to a hard disk. On the other hand, it is not necessary to install an additional database server, which keeps the example application easy. The database runs in the respective Java application.

Spring Data REST

The microservices use Spring Data REST[2] in order to provide the domain objects with little effort via REST and to write them into the database. Handing objects out directly means that the internal data representation leaks into the interface between the services. Changing the data structures is very difficult as the clients need to be adjusted as well. However, Spring Data REST can hide certain data elements and can be configured flexibly so that the tight coupling between the internal model and the interface can be decoupled if necessary.

Spring Boot

Spring Boot[3] facilitates Spring further. Spring Boot makes the generation of a Spring system very easy: with Spring Boot starters predefined packages are available that contain everything that is necessary for a certain type of application. Spring Boot can generate WAR files, which can be installed on a Java application or web server. In addition, it is possible to run the application without an application or web server. The result of the build is a JAR file in that case, which can be run with a Java Runtime Environment (JRE). The JAR file contains everything for running the application and also the necessary code to deal with HTTP requests. This approach is by far less demanding and simpler than the use of an application server (https://jaxenter.com/java-application-servers-dead-112186.html).

A simple example for a Spring Boot application is shown in Listing 13.1. The main program `main` hands control over to Spring Boot. The class is passed in as a parameter so that the application can be called. The annotation `@SpringBootApplication`

---

2. http://projects.spring.io/spring-data-rest/
3. http://projects.spring.io/spring-boot/

makes sure that Spring Boot generates a suitable environment. For example, a web server is started, and an environment for a Spring web application is generated as the application is a web application. Because of @RestController the Spring Framework instantiates the class and calls methods for the processing of REST requests. @RequestMapping shows which method is supposed to handle which request. Upon request of the URL "/" the method hello() is called, which returns as result the sign chain "hello" in the HTTP body. In an @RequestMapping annotation, URL templates such as "/customer/{id}" can be used. Then a URL like "/customer/42" can be cut into separate parts and the 42 bound to a parameter annotated with @PathVariable. As dependency the application uses only spring-boot-starter-web pulling all necessary libraries for the application along—for instance the web server, the Spring Framework, and additional dependent classes. Section 13.3 will discuss this topic in more detail.

Listing 13.1 *A simple Spring Boot REST Service*

```
@RestController
@SpringBootApplication
public class ControllerAndMain {

 @RequestMapping("/")
 public String hello() {
  return "hello";
 }

 public static void main(String[] args) {
  SpringApplication.run(ControllerAndMain.class, args);
 }

}
```

Spring Cloud

Finally, the example application uses Spring Cloud[4] to gain easy access to the Netflix Stack. Figure 13.2 shows an overview.

Spring Cloud offers via the Spring Cloud Connectors access to the PaaS (platform as a service) Heroku and Cloud Foundry. Spring Cloud for Amazon Web Services offers an interface for services from the Amazon Cloud. This part of Spring Cloud is responsible for the name of the project but is not helpful for the implementation of microservices.

---

4. http://projects.spring.io/spring-cloud/

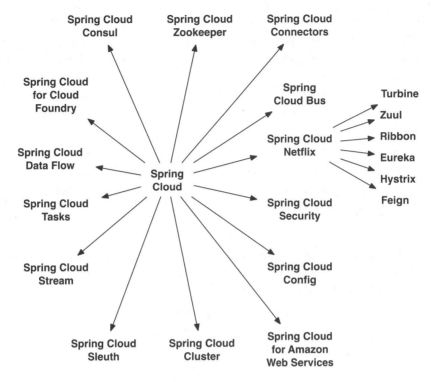

Figure 13.2 *Overview of Spring Cloud*

However, the other sub-projects of Spring Cloud provide a very good basis for the implementation of microservices:

- **Spring Cloud Security** supports the implementation of security mechanisms as typically required for microservices, among those single sign on into a microservices environment. That way a user can use each of the microservices without having to log in anew every time. In addition, the user token is transferred automatically for all calls to other REST services to ensure that those calls can also work with the correct user rights.

- **Spring Cloud Config** can be used to centralize and dynamically adjust the configuration of microservices. Section 11.4 already presented technologies, which configure microservices during deployment. To be able to reproduce the state of a server at any time, a new server should be started with a new microservice instance in case of a configuration change instead of dynamically adjusting an existing server. If a server is dynamically adjusted, there is no guarantee that new servers are generated with the right configuration as they are configured in a different way. Because of these disadvantages the example application refrains from using this technology.

- **Spring Cloud Bus** can send dynamic configuration changes for Spring Cloud Config. Moreover, the microservices can communicate via Spring Cloud Bus. However, the example application does not use this technology because Spring Cloud Config is not used, and the microservices communicate via REST.

- **Spring Cloud Sleuth** enables distributed tracing with tools like Zipkin or Htrace. It can also use a central log storage with ELK (see section 11.2).

- **Spring Cloud Zookeeper** supports Apache Zookeeper (see section 7.10). This technology can be used to coordinate and configure distributed services.

- **Spring Cloud Consul** facilitates Services Discovery using Consul (see section 7.11).

- **Spring Cloud Cluster** implements leader election and stateful patterns using technologies like Zookeeper or Consul. It can also use the NoSQL data store Redis or the Hazelcast cache.

- **Spring Cloud for Cloud Foundry** provides support for the Cloud Foundry PaaS. For example, single sign on (SSO) and OAuth2 protected resources are supported as well as creating managed service for the Cloud Foundry service broker.

- **Spring Cloud Connectors** support access to services provided by PaaS like Heroku or Cloud Foundry.

- **Spring Cloud Data Flow** helps with the implementation of applications and microservices for Big Data analysis.

- **Spring Cloud Tasks** provides features for short lived microservices.

- Finally, **Spring Cloud Stream** supports messaging using Redis, Rabbit, or Kafka.

Spring Cloud Netflix

Spring Cloud Netflix offers simple access to Netflix Stack, which has been especially designed for the implementation of microservices. The following technologies are part of this stack:

- **Zuul** can implement routing of requests to different services.
- **Ribbon** serves as a load balancer.

- **Hystrix** assists with implementing resilience in microservices.

- **Turbine** can consolidate monitoring data from different Hystrix servers.

- **Feign** is an option for an easier implementation of REST clients. It is not limited to microservices. It is not used in the example application.

- **Eureka** can be used for Service Discovery.

These technologies are the ones that influence the implementation of the example application most.

Try and Experiment

For an introduction into Spring it is worthwhile to check out the Spring Guides at https://spring.io/guides/. They show in detail how Spring can be used to implement REST services or to realize messaging solutions via JMS. An introduction into Spring Boot can be found at https://spring.io/guides/gs/spring-boot/. Working your way through these guides provides you with the necessary know-how for understanding the additional examples in this chapter.

13.3 Build

The example project is built with the tool Maven.[5] The installation of the tool is described at https://maven.apache.org/download.cgi. The command **mvn package** in the directory **microservice/microservice-demo** can be used to download all dependent libraries from the Internet and to compile the application.

The configuration of the projects for Maven is saved in files named **pom.xml**. The example project has a Parent-POM in the directory **microservice-demo**. It contains the universal settings for all modules and in addition a list of the example project modules. Each microservice is such a module, and some infrastructure servers are modules as well. The individual modules have their own **pom.xml**, which contains the module name among other information. In addition, they contain the dependencies, i.e., the Java libraries they use.

---

5. http://maven.apache.org/

Listing 13.2 *Part of pom.xml Including Dependencies*

```
. . .
<dependencies>

 <dependency>
   <groupId>org.springframework.cloud</groupId>
   <artifactId>spring-cloud-starter-eureka</artifactId>
 </dependency>

 <dependency>
   <groupId>org.springframework.boot</groupId>
   <artifactId>
       spring-boot-starter-data-jpa
     </artifactId>
 </dependency>
```

Listing 13.2 shows a part of a **pom.xml**, which lists the dependencies of the module. Depending on the nature of the Spring Cloud features the project is using, additional entries have to be added in this part of the **pom.xml** usually with the `groupId` `org.springframework.cloud`.

The build process results in one JAR file per microservice, which contains the compiled code, the configuration, and all necessary libraries. Java can directly start such JAR files. Although the microservices can be accessed via HTTP, they do not have to be deployed on an application or web server. This part of the infrastructure is also contained in the JAR file.

As the projects are built with Maven, they can be imported into all usual Java IDEs (integrated development environment) for further development. IDEs simplify code changes tremendously.

Try and Experiment

- Download and compile the example:

  Download the example provided at https://github.com/ewolff/microservice. Install Maven; see https://maven.apache.org/download.cgi. In the subdirectory **microservices-demo** execute the command **mvn package**. This will build the complete project.

- Create a continuous integration server for the project:

  https://github.com/ewolff/user-registration-V2 is an example project for a continuous delivery project. This contains in subdirectory **ci-setup** a

> setup for a continuous integration server (Jenkins) with static code analysis (Sonarqube) and Artifactory for the handling of binary artifacts. Integrate the microservices project into this infrastructure so that a new build is triggered upon each change.
>
> The next section (13.4) will discuss Vagrant in more detail. This tool is used for the continuous integration servers. It simplifies the generation of test environments greatly.

13.4 Deployment Using Docker

Deploying microservices is very easy:

- Java has to be installed on the server.
- The JAR file, which resulted from the build, has to be copied to the server.
- A separate configuration file **application.properties** can be created for further configurations. It is automatically read out by Spring Boot and can be used for additional configurations. An **application.properties** containing default values is comprised in the JAR file.
- Finally, a Java process has to start the application out of the JAR file.

Each microservice starts within its own Docker container. As discussed in section 11.7, Docker uses Linux containers. In this manner the microservice cannot interfere with processes in other Docker containers and has a completely independent file system. The Docker image is the basis for this file system. However, all Docker containers share the Linux kernel. This saves resources. In comparison to an operating system process a Docker container has virtually no additional overhead.

Listing 13.3 *Dockerfile for a Microservice Used in the Example Application*

```
FROM java
CMD /usr/bin/java -Xmx400m -Xms400m \
  -jar /microservice-demo/microservice-demo-catalog\
  /target/microservice-demo-catalog-0.0.1-SNAPSHOT.jar
EXPOSE 8080
```

A file called **Dockerfile** defines the composition of a Docker container. Listing 13.3 shows a Dockerfile for a microservice used in the example application:

- FROM determines the base image used by the Docker container. A Dockerfile for the image java is contained in the example project. It generates a minimal Docker image with only a JVM installed.

- CMD defines the command executed at the start of the Docker container. In the case of this example it is a simple command line. This line starts a Java application out of the JAR file generated by the build.

- Docker containers are able to communicate with the outside via network ports. EXPOSE determines which ports are accessible from outside. In the example the application receives HTTP requests via port 8080.

13.5 Vagrant

Docker runs exclusively under Linux, because it uses Linux containers. However, there are solutions for other operating systems, which start a virtual Linux machine and thus enable the use of Docker. This is largely transparent so that the use is practically identical to the use under Linux. But in addition all Docker containers need to be built and started.

To make installing and handling Docker as easy as possible, the example application uses Vagrant. Figure 13.3 shows how Vagrant works:

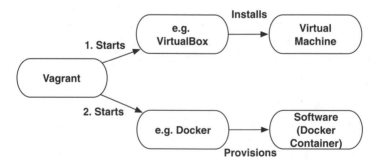

Figure 13.3 *How Vagrant Works*

To configure Vagrant a single file is necessary, the Vagrantfile. Listing 13.4 shows the Vagrantfile of the example application:

Listing 13.4 *Vagrantfile from the Example Application*

```
Vagrant.configure("2") do |config|
  config.vm.box = " ubuntu/trusty64"
  config.vm.synced_folder ."./microservice-demo",
    "/microservice-demo", create: true
  config.vm.network "forwarded_port",
    guest: 8080, host: 18080
  config.vm.network "forwarded_port",
    guest: 8761, host: 18761
  config.vm.network "forwarded_port",
      guest: 8989, host: 18989

config.vm.provision "docker" do |d|
  d.build_image "--tag=java /vagrant/java"
  d.build_image "--tag=eureka /vagrant/eureka"
  d.build_image
      "--tag=customer-app /vagrant/customer-app"
  d.build_image "
      "--tag=catalog-app /vagrant/catalog-app"
  d.build_image "--tag=order-app /vagrant/order-app"
  d.build_image "--tag=turbine /vagrant/turbine"
  d.build_image "--tag=zuul /vagrant/zuul"
end
config.vm.provision "docker", run: "always" do |d|
  d.run "eureka",
    args: "-p 8761:8761"+
        "-v /microservice-demo:/microservice-demo"
  d.run "customer-app",
    args: "-v /microservice-demo:/microservice-demo"+
        "--link eureka:eureka"
  d.run "catalog-app",
    args: "-v /microservice-demo:/microservice-demo"+
        "--link eureka:eureka"
  d.run "order-app",
    args: "-v /microservice-demo:/microservice-demo"+
        "--link eureka:eureka"
```

```
d.run "zuul",
  args: "-v /microservice-demo:/microservice-demo"+
      " -p 8080:8080 --link eureka:eureka"
d.run "turbine",
 args: "-v /microservice-demo:/microservice-demo"+
      " --link eureka:eureka"
end

end
```

- `config.vm.box` selects a base image—in this case an Ubuntu-13.04 Linux installation (Trusty Tahr).

- `config.vm. synced_folder` mounts the directory containing the results of the Maven build into the virtual machine. In this manner the Docker containers can directly make use of the build results.

- The ports of the virtual machine can be linked to the ports of the computer running the virtual machine. The `config.vm.network` settings can be used for that. In this manner applications in the Vagrant virtual machine become accessible as if running directly on the computer.

- `config.vm.provision` starts the part of the configuration that deals with the software provisioning within the virtual machine. Docker serves as provisioning tool and is automatically installed within the virtual machine.

- `d.build_image` generates the Docker images using Dockerfiles. First the base image java is created. Images for the three microservices customer-app, catalog-app and order-app follow. The images for the Netflix technologies servers belong to the infrastructure: Eureka for Service Discovery, Turbine for monitoring, and Zuul for routing of client requests.

- Vagrant starts the individual images using `d.run`. This step is not only performed when provisioning the virtual machine, but also when the system is started anew (`run: "always"`). The option `-v` mounts the directory **/microservice-demo** into each Docker container so that the Docker container can directly execute the compiled code. `-p` links a port of the Docker container to a port of virtual machine. This link provides access to the Docker container Eureka under the host name eureka from within the other Docker containers.

In the Vagrant setup the JAR files containing the application code are not contained in the Docker image. The directory **/microservice-demo** does not belong to the Docker container. It resides on the host running the Docker containers, that is, the Vagrant VM. It would also be possible to copy these files into the Docker image. Afterwards the resulting image could be copied on a repository server and

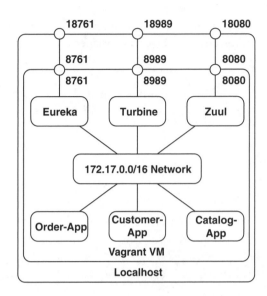

Figure 13.4 *Network and Ports of the Example Application*

downloaded from there. Then the Docker container would contain all necessary files to run the microservice. A deployment in production then only needs to start the Docker images on a production server. This approach is used in the Docker Machine setup (see section 13.6).

Networking in the Example Application

Figure 13.4 shows how the individual microservices of the example application communicate via the network. All Docker containers are accessible in the network via IP addresses from the 172.17.0.0/16 range. Docker generates such a network automatically and connects all Docker containers to the network. Within the network all ports are accessible that are defined in the Dockerfiles using EXPOSE. The Vagrant virtual machine is also connected to this network. Via the Docker links (see Listing 13.4) all Docker containers know the Eureka container and can access it under the host name **eureka**. The other microservices have to be looked up via Eureka. All further communication takes place via the IP address.

In addition, the -p option in the **d.run** entries for the Docker containers in Listing 13.4 has connected the ports to the Vagrant virtual machine. These containers can be accessed via these ports of the Vagrant virtual machine. To reach them also from the computer running the Vagrant virtual machine there is a port mapping that links the ports to the local computer. This is accomplished via the config. vm. network entries in Vagrantfile. The port 8080 of the Docker container "zuul" can, for instance, be accessed via the port 8080 in the Vagrant virtual machine.

This port can be reached from the local computer via the port 18080. So the URL http://localhost:18080/ accesses this Docker container.

Try and Experiment

- **Run the Example Application**

  The example application does not need much effort to make it run. A running example application lays the foundation for the experiments described later in this chapter.

  One remark: The **Vagrantfile** defines how much RAM and how many CPUs the virtual machines gets. The settings `v.memory` and `v.cpus`, which are not shown in the listing, deal with this. Depending on the computer used, the values should be increased if a lot of RAM or many CPUs are present. Whenever the values can be increased, they should be elevated in order to speed the application up.

  The installation of Vagrant is described in https://www.vagrantup.com/docs/installation/index.html. Vagrant needs a virtualization solution like VirtualBox. The installation of VirtualBox is explained at https://www.virtualbox.org/wiki/Downloads. Both tools are free.

  The example can only be started once the code has been compiled. Instructions how to compile the code can be found in the experiment described in section 13.3. Afterwards you can change into the directory **docker-vagrant** and start the example demo using the command `vagrant up`.

  To interact with the different Docker containers, you have to log into the virtual machine via the command `vagrant ssh`. This command has to be executed within the subdirectory **docker-vagrant**. For this to be possible an ssh client has to be installed on the computer. On Linux and Mac OS X such a client is usually already present. In Windows installing git will bring an ssh client along as described at http://git-scm.com/download/win. Afterwards `vagrant ssh` should work.

- **Investigate Docker Containers**

  Docker contains several useful commands:

  - `docker ps` provides an overview of the running Docker containers.

  - The command `docker log "name of Docker container"` shows the logs.

- docker log -f "*name of Docker Container*" provides incessantly the up-to-date log information of the container.

- docker kill "*name of the Docker Container*" terminates a Docker container.

- docker rm "*name of the Docker Container*" deletes all data. For that all containers first needs to be stopped. After starting the application, the log files of the individual Docker containers can be looked at.

- **Update Docker Containers**

  A Docker container can be terminated (docker kill) and the data of the container deleted (docker rm). The commands have to be executed inside the Vagrant virtual machine. vagrant provision starts the missing Docker containers again. This command has to be executed on the host running Vagrant. If you want to change the Docker container, simply delete it, compile the code again and generate the system anew using vagrant provision. Additional Vagrant commands include the following:

  - vagrant halt terminates the virtual machine.

  - vagrant up starts it again.

  - vagrant destroy destroys the virtual machine and all saved data.

- **Store Data on Disk**

  Right now the Docker container does not save the data so that it is lost upon restarting. The used HSQLDB database can also save the data into a file. To achieve that a suitable HSQLDB URL has to be used, see http://hsqldb .org/doc/guide/dbproperties-chapt.html#dpc_connection_url. Spring Boot can read the JDBC URL out of the **application.properties** file; see http:// docs.spring.io/spring-boot/docs/current/reference/html/boot-features-sql .html#boot-features-connect-to-production-database. Now the container can be restarted without data loss. But what happens if the Docker container has to be generated again? Docker can save data also outside of the container itself; compare https://docs.docker.com/userguide/dockervolumes/. These options provide a good basis for further experiments. Also another database than HSQLDB can be used, such as MySQL. For that purpose another Docker container has to be installed that contains the database.

  (continued)

In addition to adjusting the JDBC URL, a JDBC driver has to be added to the project.

- **How is the Java Docker Image Built?**

  The Docker file is more complex than the ones discussed here. https://docs. docker.com/reference/builder/ demonstrates which commands are available in Dockerfiles. Try to understand the structure of the Dockerfiles.

13.6 Docker Machine

Vagrant serves to install environments on a developer laptop. In addition to Docker, Vagrant can use simple shell scripts for deployment. However, for production environments this solution is unsuitable. Docker Machine[6] is specialized in Docker. It supports many more virtualization solutions as well as some cloud providers.

Figure 13.5 demonstrates how Docker Machine builds a Docker environment: First, using a virtualization solution like VirtualBox, a virtual machine is installed. This virtual machine is based on boot2docker, a very lightweight version of Linux designed specifically as a running environment for Docker containers. On that Docker Machine installs a current version of Docker. A command like `docker-machine create --driver virtualbox dev` generates, for instance, a new environment with the name dev running on a VirtualBox computer.

The Docker tool now can communicate with this environment. The Docker command line tools use a REST interface to communicate with the Docker server. Accordingly, the command line tool just has to be configured in a way that enables

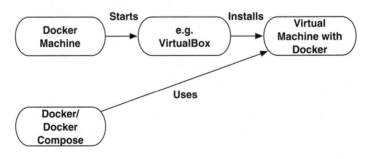

Figure 13.5 *Docker Machine*

---

6. https://docs.docker.com/machine/

it to communicate with the server in a suitable manner. In Linux or Mac OS X, the command `eval "$(docker-machine env dev)"` is sufficient to configure the Docker appropriately. For Windows PowerShell, the command `docker-machine.exe env --shell powershell dev` must be used and in Windows cmd `docker-machine.exe env --shell cmd dev`.

Docker Machine thus renders it very easy to install one or several Docker environments. All the environments can be handled by Docker Machine and accessed by the Docker command line tool. As Docker Machine also supports technologies like Amazon Cloud or VMware vSphere, it can be used to generate production environments.

Try and Experiment

The example application can also run in an environment created by Docker Machine.

The installation of Docker Machine is described at https://docs.docker.com/machine/#installation. Docker Machine requires a virtualization solution like VirtualBox. How to install VirtualBox can be found at https://www.virtualbox.org/wiki/Downloads. Using `docker-machine create --virtualbox-memory "4096" --driver virtualbox dev` a Docker environment called **dev** can now be created on a Virtual Box. Without any further configuration the storage space is set to 1 GB, which is not sufficient for a larger number of Java Virtual Machines.

`docker-machine` without parameters displays a help text, and `docker-machine create` shows the options for the generation of a new environment. https://docs.docker.com/machine/get-started-cloud/ demonstrates how Docker Machine can be used in a Cloud. This means that the example application can also easily be started in a cloud environment.

At the end of your experiments, `docker-machine rm` deletes the environment.

13.7 Docker Compose

A microservice-based system comprises typically several Docker containers. These have to be generated together and need to be put into production simultaneously.

This can be achieved with Docker Compose.[7] It enables the definition of Docker containers, which each house one service. YAML serves as format.

---

7. http://docs.docker.com/compose/

Listing 13.5 *Docker Compose Configuration for the Example Application*

```
version: '2'
services:
  eureka:
    build: ../microservice-demo/microservice-demo-eureka-server
    ports:
      - "8761:8761"
  customer:
    build: ../microservice-demo/microservice-demo-customer
    links:
     - eureka
  catalog:
    build: ../microservice-demo/microservice-demo-catalog
    links:
     - eureka
  order:
    build: ../microservice-demo/microservice-demo-order
    links:
     - eureka
  zuul:
    build: ../microservice-demo/microservice-demo-zuul-server
    links:
     - eureka
    ports:
      - "8080:8080"
  turbine:
    build: ../microservice-demo/microservice-demo-turbine-
server
    links:
     - eureka
    ports:
      - "8989:8989"
```

Listing 13.5 shows the configuration of the example application. It consists of the different services. `build` references the directory containing the Dockerfile. The Dockerfile is used to generate the image for the service. `links` defines which additional Docker containers the respective container should be able to access. All containers can access the Eureka container under the name `eureka`. In contrast to the Vagrant configuration there is no Java base image, which contains only a Java installation. This is because Docker Compose supports only containers that really offer a service. Therefore, this base image has to be downloaded from the Internet. Besides, in case of the Docker Compose containers the JAR files are copied into the Docker images so that the images contain everything for starting the microservices.

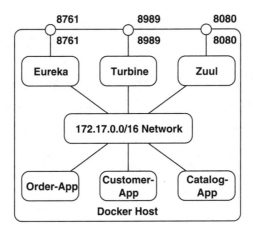

Figure 13.6 *Network and Ports of the Example Application*

The resulting system is very similar to the Vagrant system (see Figure 13.6). The Docker containers are linked via their own private network. From the outside, only Zuul can be accessed for the processing of requests and Eureka for the dashboard. They are running directly on a host that then can be accessed from the outside.

Using `docker-compose build` the system is created based on the Docker Compose configuration. Thus the suitable images are generated. `docker-compose up` then starts the system. Docker Compose uses the same settings as the Docker command line tool so it can also work together with Docker Machine. Thus it is transparent whether the system is generated on a local virtual machine or somewhere in the Cloud.

Try and Experiment

- **Run the Example with Docker Compose**

  The example application possesses a suitable Docker Compose configuration. Upon the generation of an environment with Docker Machine, Docker Compose can be used to create the Docker containers. README.md in the directory docker describes the necessary procedure.

- **Scale the Application**

  Have a look at the `docker-compose scale` command. It can scale the environment. Services can be restarted and logs can be analyzed and

  (continued)

> finally stopped. Once you have started the application, you can test these functionalities.
>
> • **Cluster Environments for Docker**
>
>   Mesos (http://mesos.apache.org/) together with Mesosphere (http://mesosphere.com/), Kubernetes (http://kubernetes.io/), or CoreOS (http://coreos.com/) offers similar options as Docker Compose and Docker Machine. However they are meant for servers and server clusters. The Docker Compose and Docker Machine configurations can provide a good basis for running the application on these platforms.

13.8 Service Discovery

Section 7.11 introduced the general principles of Service Discovery. The example application uses Eureka[8] for Service Discovery.

Eureka is a REST-based server, which enables services to register themselves so that other services can request their location in the network. In essence, each service can register a URL under its name. Other services can find the URL by the name of the service. Using this URL other services can then send REST messages to this service.

Eureka supports replication onto several servers and caches on the client. This makes the system fail-safe against the failure of individual Eureka servers and enables rapid answer requests. Changes to data have to be replicated to all servers. Accordingly, it can take some time until they are really updated everywhere. During this time the data is inconsistent: Each server has a different version of the data.

In addition, Eureka supports Amazon Web Services because Netflix uses it in this environment. Eureka can, for instance, quite easily be combined with Amazon's scaling.

Eureka monitors the registered services and removes them from the server list if they cannot be reached anymore by the Eureka server.

Eureka is the basis for many other services of the Netflix Stack and for Spring Cloud. Through a uniform Service Discovery, other aspects such as routing can easily be implemented.

Eureka Client

For a Spring Boot application to be able to register with a Eureka server and to find other microservices, the application has to be annotated with `@Enable DiscoveryClient` or `@EnableEurekaClient`. In addition, a dependency from

---

8. https://github.com/Netflix/Eureka

spring-cloud-starter-eureka has to be included in the file **pom.xml**. The application registers automatically with the Eureka server and can access other microservices. The example application accesses other microservices via a load balancer. This is described in detail in section 13.11.

Configuration

Configuring the application is necessary to define, for instance, the Eureka server to be used. The file **application.properties** (see Listing 13.6) is used for that. Spring Boot reads it out automatically in order to configure the application. This mechanism can also be used to configure one's own code. In the example application the values serve to configure the Eureka client:

- The first line defines the Eureka server. The example application uses the Docker link, which provides the Eureka server under the host name "eureka."

- leaseRenewalIntervalInSeconds determines how often data is updated between client and server. As the data has to be held locally in a cache on each client, a new service first needs to create its own cache and replicate it onto the server. Afterwards the data is replicated onto the clients. Within a test environment it is important to track system changes rapidly so that the example application uses five seconds instead of the preset value of 30 seconds. In production with many clients, this value should be increased. Otherwise the updates of information will use a lot of resources, even though the information remains essentially unchanged.

- spring.application.name serves as the name for the service during the registration at Eureka. During registration the name is converted into capital letters. This service would thus be known by Eureka under the name "CUSTOMER."

- There can be several instances of each service to achieve fail over and load balancing. The instanceId has to be unique for each instance of a service. Because of that it contains a random number, which ensures unambiguousness.

- preferIpAddress makes sure that microservices register with their IP addresses and not with their host names. Unfortunately in a Docker environment host names are not easily resolvable by other hosts. This problem is circumvented by the use of IP addresses.

Listing 13.6 *Part of application.properties with Eureka Configuration*

```
eureka.client.serviceUrl.defaultZone=http://eureka:8761/eureka/
eureka.instance.leaseRenewalIntervalInSeconds=5
spring.application.name=catalog
eureka.instance.metadataMap.instanceId=catalog:${random.value}
eureka.instance.preferIpAddress=true
```

Eureka Server

The Eureka server (Listing 13.7) is a simple Spring Boot application, which turns into a Eureka server via the `@EnableEurekaServer` annotation. In addition, the server needs a dependency on `spring-cloud-starter-eureka-server`.

Listing 13.7 *Eureka Server*

```
@EnableEurekaServer
@EnableAutoConfiguration
public class EurekaApplication {
  public static void main(String[] args) {
    SpringApplication.run(EurekaApplication.class, args);
  }
}
```

The Eureka server offers a dashboard that shows the registered services. In the example application, this can be found at http://localhost:18761/ (Vagrant) or on Docker host under port 8761 (Docker Compose). Figure 13.7 shows a screenshot of

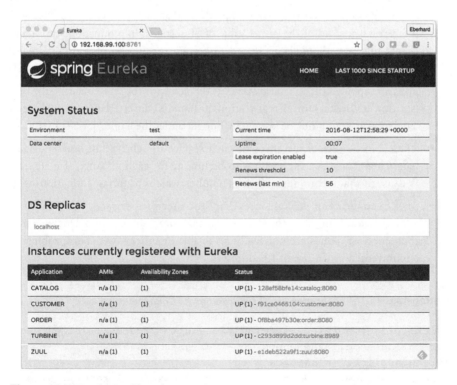

Figure 13.7 *Eureka Dashboard*

the Eureka dashboards for the example application. The three microservices and the Zuul-Proxy, which is discussed in the next section, are present on the dashboard.

13.9 Communication

Chapter 8, "Integration and Communication," explains how microservices communicate with each other and can be integrated. The example application uses REST for internal communication. The REST end points can be contacted from outside; however, the web interface the system offers is of far greater importance. The REST implementation uses HATEOAS. The list containing all orders, for instance, contains links to the individual orders. This is automatically implemented by Spring Data REST. However, there are no links to the customer and the items of the order.

Using HATEOAS can go further: the JSON can contain a link to an HTML document for each order—and vice versa. In this way a JSON-REST-based service can generate links to HTML pages to display or modify data. Such HTML code can, for instance, present an item in an order. As the "Catalog" team provides the HTML code for the item, the catalog team itself can introduce changes to the presentation—even if the items are displayed in another module.

REST is also of use here: HTML and JSON are really only representations of the same resource that can be addressed by a URL. Via Content Negotiation the right resource representation as JSON or HTML can be selected (see section 8.2).

Zuul: Routing

The Zuul[9] proxy transfers incoming requests to the respective microservices. The Zuul proxy is a separate Java process. To the outside only one URL is visible; however, internally the calls are processed by different microservices. This enables the system to internally change the structure of the microservices while still offering a URL to the outside. In addition, Zuul can provide web resources. In the example in Figure 13.8, Zuul provides the first HTML page viewed by the user.

Zuul needs to know which requests to transfer to which microservice. Without additional configuration Eureka will forward a request to a URL starting with "/customer" to the microservice called CUSTOMER. This renders the internal microservice names visible to the outside. However, this routing can also be configured differently. Moreover, Zuul filters can change the requests in order to implement general aspects in the system. There is, for instance, an integration with Spring Cloud Security to pass on security tokens to the microservices. Such filters can also be used to pass on certain requests to specific servers. This makes it possible, for instance,

---

9. https://github.com/Netflix/zuul

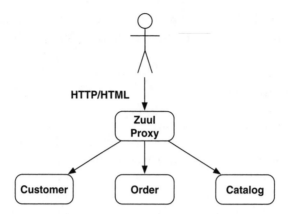

Figure 13.8 *Zuul Proxy in the Example Application*

to transfer requests to servers having additional analysis options for investigating error situations. In addition, a part of a microservice functionality can be replaced by another microservice.

Implementing the Zuul proxy server with Spring Cloud is very easy and analogous to the Eureka server presented in Listing 13.7. Instead of `@EnableEurekaServer` it is `@EnableZuulProxy`, which activates the Zuul-Proxy. As an additional dependency, `spring-cloud-starter-zuul` has to be added to the application, for instance, within the Maven build configuration, which then integrates the remaining dependencies of Zuul into the application.

A Zuul server represents an alternative to a Zuul proxy. It does not have routing built in, but uses filters instead. A Zuul server is activated by `@EnableZuulServer`.

Try and Experiment

- **Add Links to Customer and Items**

  Extend the application so that an order contains also links to the customer and to the items and thus implements HATEOAS better. Supplement the JSON documents for customers, items, and orders with links to the forms.

- **Use the "Catalog" Service to Show Items in Orders**

  Change the order presentation so that HTML from the "Catalog" service is used for items. To do so, you have to insert suitable JavaScript code into the order component, which loads HTML code from the "Catalog."

- **Implement Zuul Filters**

  Implement your own Zuul filter (see https://github.com/Netflix/zuul/wiki/Writing-Filters). The filter can, for instance, only release the requests. Introduce an additional routing to an external URL. For instance, /google could redirect to http://google.com/. Compare the Spring Cloud reference documentation.[10]

- **Authentication and Authorization**

  Insert an authentication and authorization with Spring Cloud Security. Compare http://cloud.spring.io/spring-cloud-security/.

  ---

  10. http://projects.spring.io/spring-cloud/docs/1.0.3/spring-cloud.html

13.10 Resilience

Resilience means that microservices can deal with the failure of other microservices. Even if a called microservice is not available, they will still work. Section 9.5 presented this topic.

The example application implements resilience with Hystrix.[11] This library protects calls so that no problems arise if a system fails. When a call is protected by Hystrix, it is executed in a different thread than the call itself. This thread is taken from a distinct thread pool. This makes it comparatively easy to implement a timeout during a call.

Circuit Breaker

In addition, Hystrix implements a *Circuit Breaker*. If a call causes an error, the *Circuit Breaker* will open after a certain number of errors. In that case subsequent calls are not directed to the called system anymore, but generate an error immediately. After a sleep window the *Circuit Breaker* closes so that calls are directed to the actual system again. The exact behavior can be configured.[12] In the configuration the error threshold percentage can be determined. That is the percentage of calls that have to cause an error within the time window for the circuit breaker to open. Also the sleep window can be defined, in which the *Circuit Breaker* is open and not sending calls to the system.

---

11. https://github.com/Netflix/Hystrix/

12. https://github.com/Netflix/Hystrix/wiki/Configuration

Hystrix with Annotations

Spring Cloud uses Java annotations from the project hystrix-javanica for the configuration of Hystrix. This project is part of hystrix-contrib.[13] The annotated methods are protected according to the setting in the annotation. Without this approach Hystrix commands would have to be written, which is a lot more effort than just adding some annotations to a Java method.

To be able to use Hystrix within a Spring Cloud application, the application has to be annotated with @EnableCircuitBreaker respectively @EnableHystrix. Moreover, the project needs to contain a dependency to spring-cloud-starter-hystrix.

Listing 13.8 shows a section from the class CatalogClient of the "Order" microservice from the example application. The method findAll() is annotated with @HystrixCommand. This activates the processing in a different thread and the *Circuit Breaker*. The *Circuit Breaker* can be configured—in the example the number of calls, which have to cause an error in order to open the *Circuit Breaker*, is set to 2. In addition, the example defines a fallbackMethod. Hystrix calls this method if the original method generates an error. The logic in findAll() saves the last result in a cache, which is returned by the fallbackMethod without calling the real system. In this way a reply can still be returned when the called microservice fails, however this reply might no longer be up-to-date.

Listing 13.8 *Example for a Method Protected by Hystrix*

```
@HystrixCommand(
 fallbackMethod = "getItemsCache",
 commandProperties = {
 @HystrixProperty(

name = "circuitBreaker.requestVolumeThreshold", value = "2") })
public Collection findAll() {
  this.itemsCache = ...
  ...
  return pagedResources.getContent();
}

private Collection getItemsCache() {
  return itemsCache;
}
```

---

13. https://github.com/Netflix/Hystrix/tree/master/hystrix-contrib

Monitoring with the Hystrix Dashboard

Whether a *Circuit Breaker* is currently open or closed gives an indication of how well a system is running. Hystrix offers data to monitor this. A Hystrix system provides such data as a stream of JSON documents via HTTP. The Hystrix Dashboard can visualize the data in a web interface. The dashboard presents all *Circuit Breakers* along with the number of requests and their state (open/closed) (see Figure 13.9). In addition, it displays the state of the thread pools.

A Spring Boot Application needs to have the annotation `@EnableHystrixDashboard` and a dependency to `spring-cloud-starter-hystrix-dashboard` to be able to display a Hystrix Dashboard. That way any Spring Boot application might in addition show a Hystrix Dashboard, or the dashboard can be implemented in an application by itself.

Turbine

In a complex microservices environment it is not useful that each instance of a microservice visualizes the information concerning the state of its Hystrix *Circuit Breaker*. The state of all *Circuit Breakers* in the entire system should be summarized on a single dashboard. To visualize the data of the different Hystrix systems on one

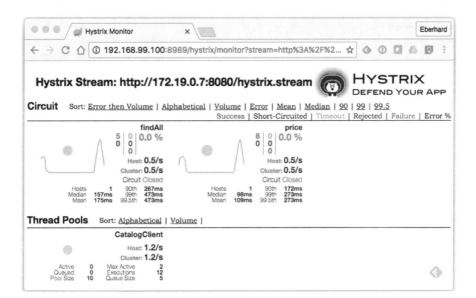

Figure 13.9 *Example for a Hystrix Dashboard*

dashboard, there is the Turbine project. Figure 13.10 illustrates the approach Turbine takes: the different streams of the Hystrix enabled microservices are provided at URLs like http://<host:port>/hystrix.stream. The Turbine server requests them and provides them in a consolidated manner at the URL http://<host:port>/turbine. stream. This URL can be used by the dashboard in order to display the information of all *Circuit Breakers* of the different microservice instances.

Turbine runs in a separate process. With Spring Boot the Turbine server is a simple application, which is annotated with `@EnableTurbine` and `@EnableEurekaClient`. In the example application it has the additional annotation `@EnableHystrixDash-board` so that it also displays the Hystrix Dashboard. It also needs a dependency on `spring-cloud-starter-turbine`.

Which data is consolidated by the Turbine server is determined by the configuration of the application. Listing 13.9 shows the configuration of the Turbine servers of the example project. It serves as a configuration for a Spring Boot application just like **application.properties** files but is written in YAML. The configuration sets the value `ORDER` for `turbine.aggregator.clusterConfig`. This is the application name in Eureka. `turbine.aggregator.appConfig` is the name of the data stream in the Turbine server. In the Hystrix Dashboard a URL like http://172.17.0.10:8989/turbine. stream?cluster=ORDER has to be used in visualize the data stream. Part of the URL is the IP address of the Turbine server, which can be found in the Eureka Dashboard. The dashboard accesses the Turbine server via the network between the Docker containers.

Listing 13.9 *Configuration application.yml*

```
turbine:
 aggregator:
  clusterConfig: ORDER
 appConfig: order
```

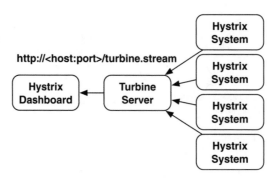

Figure 13.10 *Turbine Consolidates Hystrix Monitoring Data*

Try and Experiment

- **Terminate Microservices**

  Using the example application generate a number of orders. Find the name of the "Catalog" Docker container using `docke ps`. Stop the "Catalog" Docker container with `docker kill`. This use is protected by Hystrix.

  What happens? What happens if the "Customer" Docker container is terminated as well? The use of this microservice is not protected by Hystrix.

- **Add Hystrix to "Customer" Microservice**

  Protect the use of the "Customer" Docker container with Hystrix also. In order to do so change the class `CustomerClient` from the "Order" project. `CatalogClient` can serve as a template.

- **Change Hystrix Configuration**

  Change the configuration of Hystrix for the "Catalog" microservice. There are several configuration options.[14] Listing 13.8 (CatalogClient from the "Order" Project) shows the use of the Hystrix annotations. Other time intervals for opening and closing of the circuit breakers are, for instance, a possible change.

---

14. https://github.com/Netflix/Hystrix/wiki/Configuration

13.11 Load Balancing

For Load Balancing the example application uses Ribbon.[15] Many load balancers are proxy based. In this model the clients send all calls to a Load Balancer. The Load Balancer runs as a distinct server and forwards the request to a web server—often depending on the current load of the web servers.

Ribbon implements a different model called client-side load balancing: The client has all the information to communicate with the right server. The client calls the server directly and distributes the load by itself to different servers. In the architecture there is no bottleneck as there is no central server all calls would have to pass. In conjunction with data replication by Eureka, Ribbon is quite resilient: As long as the client runs, it can send requests. The failure of a proxy load balancer would stop all calls to the server.

---

15. https://github.com/Netflix/ribbon/wiki

Dynamic scaling is very simple within this system: A new instance is started, enlists itself at Eureka, and then the Ribbon Clients redirect load to the instance.

As already discussed in the section dealing with Eureka (section 13.8), data can be inconsistent over the different servers. Because data is not up to date, servers can be contacted, which really should be left out by the Load Balancing.

Ribbon with Spring Cloud

Spring Cloud simplifies the use of Ribbon. The application has to be annotated with @RibbonClient. While doing so, a name for the application can be defined. In addition, the application needs to have a dependency on spring-cloud-starter-ribbon. In that case an instance of a microservice can be accessed using code like that in Listing 13.10. For that purpose, the code uses the Eureka name of the microservice.

Listing 13.10 *Determining a Server with Ribbon Load Balancing*

```
ServiceInstance instance
 = loadBalancer.choose("CATALOG");
String url = "http://" + instance.getHost() + ":" +
 instance.getPort() + "/catalog/";
```

The use can also be transparent to a large extent. To illustrate this Listing 13.11 shows the use of RestTemplates with Ribbon. This is a Spring class, which can be used to call REST services. In the Listing the RestTemplate of Spring is injected into the object as it is annotated with @Autowired. The call in callMicroservice() looks like it is contacting a server called "stores." In reality this name is used to search a server at Eureka, and the REST call is sent to this server. This is done via Ribbon so that the load is also distributed across the available servers.

Listing 13.11 *Using Ribbon with RestTemplate*

```
@RibbonClient(name = "ribbonApp")
 … // Left out other Spring Cloud / Boot Annotations
public class RibbonApp {

 @Autowired
  private RestTemplate restTemplate;

  public void callMicroservice() {
    Store store = restTemplate.
     getForObject("http://stores/store/1", Store.class);
  }
}
```

Try and Experiment

- **Load Balance to an Additional Service Instance**

  The "Order" microservice distributes the load onto several instances of the "Customer and Catalog" microservice—if several instances exist. Without further measures, only a single instance is started. The "Order" microservice shows in the log which "Catalog" or "Customer" microservice it contacts. Initiate an order and observe which services are contacted.

  Afterwards start an additional "Catalog" microservice. You can do that using the command: `docker run -v /microservice-demo:/microservice-demo --link eureka:eureka catalog-app` in Vagrant. For Docker Compose `docker-compose scale catalog=2` should be enough. Verify whether the container is running and observe the log output.

  For reference: "Try and Experiment" in section 13.4 shows the main commands for using Docker. Section 13.7 shows how to use Docker Compose.

- **Create Data**

  Create a new dataset with a new item. Is the item always displayed in the selection of items? Hint: The database runs within the process of the microservice—that is, each microservice instance possesses its own database.

13.12 Integrating Other Technologies

Spring Cloud and the entire Netflix Stack are based on Java. Thus, it seems impossible for other programming languages and platforms to use this infrastructure. However, there is a solution: the application can be supplied with a sidecar. The sidecar is written in Java and uses Java libraries to integrate into a Netflix-based infrastructure. The sidecar, for instance, takes care of registration and finding other microservices in Eureka. Netflix itself offers for this purpose the Prana project.[16] The Spring Cloud solution is explained in the documentation.[17] The sidecar runs in a distinct process and serves as an interface between the microservice itself and the microservice infra-

---

16. http://github.com/Netflix/Prana/
17. http://cloud.spring.io/spring-cloud-static/Brixton.SR5/#_polyglot_support_with_sidecar

structure. In this manner other programming languages and platforms can be easily integrated into a Netflix or Spring Cloud environment.

13.13 Tests

The example application contains test applications for the developers of microservices. These do not need a microservice infrastructure or additional microservices—in contrast to the production system. This enables developers to run each microservice without a complex infrastructure.

The class **OrderTestApp** in the "Order" project contains such a test application. The applications contain their own configuration file **application-test. properties** with specific settings within the directory **src/test/resources**. The settings prevent that the applications register with the Service Discovery Eureka. Besides, they contain different URLs for the dependent microservices. This configuration is automatically used by the test application as it uses a Spring profile called "test." All JUnit tests use these settings as well so that they can run without dependent services.

Stubs

The URLs for the dependent microservices in the test application and the JUnit tests point to stubs. These are simplified microservices, which only offer a part of the functionalities. They run within the same Java process as the real microservices or JUnit tests. Therefore, only a single Java process has to be started for the development of a microservice, analogous to the usual way of developing with Java. The stubs can be implemented differently—for instance, using a different programming language or even a web server, which returns certain static documents representing the test data (see section 10.6). Such approaches might be better suited for real-life applications.

Stubs facilitate development. If each developer needs to use a complete environment including all microservices during development, a tremendous amount of hardware resources and a lot of effort to keep the environment continuously up to date would be necessary. The stubs circumvent this problem as no dependent microservices are needed during development. Due to the stubs the effort to start a microservice is hardly bigger than the one for a regular Java application.

In a real project the teams can implement stubs together with the real microservices. The "Customer" team can implement a stub for the "Customer" microservice in addition to the real service, which is used by the other microservices for development. This ensures that the stub largely resembles the microservice and is updated if the original service is changed. The stub can be taken care of in a different Maven projects, which can be used by the other teams.

Consumer-Driven Contract Test

It has to be ensured that the stubs behave like the microservices they simulate. In addition, a microservice has to define the expectations regarding the interface of a different microservice. This is achieved by consumer-driven contract tests (see section 10.7). These are written by the team that uses the microservices. In the example this is the team that is responsible for the "Order" microservice. In the "Order" microservice the consumer-driven contract tests are found in the classes **Catalog-ConsumerDrivenContractTest** and **CustomerConsumerDrivenContract-Test**. They run there to test the stubs of the "Customer and Catalog" microservice for correctness.

Even more important than the correct functioning of the stubs is the correct functioning of the microservices themselves. For that reason, the consumer-driven contract tests are also contained in the "Customer and Catalog" project. There they run against the implemented microservices. This ensures that the stubs as well as the real microservices are in line with this specification. In case the interface is supposed to be changed, these tests can be used to confirm that the change does not break the calling microservice. It is up to the used microservices—"Customer and Catalog" in the example—to comply with these tests. In this manner the requirements of the "Order" microservice in regard to the "Customer and Catalog" microservice can be formally defined and tested. The consumer-driven contract tests serve in the end as formal definition of the agreed interface.

In the example application the consumer-driven contract tests are part of the "Customer and Catalog" projects in order to verify that the interface is correctly implemented. Besides they are part of the "Order" project for verifying the correct functioning of the stubs. In a real project copying the tests should be prevented. The consumer-driven contract tests can be located in one project together with the tested microservices. Then all teams need to have access to the microservice projects to be able to alter the tests. Alternatively, they are located within the projects of the different teams that are using the microservice. In that case the tested microservice has to collect the tests from the other projects and execute them.

In a real project it is not really necessary to protect stubs by consumer-driven contract tests, especially as it is the purpose of the stubs to offer an easier implementation than the real microservices. Thus the functionalities will be different and conflict with consumer-driven contract tests.

Try and Experiment

- Insert a field into "Catalog" or "Customer" data. Is the system still working? Why?

- Delete a field in the implementation of the server for "Catalog" or "Customer." Where is the problem noticed? Why?

- Replace the home-grown stubs with stubs, that use a tool from Section 10.6.

- Replace the consumer-driven contract tests with tests that use a tool from Section 10.7.

13.14 Experiences with JVM-Based Microservices in the Amazon Cloud (Sascha Möllering)

By Sascha Möllering, zanox AG

During the last months zanox has implemented a lightweight microservices architecture in Amazon Web Services (AWS), which runs in several AWS regions. Regions divide the Amazon Cloud into sections like US-East or EU-West, which each have their own data centers. They work completely independently of each other and do not exchange any data directly. Different AWS regions are used because latency is very important for this type of application and is minimized by latency-based routing. In addition, it was a fundamental aim to design the architecture in an event-driven manner. Furthermore, the individual services were intended not to communicate directly but rather to be separated by message queues respectively bus systems. An Apache Kafka cluster as message bus in the zanox data center serves as central point of synchronization for the different regions. Each service is implemented as a stateless application. The state is stored in external systems like the bus systems, Amazon ElastiCache (based on the NoSQL database Redis), the data stream processing technology Amazon Kinesis, and the NoSQL database Amazon DynamoDB. The JVM serves as basis for the implementation of the individual services. We chose Vert.x and the embedded web server Jetty as frameworks. We developed all applications as self-contained services so that a Fat JAR, which can easily be started via `java -jar`, is generated at the end of the build process.

There is no need to install any additional components or an application server. Vert.x serves as basis framework for the HTTP part of the architecture. Within the application work is performed almost completely asynchronously to achieve high performance. For the remaining components we use Jetty as framework: These act either as Kafka/Kinesis consumer or update the Redis cache for the HTTP layer. All called applications are delivered in Docker containers. This enables the use of a uniform deployment mechanism independent of the utilized technology. To be able to deliver the services independently in the different regions, an individual Docker Registry storing the Docker images in a S3 bucket was implemented in each region. S3 is a service that enables the storage of large file on Amazon server.

If you intend to use Cloud Services, you have to address the question of whether you want to use the managed services of a cloud provider or develop and run the infrastructure yourself. zanox decided to use the managed services of a cloud provider because building and administrating proprietary infrastructure modules does not provide any business value. The EC2 computers of the Amazon portfolio are pure infrastructure. IAM, on the other hand, offers comprehensive security mechanisms. In the deployed services the AWS Java SDK is used, which enables it, in combination with IAM roles for EC2,[18] to generate applications that are able to access the managed services of AWS without using explicit credentials. During initial bootstrapping an IAM role containing the necessary permissions is assigned to an EC2 instance. Via the Metadata Service[19] the AWS SDK is given the necessary credentials. This enables the application to access the managed services defined in the role. Thus, an application can be that sends metrics to the monitoring system Amazon Cloud Watch and events to the data streaming processing solution Amazon Kinesis without having to roll out explicit credentials together with the application.

All applications are equipped with REST interfaces for heartbeats and health checks so that the application itself as well as the infrastructure necessary for the availability of the application can be monitored at all times: Each application uses health checks to monitor the infrastructure components it uses. Application scaling is implemented via Elastic Load Balancing (ELB) and AutoScaling[20] to be able to achieve a fine-grained application depending on the concrete load. AutoScaling starts additional EC2 instances if needed. ELB distributes the load between the instances. The AWS ELB service is not only suitable for web applications working with HTTP protocols but for all types of applications. A health check can also be implemented based on a TCP protocol without HTTP. This is even simpler than an HTTP healthcheck.

Still the developer team decided to implement the ELB healthchecks via HTTP for all services to achieve the goal that they all behave exactly the same, independent of the implemented logic, the used frameworks, and the language. It is also quite

---

18. https://docs.aws.amazon.com/AWSEC2/latest/UserGuide/iam-roles-for-amazon-ec2.html

19. https://docs.aws.amazon.com/AWSEC2/latest/UserGuide/ec2-instance-metadata.html

20. https://docs.aws.amazon.com/AutoScaling/latest/DeveloperGuide/as-add-elb-healthcheck.html

possible that in the future applications that do not run on JVM and, for instance, use Go or Python as programming languages, are deployed in AWS.

For the ELB healthcheck zanox uses the application heartbeat URL. As a result, traffic is only directed to the application respectively potentially necessary infrastructure scaling operations are only performed once the EC2 instance with the application has properly been started and the heartbeat was successfully monitored.

For application monitoring Amazon CloudWatch is a good choice as CloudWatch alarms can be used to define scaling events for the AutoScaling Policies, that is, the infrastructure scales automatically based on metrics. For this purpose, EC2 basis metrics like CPU can be used, for instance. Alternatively, it is possible to send your own metrics to CloudWatch. For this purpose, this project uses a fork of the project jmxtrans-agent,[21] which uses the CloudWatch API to send JMX metrics to the monitoring system. JMX (Java Management Extension) is the standard for monitoring and metrics in the Java world. Besides metrics are sent from within the application (i.e., from within the business logic) using the library Coda Hale Metrics[22] and a module for the CloudWatch integration by Blacklocus.[23]

A slightly different approach is chosen for the logging: In a cloud environment it is never possible to rule out that a server instance is abruptly terminated. This often causes the sudden loss of data that are stored on the server. Log files are an example for that. For this reason, a logstash-forwarder[24] runs in parallel to the core application on the server for sending the log entries to our ELK-Service running in our own data center. This stack consists of Elasticsearch for storage, Logstash for parsing the log data, and Kibana for UI-based analysis. ELK is an acronym for Elasticsearch, Logstash, und Kibana. In addition, a UUID is calculated for each request respectively each event in our HTTP layer so that log entries can still be assigned to events after EC2 instances have ceased to exist.

Conclusion

The pattern of microservices architectures fits well to the dynamic approach of Amazon Cloud if the architecture is well designed and implemented. The clear advantage over implementing in your own data center is the infrastructure flexibility. This makes it possible to implement a nearly endlessly scalable architecture, which is, in addition, very cost efficient.

---

21. https://github.com/SaschaMoellering/jmxtrans-agent
22. https://dropwizard.github.io/metrics/
23. https://github.com/blacklocus/metrics-cloudwatch
24. https://github.com/elastic/logstash-forwarder

13.15 Conclusion

The technologies used in the example provide a very good foundation for implementing a microservices architecture with Java. Essentially, the example is based on the Netflix Stack, which has demonstrated its efficacy for years already in one of the largest websites.

The example demonstrates the interplay of different technologies for Service Discovery, Load Balancing, and resilience—as well as an approach for testing microservices and for their execution in Docker containers. The example is not meant to be directly useable in a production context but is first of all designed to be very easy to set up and get running. This entails a number of compromises. However, the example serves very well as the foundation for further experiments and the testing of ideas.

In addition, the example demonstrates a Docker-based application deployment, which is a good foundation for microservices.

Essential Points

- Spring, Spring Boot, Spring Cloud, and the Netflix Stack offer a well-integrated stack for Java-based microservices. These technologies solve all typical challenges posed during the development of microservices.

- Docker-based deployment is easy to implement, and in conjunction with Docker Machine and Docker Compose, can be used for deployment in the Cloud, too.

- The example application shows how to test microservices using consumer-driven contract tests and stubs without special tools. However, for real-life projects tools might be more useful.

Try and Experiment

Add Log Analysis

The log analysis of all log files is important for running a microservice system. At https://github.com/ewolff/user-registration-V2 an example project is provided. The subdirectory **log-analysis** contains a setup for an ELK (Elasticsearch, Logstash und Kibana) stack-based log analysis. Use this approach to add a log analysis to the microservice example.

(continued)

Add Monitoring

In addition, the example project from the continuous delivery book contains graphite an installation of Graphite for monitoring in the subdirectory. Adapt this installation for the microservice example.

Rewrite a Service

Rewrite one of the services in a different programming language. Use the consumer-driven contract tests (see sections 13.13 and 10.7) to protect the implementation. Make use of a sidecar for the integration into the technology stack (see section 13.12).

Chapter 14

Technologies for Nanoservices

Section 14.1 discusses the advantages of nanoservices and why nanoservices can be useful. Section 14.2 defines nanoservices and distinguishes them from microservices. Section 14.3 focuses on Amazon Lambda, a cloud technology that can be used with Python, JavaScript, or Java. Here each function call is billed instead of renting virtual machines or application servers. OSGi (section 14.4) modularizes Java applications and also provides services. Another Java technology for nanoservices is Java EE (section 14.5), if used correctly. Vert.x, another option, (section 14.6) also runs on the JVM but supports a broad variety of programming languages in addition to Java. Section 14.7 focuses on the programming language Erlang, which is quite old. The architecture of Erlang enables the implementation of nanoservices. Seneca (section 14.8) has a similar approach as Erlang but is based on JavaScript and has been specially designed for the development of nanoservices.

The term "microservice" is not uniformly defined. Some people believe microservices should be extremely small services—that is, ten to a hundred lines of code (LoC). This book calls such services "nanoservices." The distinction between microservices and nanoservices is the focus of this chapter. A suitable technology is an essential prerequisite for the implementation of small services. If the technology, for instance, combines several services into one operating system process, the resource utilization per service can be decreased and the service rollout in production facilitated. This decreases the expenditure per service, which enables support of a large number of small nanoservices.

14.1 Why Nanoservices?

Nanoservices are well in line with the previously discussed size limits of microservices: Their size is below the maximum size, which was defined in section 3.1 and depends, for instance, on the number of team members. In addition, a microservice should be small enough to still be understood by a developer. With suitable technologies the technical limits for the minimal size of a microservice, which were discussed in section 3.1, can be further reduced.

Very small modules are easier to understand and therefore easier to maintain and change. Besides, smaller microservices can be replaced more easily by new implementations or a rewrite. Accordingly, systems consisting of minimally sized nanoservices can more easily be developed further.

There are systems that successfully employ nanoservices. In fact, in practice it is rather the too large modules that are the source of problems and prevent the successful further development of a system. Each functionality could be implemented in its own microservice—each class or function could become a separate microservice. Section 9.2 demonstrated that it can be sensible for CQRS to implement a microservice that only reads data of a certain type. Writing the same type of data can already be implemented in another microservice. So microservices can really have a pretty small scope.

Minimum Size of Microservices is Limited

What are reasons against very tiny microservices? Section 3.1 identified factors that render microservices below a certain size not practicable:

- The expenditure for infrastructure increases. When each microservice is a separate process and requires infrastructure, such as an application server and monitoring, the expenditure necessary for running hundreds or even thousands of microservices becomes too large. Therefore, nanoservices require technologies that make it possible to keep the expenditure for infrastructure per individual service as small as possible. In addition, a low resource utilization is desirable. The individual services should consume as little memory and CPU as possible.

- In the case of very small services a lot of communication via the network is required. That has a negative influence on system performance. Consequently, when working with nanoservices communication between the services should not occur via the network. This might result in less technological freedom. When all nanoservices run in a single process, they are usually required to employ the same technology. Such an approach also affects system robustness. When several services run in the same process, it is much more difficult to isolate them from each other. A nanoservice can use up so many resources that other nanoservices do not operate error free anymore. When two nanoservices run in the same process, the operating system cannot intervene in such situations. In addition, a crash of a nanoservice can result in the failure of additional nanoservices. If the processes crash, their crash will affect all nanoservices running in the same process.

The technical compromises can have a negative effect on the properties of nanoservices. In any case the essential feature of microservices has to be maintained—namely, the independent deployment of the individual services.

Compromises

In the end the main task is to identify technologies that minimize the overhead per nanoservice and at the same time preserve as many advantages of microservices as possible.

In detail the following points need to be achieved:

- The expenditure for infrastructure such as monitoring and deployment has to be kept low. It has to be possible to bring a new nanoservice into production without much effort and to have it immediately displayed in monitoring.

- Resource utilization, for instance in regard to memory, should be as low as possible to enable a large number of nanoservices with little hardware. This does not only make the production environment cheaper but also facilitates the generation of test environments.

- Communication should be possible without the network. This does not only improve latency and performance but increases the reliability of the communication between nanoservices because it is not influenced by network failures.

- Concerning isolation, a compromise has to be found. The nanoservices should be isolated from each other so that one nanoservice cannot cause another nanoservice to fail. Otherwise, a single nanoservice might cause the entire system to break down. However, achieving a perfect isolation might be less important than having a lower expenditure for infrastructure, a low resource utilization, and the other advantages of nanoservices.

- Using nanoservices can limit the choice of programming languages, platforms, and frameworks. Microservices, on the other hand, enable, in principle, a free choice of technology.

Desktop Applications

Nanoservices enable the use of microservice approaches in areas in which microservices themselves are hardly useable. One example is the possibility of dividing a desktop application in nanoservices. OSGi (section 14.4) is, for instance, used for desktop and even for embedded applications. A desktop application consisting of microservices is, on the other hand, probably too difficult to deploy to really use it for desktop applications. Each microservice has to be deployed by itself, and that is hardly possible for a large number of desktop clients—some of which might even be located in other companies. Moreover, the integration of several microservices into a coherent desktop application is hard—in particular if they are implemented as completely separated processes.

14.2 Nanoservices: Definition

A nanoservice differs from a microservice. It compromises in certain areas. One of these areas is isolation: multiple nanoservices run on a single virtual machine or in a single process. Another area is technology freedom: nanoservices use a shared platform or programming language. Only with these limitations does the use of nanoservices become feasible. The infrastructure can be so efficient that a much larger number of services is possible. This enables the individual services to be smaller. A nanoservice might comprise only a few lines of code.

However, by no means may the technology require a joint deployment of nanoservices, for independent deployment is the central characteristic of microservices and also nanoservices. Independent deployment constitutes the basis for the essential advantages of microservices: Teams that can work independently, a strong modularization, and as consequence a sustainable development.

Therefore, nanoservices can be defined as follows:

- Nanoservices *compromise* in regard to some microservice properties such as isolation and technology freedom. However, nanoservices still have to be independently deployable.

- The compromises enable a *larger number* of services and therefore for *smaller services*. Nanoservices can contain just a few lines of code.

- To achieve this, nanoservices use *highly efficient runtime environments*. These exploit the restrictions of nanoservices in order to enable more and smaller services.

Thus, nanoservices depend a lot on the employed technologies. The technology enables certain compromises in nanoservices and therefore nanoservices of a certain size. Therefore, this chapter is geared to different technologies to explain the possible varieties of nanoservices.

The objective of nanoservices is to amplify a number of advantages of microservices. Having even smaller deployment units decreases the deployment risk further, facilitates deployment even more, and achieves better, understandable, and replaceable services. In addition, the domain architecture will change: A *Bounded Context* that might consist of one or a few microservices will now comprise a multitude of nanoservices that each implement a very narrowly defined functionality.

The difference between microservices and nanoservices is not strictly defined: If two microservices are deployed in the same virtual machine, efficiency increases, and isolation is compromised. The two microservices now share an operating system instance and a virtual machine. When one of the microservices uses up the resources of the virtual machine, the other microservice running on the same virtual machine will also fail. This is the compromise in terms of isolation. So in a sense these microservices are already nanoservices.

By the way, the term "nanoservice" is not used very much. This book uses the term "nanoservice" to make it plain that there are modularizations that are similar to microservices but differ when it comes to detail, thereby enabling even smaller services. To distinguish these technologies with their compromises clearly from "real" microservices the term "nanoservice" is useful.

14.3 Amazon Lambda

Amazon Lambda[1] is a service in the Amazon Cloud. It is available worldwide in all Amazon computing centers.

Amazon Lambda can execute individual functions that are written in Python, JavaScript with Node.js, or Java 8 with OpenJDK. The code of these functions does not have dependencies on Amazon Lambda. Access to the operating system is possible. The computers the code is executed on contain the Amazon Web Services SDK as well as ImageMagick for image manipulations. These functionalities can be used by Amazon Lambda applications. Besides, additional libraries can be installed.

Amazon Lambda functions have to start quickly because it can happen that they are started for each request. Therefore, the functions also may not hold a state.

---

1. http://aws.amazon.com/lambda

Thus there are no costs when there are no requests that cause an execution of the functions. Each request is billed individually. Currently, the first million requests are free. The price depends on the required RAM and processing time.

Calling Lambda Functions

Lambda functions can be called directly via a command line tool. The processing occurs asynchronously. The functions can return results via different Amazon functionalities. For this purpose, the Amazon Cloud contains messaging solutions such as Simple Notification Service (SNS) or Simple Queue Service (SQS).

The following events can trigger a call of a Lambda function:

- In Simple Storage Service (S3) large files can be stored and downloaded. Such actions trigger events to which an Amazon Lambda function can react.

- Amazon Kinesis can be used to administrate and distribute data streams. This technology is meant for the real time processing of large data amounts. Lambda can be called as reaction to new data in these streams.

- With Amazon Cognito it is possible to use Amazon Lambda to provide simple back ends for mobile applications.

- The API Gateway provides a way to implement REST APIs using Amazon Lambda.

- Furthermore, it is possible to have Amazon Lambda functions be called at regular intervals.

- As a reaction to a notification in Simple Notification Service (SNS), an Amazon Lambda function can be executed. As there are many services which can provide such notifications, this makes Amazon Lambda useable in many scenarios.

- DynamoDB is a database within the Amazon Cloud. In case of changes to the database it can call Lambda functions. So Lambda functions essentially become database triggers.

Evaluation for Nanoservices

Amazon Lambda enables the independent deployment of different functions without problems. They can also bring their own libraries along.

The technological expenditure for infrastructure is minimal when using this technology: A new version of an Amazon Lambda function can easily be deployed with a command line tool. Monitoring is also simple: the functions are immediately integrated into Cloud Watch. Cloud Watch is offered by Amazon to create metrics of Cloud applications and to consolidate and monitor log files. In addition, alarms can be defined based on these data that can be forwarded by SMS or email. Since all Amazon services can be contacted via an API, monitoring or deployment can be automated and integrated into their own infrastructures.

Amazon Lambda provides integration with the different Amazon services such as S3, Kinesis, and DynamoDB. It is also easily possible to contact an Amazon Lambda function via REST using the API Gateway. However, Amazon Lambda exacts that Node.js, Python, or Java are used. This profoundly limits the technology freedom.

Amazon Lambda offers an excellent isolation of functions. This is also necessary since the platform is used by many different users. It would not be acceptable for a Lambda function of one user to negatively influence the Lambda functions of other users.

Conclusion

Amazon Lambda enables you to implement extremely small services. The overhead for the individual services is very small. Independent deployment is easily possible. A Python, JavaScript, or Java function is the smallest deployment unit supported by Amazon Lambda—it is hardly possible to make them any smaller. Even if there is a multitude of Python, Java, or JavaScript functions, the expenditure for the deployments remains relatively low.

Amazon Lambda is a part of the Amazon ecosystem. Therefore, it can be supplemented by technologies like Amazon Elastic Beanstalk. There, microservices can run that can be larger and written in other languages. In addition, a combination with Elastic Computing Cloud (EC2) is possible. EC2 offers virtual machines on which any software can be installed. Moreover, there is a broad choice in regard to databases and other services that can be used with little additional effort. Amazon Lambda defines itself as a supplement of this tool kit. In the end one of the crucial advantages of the Amazon Cloud is that nearly every possible infrastructure is available and can easily be used. Thus developers can concentrate on the development of specific functionalities while most standard components can just be rented.

Try and Experiment

- There is a comprehensive tutorial[2] that illustrates how to use Amazon Lambda. It does not only demonstrate simple scenarios, but it also shows how to use complex mechanisms such as different Node.js libraries, implementing REST services, or how to react to different events in the Amazon system. Amazon offers cost-free quotas of most services to new customers. In case of Lambda each customer gets such a large free quota that it is fully sufficient for tests and first getting to know the technology. Also note that the first million calls during a month are free. However, you should check the current pricing.[3]

---

2. http://aws.amazon.com/lambda/getting-started/
3. https://aws.amazon.com/lambda/pricing/

14.4 OSGi

OSGi[4] is a standard with many different implementations.[5] Embedded systems often use OSGi. Also the development environment Eclipse is based on OSGi, and many Java desktop applications use the Eclipse framework. OSGi defines a modularization within the JVM (Java Virtual Machine). Even though Java enables a division of code into classes or packages, there is no modular concept for larger units.

The OSGi Module System

OSGi supplements Java by such a module system. To do so OSGi introduces bundles into the Java world. Bundles are based on Java's JAR files, which comprise code of multiple classes. Bundles have a number of additional entries in the file **META-INF/ MANIFEST.MF**, which each JAR file should contain. These entries define which classes and interfaces the bundle exports. Other bundles can import these classes and interfaces. Therefore OSGi extends Java with a quite sophisticated module concept without inventing entirely new concepts.

---

4. http://www.osgi.org/
5. http://en.wikipedia.org/wiki/OSGi#Current_framework_implementations

Listing 14.1 *OSGi MANIFEST.MF*

```
Bundle-Name: A service
Bundle-SymbolicName: com.ewolff.service
Bundle-Description: A small service
Bundle-ManifestVersion: 2
Bundle-Version: 1.0.0
Bundle-Acltivator: com.ewolff.service.Activator
Export-Package: com.ewolff.service.interfaces;version="1.0.0"
Import-Package: com.ewolff.otherservice.interfaces;
version="1.3.0"
```

Listing 14.1 shows an example of a **MANIFEST.MF** file. It contains the description and name of the bundle and the bundle activator. This Java class is executed upon the start of the bundle and can initialize the bundle. `Export-Package` indicates which Java packages are provided by this bundle. All classes and interfaces of these packages are available to other bundles. `Import-Package` serves to import packages from another bundle. The packages can also be versioned.

In addition to interfaces and classes bundles can also export services. However, an entry in **MANIFEST.MF** is not sufficient for this. Code has to be written. Services are only Java objects in the end. Other bundles can import and use the services. Also calling the services happens in the code.

Bundles can be installed, started, stopped, and uninstalled at runtime. Therefore, bundles are easy to update: Stop and uninstall the old version, then install a new version and start. However, if a bundle exports classes or interfaces and another bundle uses these, an update is not so simple anymore. All bundles that use classes or interfaces of the old bundle and now want to use the newly installed bundle have to be restarted.

Handling Bundles in Practice

Sharing code is by far not as important for microservices as the use of services. Nevertheless at least the interface of the services has to be offered to other bundles.

In practice a procedure has been established where a bundle only exports the interface code of the service as classes and Java interfaces. Another bundle contains the implementation of the service. The classes of the implementation are not exported. The service implementation is exported as OSGi service. To use the service a bundle has to import the interface code from the one bundle and the service from the other bundle (see Figure 14.1).

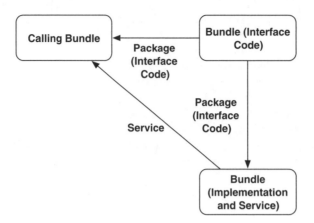

Figure 14.1 *OSGi Service, Implementation, and Interface Code*

OSGi enables restarting services. With the described approach the implementation of the service can be exchanged without having to restart other bundles. These bundles only import the Java interfaces and classes of the interface code. That code does not change for a new service implementation so that restarting is not necessary anymore. That way the access to services can be implemented in such a manner that the new version of the service is, in fact, used.

With the aid of OSGi blueprints[6] or OSGi declarative services[7] these details can be abstracted away when dealing with the OSGi service model. This facilitates the handling of OSGi. These technologies, for instance, render it much easier to handle the restart of a service or its temporary failure during the restart of a bundle.

An independent deployment of services is possible but also laborious since interface code and service implementation have to be contained in different bundles. This model allows only changes to the implementation. Modifications of the interface code are more complex. In such a case the bundles using a service have to be restarted because they have to reload the interface.

In reality OSGi systems are often completely reinstalled for these reasons instead of modifying individual bundles. An Eclipse update, for instance, often entails a restart. A complete reinstallation also facilitates the reproduction of the environment. When an OSGi system is dynamically changed, at some point it will be in a state that nobody is able to reproduce. However, modifying individual bundles is an essential prerequisite for implementing the nanoservice approach with OSGi.

---

6. https://osgi.org/download/r6/osgi.cmpn-6.0.0.pdf

7. https://osgi.org/download/r6/osgi.cmpn-6.0.0.pdf

Independent deployment is an essential property of a nanoservice. OSGi compromises this essential property.

Evaluation for Nanoservices

OSGi has a positive effect on Java projects in regard to architecture. The bundles are usually relatively small so that the individual bundles are easy to understand. In addition, the split into bundles forces the developers and architects to think about the relationships between the bundles and to define them in the configurations of the bundles. Other dependencies between bundles are not possible within the system. Normally, this leads to a very clean architecture with clear and intended dependencies.

However, OSGi does not offer technological freedom: It is based on the JVM and therefore can only be used with Java or JVM-based languages. For example, it is nearly impossible that an OSGi bundle brings along its own database because databases are normally not written in Java. For such cases additional solutions alongside the OSGi infrastructure have to be found.

For some Java technologies an integration with OSGi is difficult since loading Java classes works differently without OSGi. Moreover, many popular Java application servers do not support OSGi for deployed applications so that changing code at runtime is not supported in such environments. The infrastructure has to be specially adapted for OSGi.

Furthermore, the bundles are not fully isolated: When a bundle uses a lot of CPU or causes the JVM to crash, the other bundles in the same JVM will be affected. Failures can occur, for instance, due to a memory leak, which causes more and more memory to be allocated due to an error until the system breaks down. Such errors easily arise due to blunders.

On the other hand, the bundles can locally communicate due to OSGi. Distributed communication is also possible with different protocols. Moreover, the bundles share a JVM, which reduces, for instance, the memory utilization.

Solutions for monitoring are likewise present in the different OSGi implementations.

Conclusion

OSGi leads, first of all, to restrictions in regard to technological freedom. It restricts the project to Java technologies. In practice the independent deployment of the bundles is hard to implement. Interface changes are especially poorly supported. Besides bundles are not well isolated from each other. On the other hand, bundles can easily interact via local calls.

Try and experiment

- Get familiar with OSGi with, for instance, the aid of a tutorial.[8]

- Create a concept for the distribution into bundles and services for a part of a system you know.

- If you had to implement the system with OSGi, which additional technologies (databases etc.) would you have to use? How would you handle this?

---

8. http://www.vogella.com/tutorials/OSGi/article.html

14.5 Java EE

Java EE[9] is a standard from the Java field. It comprises different APIs such as JSF (Java ServerFaces), Servlet, and JSP (Java Server Pages) for web applications; JPA (Java Persistence API) for persistence; or JTA (Java Transaction API) for transactions. Additionally, Java EE defines a deployment model. Web applications can be packaged into WAR files (Web ARchive), JAR files (Java ARchive) can contain logic components like Enterprise Java Beans (EJBs), and EARs (Enterprise ARchives) can comprise a collection of JARs and WARs. All these components are deployed in one application server. The application server implements the Java EE APIs and offers, for instance, support for HTTP, threads, and network connections and also support for accessing databases.

This section deals with WARs and the deployment model of Java EE application servers. Chapter 13, "Example of a Microservice-Based Architecture," already described in detail a Java system that does not require an application server. Instead it directly starts a Java application on the Java Virtual Machine (JVM). The application is packaged in a JAR file and contains the entire infrastructure. This deployment is called Fat JAR deployment, because the application, including the entire infrastructure, is contained in one single JAR. The example from Chapter 13 uses Spring Boot, which also supports a number of Java EE APIs such as JAX-RS for REST. Dropwizard[10] also offers such a JAR model. It is actually focused on JAX RS-based REST web services; however, it can also support other applications. Wildfly Swarm[11] is a variant of the Java EE server Wildfly, which also supports such a deployment model.

---

9. http://www.oracle.com/technetwork/java/javaee/overview/index.html

10. https://dropwizard.github.io/dropwizard/

11. http://github.com/wildfly-swarm/

Nanoservices with Java EE

A Fat JAR deployment utilizes too many resources for nanoservices. In a Java EE application server, multiple WARs can be deployed, thereby saving resources. Each WAR can be accessed via its own URL. Furthermore, each WAR can be individually deployed. This enables bringing each nanoservice individually into production.

However, the separation between WARs is not optimal:

- Memory and CPU are collectively used by all nanoservices. When a nanoservice uses a lot of CPU or memory, this can interfere with other nanoservices. A crash of one nanoservice propagates to all other nanoservices.

- In practice, redeployment of a WAR causes memory leaks if it is not possible to remove the entire application from memory. Therefore, in practice the independent deployment of individual nanoservices is hard to achieve.

- In contrast to OSGi the ClassLoaders of the WARs are completely separate. There is no possibility for accessing the code of other nanoservices.

- Because of the separation of the code, WARs can only communicate via HTTP or REST. Local method calls are not possible.

Since multiple nanoservices share an application server and a JVM, this solution is more efficient than the Fat JAR deployment of individual microservices in their own JVM as described in Chapter 13. The nanoservices use a shared heap and therefore use less memory. However, scaling works only by starting more application servers. Each of the application servers contains all nanoservices. All nanoservices have to be scaled collectively. It is not possible to scale individual nanoservices.

The technology choice is restricted to JVM technologies. Besides all technologies are excluded that do not work with the servlet model, such as Vert.x (section 14.6) or Play.

Microservices with Java EE?

For microservices Java EE can also be an option: Theoretically it would be possible to run each microservice in its own application server. In this case an application server has to be installed and configured in addition to the application. The version of the application server and its configuration have to fit to the version of the application. For Fat JAR deployment there is no need for a specific configuration of the application server because it is part of the Fat JAR and therefore configured just like the application. This additional complexity of the application server is not counterbalanced by any advantage. Since deployment and monitoring of the application server only work for Java applications, these features can only be used in a microservices-based architecture when the technology choice is restricted to Java technologies. In general, application servers have hardly any advantages[12]—especially for microservices.

An Example

The application from Chapter 13 is also available with the Java EE deployment model.[13] Figure 14.2 provides an overview of the example: There are three WARs, which comprise "Order," "Customer," and "Catalog." They communicate with each other via REST. When "Customer" fails, "Order" would also fail in the host since "Order" communicates only with this single "Customer" instance. To achieve better availability, the access would have to be rerouted to other "Customer" instances.

A customer can use the UI of the nanoservices from the outside via HTML/HTTP. The code contains only small modifications compared to the solution from Chapter 13. The Netflix libraries have been removed. On the other hand, the application has been extended with support for servlet containers.

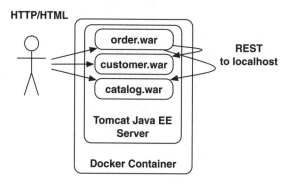

Figure 14.2 *Example Application with Java EE Nanoservices*

12. http://jaxenter.com/java-application-servers-dead-1-111928.html

13. https://github.com/ewolff/war-demo

14.6 Vert.x

Vert.x [15] is a framework containing numerous interesting approaches. Although it runs on the Java Virtual Machine, it supports many different programming languages—such as Java, Scala, Clojure, Groovy, and Ceylon as well as JavaScript, Ruby, or Python. A Vert.x system is built from Verticles. They receive events and can return messages.

---

15. http://vertx.io/

Listing 14.2 shows a simple Vert.x Verticle, which only returns the incoming messages. The code creates a server. When a client connects to the server, a callback is called, and the server creates a pump. The pump serves to transfer data from a source to a target. In the example source and target are identical.

The application only becomes active when a client connects, and the callback is called. Likewise, the pump only becomes active when new data are available from the client. Such events are processed by the event loop, which calls the Verticles. The Verticles then have to process the events. An event loop is a thread. Usually one event loop is started per CPU core so that the event loops are processed in parallel. An event loop and thus a thread running on a single CPU core can support an arbitrary number of network connections. Events of all connections can be processed in a single event loop. Therefore, Vert.x is also suitable for applications that have to handle a large number of network connections.

Listing 14.2 *Simple Java Vert.x Echo Verticle*

```
public class EchoServer extends Verticle {

  public void start() {
    vertx.createNetServer().connectHandler(new Handler() {
      public void handle(final NetSocket socket) {
        Pump.createPump(socket, socket).start();
      }
    }).listen(1234);
  }
}
```

As described Vert.x supports different programming languages. Listing 14.3 shows the same Echo Verticle in JavaScript. The code adheres to JavaScript conventions and uses, for instance, a JavaScript function for callback. Vert.x has a layer for each programming language that adapts the basic functionality in such a way that it seems like a native library for the respective programming language.

Listing 14.3 *Simple JavaScript Vert.x Echo Verticle*

```
var vertx = require('vertx')

vertx.createNetServer().connectHandler(function(sock) {
  new vertx.Pump(sock, sock).start();
}).listen(1234);
```

Vert.x modules can contain multiple Verticles in different languages. Verticles and modules can communicate with each other via an event bus. The messages on the event bus use JSON as data format. The event bus can be distributed onto multiple servers. In this manner Vert.x supports distribution and can implement high availability by starting modules on other servers. Besides the Verticles and modules are loosely coupled since they only exchange messages. Vert.x also offers support for other messaging systems and can also communicate with HTTP and REST. Therefore, it is relatively easy to integrate Vert.x systems into microservice-based systems.

Modules can be individually deployed and also removed again. Since the modules communicate with each other via events, modules can easily be replaced by new modules at runtime. They only have to process the same messages. A module can implement a nanoservice. Modules can be started in new nodes so that the failure of a JVM can be compensated.

Vert.x also supports Fat JARs where the application brings all necessary libraries along. This is useful for microservices since this means that the application brings all dependencies along and is easier to deploy. For nanoservices this approach is not so useful because the approach consumes too many resources—deploying multiple Vert.x modules in one JVM is a better option for nanoservices.

Conclusion

Via the independent module deployment and the loose coupling by the event bus Vert.x supports multiple nanoservices within a JVM. However, a crash of the JVM, a memory leak, or blocking the event loop would affect all modules and Verticles in the JVM. On the other hand, Vert.x supports many different programming languages—in spite of the restriction to JVM. This is not only a theoretical option. In fact, Vert.x aims at being easily useable in all supported languages. Vert.x presumes that the entire application is written in a nonblocking manner. However, there is the possibility to execute blocking tasks in Worker Verticles. They use separate thread pools so that they do not influence the nonblocking Verticles. Therefore even code that does not support the Vert.x nonblocking approach can still be used in a Vert.x system. This enables even greater technological freedom.

Try and Experiment

The Vert.x homepage[16] offers an easy start to developing with Vert.x. It demonstrates how a web server can be implemented and executed with different programming languages. The modules in the example use Java and Maven.[17] There are also complex examples in other programming languages.[18]

---

16. http://vertx.io/
17. https://github.com/vert-x3/vertx-examples/tree/master/maven-simplest
18. https://github.com/vert-x/vertx-examples

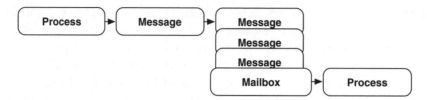

Figure 14.3 *Communication between Erlang Processes*

14.7 Erlang

Erlang[19] is a functional programming language that is, first of all, used in combination with the Open Telecom Platform (OTP) framework. Originally, Erlang was developed for telecommunication. In this field applications have to be very reliable. Meanwhile Erlang is employed in all areas that profit from its strengths. Erlang uses a virtual machine similar to Java as a runtime environment, which is called BEAM (Bogdan/ Björn's Erlang Abstract Machine).

Erlang's strengths are, first of all, its resilience against failures and the possibility to let systems run for years. This is only possible via dynamic software updates. At the same time, Erlang has a lightweight concept for parallelism. Erlang uses the concept of processes for parallel computing. These processes are not related to operating system processes and are even more lightweight than operating system threads. In an Erlang system millions of processes can run that are all isolated from each other.

Another factor contributing to the isolation is the asynchronous communication. Processes in an Erlang system communicate with each other via messages. Messages are sent to the mailbox of a process (see Figure 14.3). In one process only one message is processed at a time. This facilitates the handling of parallelism: there is parallel execution because many messages can be handled at the same time. But each process takes care of only one message at a time. Parallelism is achieved because there are multiple processes. The functional approach of the language, which attempts to get by without a state, fits well to this model. This approach corresponds to the Verticles in Vert.x and their communication via the event bus.

Listing 14.4 shows a simple Erlang server that returns the received message. It is defined in its own module. The module exports the function `loop`, which does not have any parameters. The function receives a message `Msg` from a node `From` and then returns the same message to this node. The operator "!" serves for sending the message. Afterwards the function is called again and waits for the next message. Exactly the same code can also be used for being called by another computer via the

---

19. http://www.erlang.org/

network. Local messages and messages via the network are processed by the same mechanisms.

Listing 14.4 *An Erlang Echo Server*

```
module(server).
-export([loop/0]).
loop() ->
    receive
        {From, Msg} ->
            From ! Msg,
            loop()
end.
```

Due to the sending of messages, Erlang systems are especially robust. Erlang makes use of "Let It Crash." An individual process is just restarted when problems occur. This is the responsibility of the supervisor, a process that is specifically dedicated to monitoring other processes and restarting them if necessary. The supervisor itself is also monitored and restarted in case of problems. This way a tree is created in Erlang that in the end prepares the system in case processes should fail (see Figure 14.4).

Since the Erlang process model is so lightweight, restarting a process is done rapidly. When the state is stored in other components, there will also be no information loss. The remainder of the system is not affected by the failure of the process: As the communication is asynchronous, the other processes can handle the higher latency caused by the restart. In practice this approach has proven very reliable. Erlang systems are very robust and still easy to develop.

This approach is based on the actor model:[20] Actors communicate with each other via asynchronous messages. As a response they can themselves send messages,

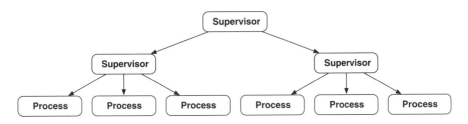

Figure 14.4 *Monitoring in Erlang Systems*

---

20. http://en.wikipedia.org/wiki/Actor_model

start new actors, or change their behavior for the next messages. Erlang's processes correspond to actors.

In addition, there are easy possibilities to monitor Erlang systems. Erlang itself has built-in functions that can monitor memory utilization or the state of the mailboxes. OTP offers for this purpose the operations and maintenance support (OAM), which can, for instance, also be integrated into SNMP systems.

Since Erlang solves typical problems arising upon the implementation of microservices like resilience, it supports the implementation of microservices[21] quite well. In that case a microservice is a system written in Erlang that internally consists of multiple processes.

However, the services can also get smaller; each process in an Erlang system could be considered as a nanoservice. It can be deployed independently of the others, even during runtime. Furthermore, Erlang supports operating system processes. In that case they are also integrated into the supervisor hierarchy and restarted in case of a breakdown. This means that any operating system process written in any language might become a part of an Erlang system and its architecture.

Evaluation for Nanoservices

As discussed an individual process in Erlang can be viewed as a nanoservice. The expenditure for the infrastructure is relatively small in that case: Monitoring is possible with built-in Erlang functions. The same is true for deployment. Since the processes share a BEAM instance, the overhead for a single process is not very high. In addition, it is possible for the processes to exchange messages without having to communicate via the network and therefore with little overhead. The isolation of processes is also implemented.

Finally, even processes in other languages can be added to an Erlang system. For this purpose, an operating system process that can be implemented in an arbitrary language is put under the control of Erlang. The operating system process can, for instance, be safeguarded by "Let It Crash." This enables integration of practically all technologies into Erlang—even if they run in a separate process.

On the other hand, Erlang is not very common. The consequent functional approach also needs getting used to. Finally, the Erlang syntax is not very intuitive for many developers.

---

21. https://www.innoq.com/en/talks/2015/01/talk-microservices-erlang-otp/

Try and Experiment

- A very simple example[22] is based on the code from this section and demonstrates how communication between nodes is possible. You can use it to get a basic understanding of Erlang.

- There is a very nice tutorial [23] for Erlang, which also treats deployment and operation. With the aid of the information from the tutorial the example [24] can be supplemented by a supervisor.

- An alternative language out of the Erlang ecosystem is Elixir.[25] Elixir has a different syntax but also profits from the concepts of OTP. Elixir is much simpler to learn than Erlang and thus lends itself to a first start.

- There are many other implementations of the actor model.[26] It is worthwhile to look more closely before deciding whether such technologies are also useful for the implementation of microservices or nanoservices and which advantages might be associated. Akka from the Scala/Java area might be of interest here.

---

22. https://github.com/ewolff/erlang-example/
23. http://learnyousomeerlang.com/
24. https://github.com/ewolff/erlang-example/
25. http://elixir-lang.org/
26. http://en.wikipedia.org/wiki/Actor_model

14.8 Seneca

Seneca[27] is based on Node.js and accordingly uses JavaScript on the server. Node.js has a programming model where one operating system process can take care of many tasks in parallel. To achieve this there is an event loop that handles the events. When a message enters the system via a network connection, the system will first wait until the event loop is free. Then the event loop processes the message. The processing has to be fast since the loop is blocked, otherwise resulting in long waiting times for all other messages. For this reason, the response of other servers may in no case be waited for in the event loop. That would block the system for too long. The interaction with other systems has to be implemented in such a way that the interaction is

---

27. http://senecajs.org/

only initiated. Then the event loop is freed to handle other events. Only when the response of the other system arrives is it processed by the event loop. Then the event loop calls a callback that has been registered upon the initiation of the interaction. This model is similar to the approaches used by Vert.x and Erlang.

Seneca introduces a mechanism in Node.js that enables processing of commands. Patterns of commands are defined that cause certain code to be executed.

Communicating via such commands is also easy to do via the network. Listing 14.5 shows a server that calls **seneca.add()**. Thereby a new pattern and code for handling events with this pattern are defined. To the command with the component **cmd: "echo"** a function reacts. It reads out the **value** from the command and puts it into the **value** parameter of the function **callback**. Then the function **callback** is called. With **seneca.listen()** the server is started and listens to commands from the network.

Listing 14.5 *Seneca Server*

```
var seneca = require("seneca")()

seneca.add( {cmd: "echo"}, function(args,callback){
    callback(null,{value:args.value})
})


seneca.listen()
```

The client in Listing 14.6 sends all commands that cannot be processed locally via the network to the server. **seneca.client().seneca.act()** creates the commands that are sent to the server. It contains **cmd: "echo"**—therefore the function of the server in Listing 14.5 is called. **"echo this"** is used as the value. The server returns this string to the function that was passed in as a callback—and in this way it is finally printed on the console. The example code can be found on GitHub.[28]

Listing 14.6 *Seneca Client*

```
var seneca=require("seneca")()

seneca.client()

seneca.act('cmd: "echo",value:"echo this", function(err,result){
    console.log( result.value )
})
```

---

28. https://github.com/ewolff/seneca-example/

Therefore, it is very easy to implement a distributed system with Seneca. However, the services do not use a standard protocol like REST for communicating. Nevertheless, REST systems also can be implemented with Seneca. Besides the Seneca protocol is based on JSON and therefore can also be used by other languages.

A nanoservice can be a function that reacts with Seneca to calls from the network—and therefore it can be very small. As already described, a Node.js system as implemented with Seneca is fragile when a function blocks the event loop. Therefore, the isolation is not very good.

For the monitoring of a Seneca application there is an admin console that at least offers a simple monitoring. However, in each case it is only available for one Node.js process. Monitoring across all servers has to be achieved by different means.

An independent deployment of a single Seneca function is only possible if there is a single Node.js process for the Seneca function. This represents a profound limitation for independent deployment since the expenditure of a Node.js process is hardly acceptable for a single JavaScript function. In addition, it is not easy to integrate other technologies into a Seneca system. In the end the entire Seneca system has to be implemented in JavaScript.

Evaluation for Nanoservices

Seneca has been especially developed for the implementation of microservices with JavaScript. In fact, it enables a very simple implementation for services that can also be contacted via the network. The basic architecture is similar to Erlang: In both approaches services send messages or. commands to each other to which functions react. In regard to the independent deployment of individual services, the isolation of services from each other and the integration of other technologies, Erlang is clearly superior. Besides, Erlang has a much longer history and has long been employed in different very demanding applications.

Try and Experiment

The code example[29] can be a first step to get familiar with Seneca. You can also use the basic tutorial.[30] In addition, it is worthwhile to look at other examples.[31] The nanoservice example can be enlarged to a comprehensive application or can be distributed to a larger number of Node.js processes.

---

29. https://github.com/ewolff/seneca-example/
30. http://senecajs.org/getting-started/
31. https://github.com/rjrodger/seneca-examples/

14.9 Conclusion

The technologies presented in this chapter show how microservices can also be implemented very differently. Since the difference is so large, the use of the separate term "nanoservice" appears justified. Nanoservices are not necessarily independent processes anymore that can only be contacted via the network but might run together in one process and use local communication mechanisms to contact each other. Thereby not only the use of extremely small services is possible, but also the adoption of microservice approaches in areas such as embedded or desktop applications.

An overview of the advantages and disadvantages of different technologies in regard to nanoservices is provided in Table 14.1. Erlang is the most interesting technology since it also enables the integration of other technologies and is able to isolate the individual nanoservices quite well from each other so that a problem in one nanoservice will not trigger the failure of the other services. In addition, Erlang has been the basis of many important systems for a long time already so that the technology as such has proven its reliability beyond doubt.

Seneca follows a similar approach, but cannot compete with other technologies in terms of isolation and the integration of other technologies than JavaScript. Vert.x has a similar approach on the JVM and supports numerous languages. However, it does not isolate nanoservices as well as Erlang. Java EE does not allow for communication without a network, and individual deployment is difficult in Java EE. In practice memory leaks occur frequently during the deployment of WARs. Therefore, during a deployment the application server is usually restarted to avoid memory leaks. Then all nanoservices are unavailable for some time. Therefore, a nanoservice

Table 14.1 *Technology Evaluation for Nanoservices*

	Lambda	OSGi	Java EE	Vert x	Erlang	Seneca
Effort for infrastructure per service	++	+	+	+	++	++
Resource consumption	++	++	++	++	++	++
Communication with network	−	++	−−	++	++	−
Isolation of services	++	−−	−−	−	++	−
Use of different technologies	−	−−	−−	+	+	−−

cannot be deployed without influencing the other nanoservices. OSGi enables the shared use of code between nanoservices, in contrast to Java EE. In addition, OSGi uses method calls for communication between services and not commands or messages like Erlang and Seneca. Commands or messages have the advantage of being more flexible. Parts of a message that a certain service does not understand are not a problem; they can just be ignored.

Amazon Lambda is especially interesting since it is integrated into the Amazon ecosystem. This makes handling the infrastructure very easy. The infrastructure can be a challenging problem in case of small nanoservices because so many more environments are needed due to the high number of services. With Amazon a database server is only an API call or a click away—alternatively, an API can be used to store data instead of a server. Servers become invisible for storing data—and this is also the case with Amazon Lambda for executing code. There is no infrastructure for an individual service but only code that is executed and can be used by other services. Because of the prepared infrastructure monitoring is also no challenge anymore.

Essential Points

- Nanoservices divide systems into even smaller services. To achieve this, they compromise in certain areas such as technology freedom or isolation.

- Nanoservices require efficient infrastructures that can handle a large number of small nanoservices.

Chapter 15

Getting Started with Microservices

As a conclusion to the book, this chapter helps you think about how to get started with microservices. Section 15.1 enumerates the different advantages of microservices once more to illustrate that there is not only a single reason to introduce microservices but several. Section 15.2 describes several ways for introducing microservices—depending on the use context and the expected advantages. Section 15.3 finally follows up on the question of whether microservices are more than just hype.

15.1 Why Microservices?

Microservices entail a number of advantages such as the following (see also Chapter 4, "Reasons for Using Microservices"):

- Microservices make it easier to implement agility for large projects since teams can work independently.

- Microservices can help to supplement and replace legacy applications stepwise.

- Microservice-based architectures make possible sustainable development since they are less susceptible to architecture decay and because individual microservices can be easily replaced. This increases the long-term maintainability of the system.

- In addition, there are technical reasons for microservices such as robustness and scalability.

To prioritize these advantages and the additional ones mentioned in Chapter 4 should be the first step when considering the adaptation of a microservice-based architecture. Likewise, the challenges discussed in Chapter 5, "Challenges," have to be evaluated and, where necessary, strategies for dealing with these challenges have to be devised.

Continuous delivery and infrastructure play a prominent role in this context. If the deployment processes are still manual, the expenditure for operating a large number of microservices is so high that their introduction is hardly feasible. Unfortunately, many organizations still have profound weaknesses, especially in the area of continuous delivery and infrastructure. In such a case continuous delivery should be introduced alongside microservices. Since microservices are much smaller than deployment monoliths, continuous delivery is also easier with microservices. Therefore, both approaches have synergies.

In addition, the organizational level (Chapter 12, "Organizational Effects of a Microservices-Based Architecture") has to be taken into account. When the scalability of agile processes constitutes an important reason for introducing microservices, the agile processes should already be well established. For example, there has to be a product owner per team who also decides about all features as well as agile planning. The teams should also be already largely self-reliant—otherwise in the end they might not make use of the independence microservices offer.

Introducing microservices can solve more than just one problem. The specific motivation for microservices will differ between projects. The large number of advantages can be a good reason for introducing microservices on its own. In the end the strategy for introducing microservices has to be adapted to the advantages that are most important in the context of a specific project.

15.2 Roads towards Microservices

There are different approaches that pave the way towards microservices:

- The most typical scenario is to start out with a monolith that is converted stepwise into a multitude of microservices. Usually, different functionalities are transferred one by one into microservices. A driving force behind this conversion is often the wish for an easier deployment. However, independent scaling and achieving a more sustainable architecture can also be important reasons.

- However, migrating from a monolith to microservices can also occur in a different manner. When, for instance, resilience is the main reason for switching to microservices, the migration can be started by first adding technologies like Hystrix to the monolith. Afterwards the system can be split into microservices.

- Starting a microservice-based system from scratch is by far the rarer scenario. Even in such a case a project can start by building a monolith. However, it is more sensible to devise a first coarse-grained domain architecture that leads to the first microservices. Thereby an infrastructure is created that supports more than just one microservice. This approach also enables teams to already work independently on features. However, a fine-granular division into microservices right from the start often does not make sense because it will probably have to be revised again later on. Introducing the necessary profound changes into an already existing microservices architecture can be highly complex.

Microservices are easy to combine with existing systems, which facilitates their introduction. A small microservice as supplement to an existing deployment monolith is rapidly written. If problems arise, such a microservice can also be rapidly removed again from the system. Other technical elements can then be introduced in a stepwise manner.

The easy combination of microservices with legacy systems is an essential reason for the fact that the introduction of microservices is quite simple and can immediately result in advantages.

15.3 Microservice: Hype or Reality?

Without a doubt microservices are an approach that is in the focus of attention right now. This does not have to be bad—yet, such approaches often are at second glance only fashionable and do not solve any real problems.

However, the interest in microservices is more than just a fashion or hype:

- As described in the introduction, Amazon has been employing microservices for many years. Likewise, many Internet companies have been following this approach for a long time. Therefore, microservices are not just fashionable but have already been used for a long time behind the scenes in many companies before they became fashionable.

- For the microservice pioneers the advantages associated with microservices were so profound that they were willing to invest a lot of money into creating the not-yet-existing necessary infrastructures. These infrastructures are nowadays available free of cost as Open Source—Netflix is a prominent example. Therefore, it is much easier nowadays to introduce microservices.

- The trend towards agility and cloud infrastructures is suitably complemented by microservices-based architectures: They enable the scaling of agility and fulfill the demands of the Cloud in regards to robustness and scalability.

- Likewise, microservices as small deployment units support continuous delivery, which is employed by many enterprises to increase software quality and to bring software more rapidly into production.

- There is more than one reason for microservices. Therefore, microservices represent an improvement for many areas. Since there is not a single reason for the introduction of microservices but a number of them, it is more likely that even very diverse projects will really benefit from switching to microservices in the end.

Presumably, everybody has already seen large, complex systems. Maybe now is the time to develop smaller systems and to profit from the associated advantages. In any case there seem to be only very few reasons arguing for monoliths—except for their lower technical complexity.

15.4 Conclusion

Introducing microservices makes sense for a number of reasons:

- There is a plethora of advantages (discussed in section 15.1 and Chapter 4).

- The way to microservices is evolutionary. It is not necessary to start adopting microservices for the whole system from the beginning. Instead, a stepwise migration is the usual way (section 15.2). Many different approaches can be chosen in order to profit as quickly as possible from the advantages microservices offer.

- The start is reversible: If microservices prove not to be suitable for a certain project, they can easily be replaced again.

- Microservices are clearly more than a hype (section 15.3). For being just a hype they have been in use for too long and have been too broadly adapted. Therefore, one should at least experiment with microservices—and this books invites the reader to do just that in many places.

Try and Experiment

Answer the following questions for an architecture/system you are familiar with:

- Which are the most important advantages of microservices in this context?

- How could a migration to microservices be achieved? Possible approaches:

  - Implement new functionalities in microservices

  - Enable certain properties (e.g., robustness or rapid deployment) via suitable technologies

- What could a project look like that tests the introduction of microservices with as little expenditure as possible?

- In which case would a first project with microservives be a success and the introduction of microservices therefore sensible?

Index